A. B Cameron

From the Garden to the Cross

A Study of our Lord's Passion

A. B Cameron

From the Garden to the Cross
A Study of our Lord's Passion

ISBN/EAN: 9783337081690

Printed in Europe, USA, Canada, Australia, Japan

Cover: Foto ©Lupo / pixelio.de

More available books at **www.hansebooks.com**

FROM THE GARDEN TO THE CROSS

A STUDY OF OUR LORD'S PASSION

BY

A. B. CAMERON M.A. D.D.

LONDON
ISBISTER & COMPANY Limited
15 & 16 Tavistock Street Covent Garden
1896

> "Thou who for me didst feel such pain,
> Whose precious blood the cross did stain,
> Let not those agonies be vain!"

To My Wife

CONTENTS

Leaving the Upper Room	9
Jesus in Gethsemane	26
The divine Mystery of the Agony	43
The Apprehension in the Garden	63
Jesus before His ecclesiastical Judges	83
Peter's Denial	110
Jesus before Pilate	132
Jesus before Herod	157
Jesus again at Pilate's judgment bar	181
Jesus at the bar of the People	199
Pilate washes his hands before the multitude	221
Jesus scourged and crowned with thorns	240
The traitor's end	262
The Via Dolorosa	284
Simon of Cyrene	302
The Daughters of Jerusalem	318

LEAVING THE UPPER ROOM.

The hour was at hand when Jesus as our High Priest and Saviour must go forth on His way of death. It wanted now but this, followed by His rising again, to complete His ministry on earth. He had lived His perfect life, borne His faithful witness to God's truth and grace, and wrought His deeds of healing power and love. To crown the whole there was needed only the sacrifice of Himself on the cross, with all that should come of it, for the world's redemption and His own glory. So now He must enter upon His *via dolorosa*, which may be said to begin with the departure from the Upper Room and to end with Calvary.

The company attending Him on setting out were the eleven. Judas had already parted from them.¹ He had gone out from the Upper Room by himself before they had risen from the table. He was now mingling with his Master's foes, and basely bargaining with them for a traitor's reward. His was to be a dark and lonely pathway through sin and shame down to depths of despair over his crime, bringing him to the most tragical end. The others were still clinging to their Master. There was not, it is true, a traitor among them, but there was not one who was not before long to prove a deserter. Jesus was really to go forward alone on His pathway to the cross. It was, however, with a song upon His lips that He went.

But whither was the company to go? Where were they to pass the night? It seemed as if in Jerusalem Jesus had not where to lay His head. On other evenings of this Passion week He had gone out to Bethany, and lodged with His friends Lazarus, Martha, and Mary. As some tell us, however, it behoved Him on this paschal night not to go beyond the bounds of the holy city.²

---

¹ Keim thinks Judas did not leave till he saw Jesus set out for Gethsemane (*Jesus of Nazara*, vol. vi. 320). Andrews, that he went out on Jesus saying to him at the Supper table, 'That thou doest do quickly' (*Life of our Lord*, p. 413). The question whether Judas partook of the Supper has often been discussed. There are weighty authorities on both sides.

² No one could leave the city after the paschal supper till next morning. But many more were at the feast than Jerusalem could accommodate. Many found shelter and sleep by night in the gardens around. See Andrews' *Life of our Lord*, p. 395.

If so, the Mount of Olives must have been regarded as lying within these bounds. There He had passed nights in retirement before. Judas, we are told, knew the place, the favourite spot, the garden there in which He was likely to be found. He had doubtless satisfied himself on that point before he left the Upper Room. To that favourite retreat Jesus directed His way, and His disciples accompanied Him with an indefinite feeling of sadness and foreboding in their hearts, it is true, but little knowing that the garden was to become for ever memorable as the scene of the agony and the arrest.

The eleven went forth with Him into the street and into the night. It was drawing towards midnight; the second watch, which began at ten o'clock, was already well advanced. The moon was at the full. Most probably it was just beginning to throw its silvery light over the city, and the hills around were appearing in sombre majesty and impressiveness. There were crowds abroad, for Jerusalem was full of pilgrims, and there were the temple services to attract them.[1] Yet Jesus and His disciples seem to have moved on unchallenged. Quietly they made their way

---

[1] Edersheim, *Life and Times of Jesus the Messiah*, vol. II., 533.

through the animated streets; they passed through the eastern gate, then down into the valley through which the brook Kedron flowed, and so onward to the enclosed garden on the slope of Olivet called Gethsemane, destined to be for ever sacred in Christian hearts and memories.

But before they left the supper table they joined in singing a hymn.[1] We have the means of knowing what they sang. It was the Hallel, the portion of the Psalter which was wont to be sung at the close of the paschal feast—that from the 115th Psalm to the end of the 118th.

It was the custom of the Jews for the father of the house or the superior present to start the singing of the Hallel, and the rest then joined in.[2] How intensely interesting and touching for us to think of the voice of Jesus blending with the voices of His disciples in the chanting of these Psalms. Think of Him singing in the Upper Room of Himself thus: "The sorrows of death compassed me about, the pains of hell gat hold upon me. I found trouble and sorrow;" and then again, "Return unto thy rest, O my soul; for Thou hast delivered my soul from death, mine eyes from tears, and my feet from falling." Or again,

---

[1] Matt. xxvi. 30.
[2] Baring Gould, *Passion of Jesus*, p. 63.

"All nations compassed me about, they compassed me about, they compassed me about like bees." "But the Lord is on my side, I will not fear. What can man do unto me?" "The Lord hath chastened me sore. He hath thrust at me that I might fall. But He hath also helped me, and He hath exalted His right hand." "The stone which the builders refused is become the headstone of the corner." "Open to me the gates of righteousness; I will go into them, and I will praise the Lord." "O, give thanks unto the Lord, for He is good; for His mercy endureth for ever."

Jesus could make those words His own as no other who had ever used them. In them He could perceive Himself, now as the suffering and again as the triumphant Redeemer. They told of His coming woes, and of the glory in which they were to end. They gave expression to His sublime faith in God. They were wonderfully suited to the lips of Him who saw God directly and personally connected with each one of the experiences through which He had to pass, from the depths of suffering to the heights of joy, from the direst apparent failure and hopelessness to the most glorious triumph. They come with thrilling force from Jesus on His way to Gethsemane and Calvary, not forgetful as He goes of the glory that is to follow. In them are expressed for us both the weeping of the night of the Garden and the Cross, and the joy of the Resurrection morning.

When modern Jews are observing this paschal meal, it is their custom that, at its close, they throw open the doors of the place in which they are assembled, and then remain in profound silence for some minutes. They are waiting for the coming of Elijah, the great Forerunner, to announce the expected Messiah and the setting up of His kingdom. The solemn silence is broken by the whole company joining in the singing of the Hallel, to which we have already referred, just as they are about to leave.[1] Never could this interesting Jewish custom have been observed with deeper significance than on this occasion when the Messiah Himself was in the midst of His followers, and when He was on the way to that cross which was to become the throne of His new and everlasting kingdom.

When they had sung the hymn, chanted those Psalms predictive of Jesus' sufferings and also of His triumph, they went out to the Mount of Olives. Doubtless there was much earnest and tender discourse by the way, like that which had

---

[1] Mill, *British Jews*, p. 201.

been heard at the table of the Supper. How much of what occupies the 14th, 15th, and 16th chapters of John was spoken in the Upper Room, and how much on the way, it would be impossible to say. It may have been the thought of their going forth as men for whom Jerusalem had no home that led Him for His own and their comfort to say, "In my Father's house are many mansions. If it were not so, I would have told you. I go to prepare a place for you."[1] Perhaps it was the sight of the moonlit vines growing in the gardens of Olivet before them that suggested the beautiful words He utters on the vine and the branches.[2] The calm resting on all nature, as it drew on to the midnight hour, may have led Him to speak of the peace He was to bequeath, which the world could not give and could not take away, and of the untroubled heart that rested on the great love of God.[3] Then the disciples walking by His side—how the approaching crisis would find them, what their future would be—these subjects could not but be touched upon. The prospect of His own woe, awful though it was, did not wholly absorb Him. He had a loving concern for

---

[1] John xiv. 2.
[2] John xv. 1.
[3] John xiv. 27.

them. The part they were to play was as clearly before Him as His own. He could tell them beforehand of the collapse of their faith and courage, which at the first onset was to take place, and of their scattering like a flock of frightened sheep when He their shepherd should be assailed and smitten.[1] He had prayed, and He would still pray for their upholding in their greatest hour of trial. He would warn them anew of their imminent peril, and of their urgent need to be specially sustained.[2]

Some are of opinion that it was on the way to the Kedron Jesus turned aside and offered up His great intercessory prayer.[3] They think that in some retired spot in the valley near the bridge over the brook—some spot from which the hill Olivet rising up on the other side and the gardens on its slope might be in full view—Jesus might have found the fitting temple of nature, where, under the open firmament of heaven lighted up by the shining moon, and with a solemnizing calm resting on all around, He could pour out His soul in holy intercession as He desired. Such an idea is certainly not out of place, and for some minds it has its attractions.

---

[1] Matt xxvi. 31.
[2] Luke xxii. 32.
[3] Lange, *Gospel of John*, p. 291.

But it is more likely that the Upper Room itself was the place.[1] It is more likely that the chamber already consecrated as the scene of the Supper was still further consecrated by being made the Holy of holies into which Jesus entered as the great High Priest, and where He pleaded with the Father for His disciples and the countless multitude that should believe on Him through their word. It seems most fitting that the place where the Church held her first communion, with her Lord visibly in her midst, should be the place in which He prayed that those might be kept who had been given unto Him, and that they might know Him, abide in His love and fellowship, and behold His glory.[2]

But while Jesus spoke of coming trial and danger, and prayed for their safeguarding, the disciples did not seem to understand Him. They did not share their Master's fears and forebodings. Peter, who spoke for them, evidently had no dread of the flock scattering. Self-confidence made him think that he for one was never likely to leave his Lord. He thought he had the love

---

[1] Geikie, *Life and Words of Christ*, p. 666. Also Edersheim (vol. II., 513, 528). Westcott thinks it may have been the temple, but that would be too crowded and noisy at this Passover time. See his *Gospel of St. John*, p. 237.

[2] John xvii.

that was stronger than any death. Measuring his assurance on this point by the intensity of his feelings at the moment he said, "Though all shall be offended because of Thee, yet will I never be offended."[1] So strongly did the tide of feeling within him run in this direction of self-assertion, that nothing for the time could arrest or abate it. Even the gentle but emphatic warning words of his Master, "Verily, I say unto thee, that this night before the cock crow, thou shalt deny me thrice,"[2] proved unavailing.

Peter knew himself, as he thought, better than his Master did. He could measure himself, he vainly imagined, against any danger. He was equal to any possible challenge to the strength or genuineness of his devotion. With his characteristic ardour and energy he said, "Though I should die with Thee yet will I not deny Thee."[3] And may we not discern just a trace of injured feeling in his mind as he let fall that passionate utterance, as if the Master were not doing justice to the strength of his attachment and the strength of his character, as if the Master were not quite trusting him as he thought he deserved?

---

[1] Matt. xxvi. 33.
[2] Matt. xxvi. 34.
[3] Matt. xxvi. 35.

But Peter did not stand alone in his declarations. His zeal and ardour proved contagious as they had often done before. "Likewise, also, said all the disciples."[1] They rightly interpreted their Master's words as a challenge to their devotion. They were ready to meet it with the warmest protestations on their part; nor were they consciously exaggerating when they said that they could willingly die for Him. The very thought that some great mysterious sorrow was impending over Him, and that He seemed to be asking for their fidelity in His hour of trial, doubtless made their Master dearer to them than ever, and intensified all their feelings towards Him.

It was not usual for Jesus to call for declarations of attachment. He was content that it should reveal itself in everyday words and deeds, in the thing done or said that showed how much He was loved. His followers were not required to be painfully introspective, to be examining again and again, as they walked with Him, into the state of their hearts, and to be making frequent avowals of their love and of their faith. We question whether Jesus saw any wisdom or virtue in that—a practice so like that of children taking up by the roots

---

[1] Matt. xxvi. 35.

now and again the things they have planted, that they may satisfy themselves as to how they are growing, with the result that they weaken, if they do not destroy, the life of the plants they are so anxious about. It was enough if the disciples walked with Jesus, and did so with true and honest hearts. Yet times there might be which might specially call for their avowals. Such a time was this when Jesus had His face steadfastly set to go to Gethsemane. In view of all that was to take place there, we can understand Jesus in so many words asking the touching question, "Will ye also go away?"

It did honour then to the disciples that they should make the avowal which they did, and that they should declare their readiness to die with Him. But they did not know themselves as their Master knew them. They were still ignorant of what the cross was which was about to come upon Him. They could not forecast that, as a trial or test of their fidelity, it would be far beyond their strength to face or to abide. They could not believe that there could be any trial great or terrible enough to make them deserters from their Master.[1] They could not understand the agony to be endured in

---

Mark xiv. 31.

the prospect of the cross, and which Gethsemane was to witness. When it revealed itself in its dread reality it proved too much for them. Their faith, their courage first faltered, and then for the time failed altogether.[1]

But could there have been found men anywhere, in that age or in ours, who as disciples would have done any better than they did? If the trial was so great, so appalling, as to cause Jesus His bloody sweat in the Garden, we may well suppose that the approach of it, and the possibility of sharing in it, would have been enough to make cowards of the bravest and the most heroic.

Once before, on a memorable occasion, Jesus had sent His disciples forth on a mission fitted to make special demands on their courage and faith.[2] That was when they were appointed to go two and two, and preach the coming of the kingdom. Then He had sent them without scrip, purse, or sword. He had bidden them go even as they were while they stood around Him, without provision for their journey and without defence save that of God, whose work they were to do. It was a trial of their faith. It needed personal fortitude and great loyalty to their Master thus to go at His command

---

[1] Matt. xxvi. 56.
[2] Luke x. 1-24, The sending forth of the Seventy.

to be the preachers of His kingdom. They were for the most part humble fishermen, and they were to perform the office of prophets with nothing to accredit them but their commission from the Man of Nazareth, and their power to work certain miracles in His name. They might well have hesitated. They might well have had their misgivings. They could not know what reception the people would give them, or what perils and sufferings might be before them; and it was trying to have to go, humanly speaking, entirely unprovided for. But they had been equal to that demand upon their faith and their loyalty. They had gone forth, and they had returned with glad tidings to their Master. They had "lacked nothing." "Even the devils had been subject to them in His name."[1]

It was, however, another and a greater trial that lay before them now. It needed all the preparation they could make for it. To use Jesus' own words, which doubtless He meant in a figurative sense, they needed purse and scrip and sword. "Now," said He, "he that hath a purse let him take it, and likewise his scrip; and he that hath no sword, let him sell his garment and buy one."[2] Better without comforts than without the needed weapons

---

[1] Luke x. 17.
[2] Luke xxii. 35-38.

and defences for the crisis. Their honour and safety could hardly be bought at too great a price. That they might be sufficiently equipped and armed, that they might have all their spiritual resources and weapons—their trust in God, their faith in their Master and His cause whatever might happen, their steadfastness and loyalty—that they might have all these at command to meet the impending trial, was of paramount importance. All these would be required, and would be well tried, when they should see their Master in the hands of His foes on the way to His cross. When the Shepherd should be smitten it would be hard, nay it was to be found impossible, for the flock to keep from scattering.

It would seem that Peter put too carnal a meaning into his Lord's words. Two swords were forthcoming after those words were uttered,[1] and Peter took possession of one of them. What blundering use he made of it we know. The stroke which cut off Malchus' ear,[2] would, but for Jesus' intervention, have proved fatal to them all. It was quite another kind of armour or defence which the coming crisis called for. It was that which the Master Himself had, and in which He placed all His trust. It

---

[1] Luke xxii. 38.
[2] John xviii. 10.

would have been well had the disciples gone to meet the crisis as He did. It would have been worth their while, "selling their garments," parting with all else, to buy such a sword as He carried, a sword which was to beat down Satan under His feet, and to win for Him the victory of redemption.

It is remarkable how Jesus rests His prophetic eye on this victory, even when He is about to enter the scene of His passion, and how He seeks to share with His disciples the comfort which the hope of it gave to Himself. While He places before them the dark picture of His agony and cross He is careful to lighten it for them by the hope of His resurrection. In a way so true to His beautiful and perfect love for them He tells them that so soon as ever He should come back from the grave He would make His way to them, that the old fellowship, broken for a while by death, might be resumed never to be broken again. "After I am risen again," He says, "I will go before you into Galilee."[1] In the old loved haunts, in the Galilee where they had walked so long with their Master and seen so much of Him, and which was dear to them as the country of

---

[1] Matt. xxvi. 32; Mark xiv 28.

their birth, their kindred and their toils, they should meet again, and their joy should be full.

With such discourse of trial and victory, of the darkness of the night and the joy of the morning that was to follow it all, Jesus beguiled the way for His disciples till they reached the garden. There they thought to pass the solemn paschal night just as probably they had passed many another before. It was, however, destined to be the scene of momentous events for which, notwithstanding all that had been or could be said, they were unprepared.

JESUS IN GETHSEMANE.

It would probably be an hour or so from midnight when Jesus and His disciples reached Gethsemane. It was one of those gardens on Olivet to which pilgrims coming up to the feast were wont to repair for meditation and repose. Never did it receive greater consecration as a sanctuary of devotion than it did when Jesus entered it, there to agonize in prayer as the great High Priest under the burden of His people's sins. It was an enclosed spot, little more than half a mile from the city, planted with olive trees in the shade of which He could find the privacy which He sought.

As to its exact locality opinions differ. The Latin Christians of Jerusalem have a place which they have walled round and planted with olive trees, and which they believe to be the veritable scene of the Passion. The monks will show you the grotto of the agony, the place where the three disciples slept, and the very spot where the betrayal and the arrest took place. But the Greek Christians have chosen another locality as the true Gethsemane, and are quite as positive about it. Thomson thinks neither locality is the true one, that both are too near the city and the public road eastwards to have afforded the seclusion Jesus desired, but that it may have been in some hollow of the hill a few hundred yards farther off.[1] Within the Latin enclosure there are some eight olive trees growing at the present day. They are very venerable, with massive trunks, partly decayed, gnarled branches and scanty foliage. It is more than doubtful, however, whether any of them are old enough to have thrown their shadows in the moonlight over the form of the Man of Sorrows in His agony. Josephus says that after the siege of Jerusalem, under Titus A.D. 70, not a single olive tree was left standing, all having been cut down by the soldiers of the tenth legion.[2]

Gethsemane means "the garden of the oil press." It is supposed by some[3] that in its enclosure

---

[1] Thomson's *Land and the Book*, p. 634. The whole question is very fully discussed in Robinson's *Palestine*, vol. I. 234, 346. Caspari (*Life of Christ* p 222) thinks something may be said for the traditional site as the tradition is very ancient.

[2] Josephus, *B. J.* v. 6. 2.

[3] Baring Gould, *Passion of Jesus*, p. 63.

there was not only an olive orchard but an olive crushing mill belonging to the temple, from which the seven-branched candlestick was supplied with oil. It is more than likely that this is but conjecture In the deepest sense, however, Gethsemane was the oil press supplying from sorest pain and conflict that which should make Jesus the true Light of the world.

Dr. Petavel is of opinion [1] that Gethsemane was the name of a country house situated on the other side of the Kedron, and on the slope of the Mount of Olives. The χωρίον λεγόμενον Γεθσημανεῖ of Matthew [2] which is rendered "the place called Gethsemane," he thinks ought to be translated, the house called Gethsemane. According to him it had enclosed ground occupied with olive trees attached to it, and it belonged to Mary the mother of John whose surname was Mark. Jesus came to it as to a favourite retreat. His eight disciples He left at the gate that they might have its shelter during the chilly night. He Himself with the chosen three went into the garden. Judas at length came as if he had only returned from business on which he had

---

[1] *Expositor*, March, 1891.
[2] Matt. xxvi. 36.

been sent by the Master. He was admitted, and the band accompanying him promptly followed, passed through the entrance, and hastened with their torches now lit and their weapons in readiness into the garden to discover Jesus and to seize Him. The tumult of this movement awakened Mark from his slumbers in the house, and throwing a sheet hastily about him the young man rushed forth to give warning to the Master and His disciples. But before he could reach them the apprehension had taken place, and he fled, leaving the sheet that covered him in the hands of some of Jesus' captors. Dr. Petavel thinks it was just because a private house with private property adjoining it had to be invaded that Judas' services as the betrayer were of the greatest value. Had Jesus and His disciples been in any other but private and enclosed ground on the slopes of Olivet, the armed band would have had no need of his help. According to Baring Gould, however, Mary's house was that in which the Upper Room gathering took place, and was therefore on the city side of the brook Kedron. To it Judas with his band first came; young Mark was awakened; and we can understand the rest.

On reaching the entrance to the garden, Jesus bade His disciples halt. "Sit ye here," said He to them, "while I go and pray yonder."[1] Probably there was some gateway under which they might thus rest as He desired. He then sought for Himself the more shaded parts of the garden for the sake of greater retirement. It would seem to have been intended that the disciples should act as sentinels to give warning of the approach of foes. Thus we can understand the significance and the need of the Master's injunction on leaving them, "Pray that ye enter not into temptation."[2]

But three were chosen to attend Him, and to be witnesses of His passion, Peter, James and John.[3] They were, we may believe, the best of the band, and the best Jesus could find among men as companions for Himself in the joys and sorrows, the work and the conflict of His earthly ministry. They showed they had the qualities which when sanctified and developed under His personal influence form the noblest Christian characters, and fit men for the highest Christian service. They brought the tribute of their great loving souls to Him, and He gratefully accepted it. They gave Him their confidence, and their devotion, and He repaid them with a boundless generosity. In the most solemn and sacred moments

---

[1] Matt. xxvi. 36.
[2] Luke xxii. 40.
[3] Mark xiv. 32.

of His life they were permitted to be with Him.
They were with Him on the Holy Mount when He
was seen in glory,[1] and in the death chamber where
He raised Jairus' daughter to life.[2] Now in the
garden the special honour and privilege were given
to them of being witnesses of the most sacred scene
of all, and of sharing, if only they could or would,
the fellowship of their Master's sufferings.

Taking these three chosen ones with Him Jesus
went some distance into the dark recesses of the
garden. There His mysterious sorrow began. A
startling change seemed to come over Him. He
who appeared so calm and even cheerful at the
Supper table began to wear a look of greatest anguish.
Putting together the accounts of it given by the
Synoptists—for the Fourth Gospel is silent on the
whole subject—we find that He began to be very
sorrowful and very heavy, to be sore amazed—
literally seized with terror—and that He exclaimed
"My soul is exceeding sorrowful even unto death."[3]
As if His sorrow were all too great to be shared,
He removed Himself from them "a stone's cast."[4]
After telling them of its overwhelming greatness

---

[1] Matt. xvii. 1.
[2] Luke viii. 51.
[3] Mark xiv. 34.
[4] Luke xxii. 41.

He was constrained to withdraw Himself from them for a little, and all alone to prostrate Himself to the earth, and pour out His agonized prayer to the Father. But so soon as the great wave of divine agony had passed over His soul, and He had uttered His supplications with strong crying and tears unto the Father, He returned to His disciples, hungering and asking for their sympathy and for all the help they, as His deeply pledged friends, could give Him by tarrying and watching with Him.[1]

Three times Jesus thus came and went, sought and quitted the companionship of the chosen three.[2] Three times in absolute seclusion in the garden He agonized in prayer with the Father. Each time He fell on His face and prayed in such words as these, "O my Father, if it be possible, let this cup pass from me: nevertheless, not as I will, but

---

[1] Matt. xxvi. 40.

[2] Keim (*Jesus of Nazara*, vol. VI, 15) thinks the evangelists are in some perplexity how to fill out their schemes of three prayers as well as three denials. Strauss rejects the narrative of the Passion in Gethsemane altogether, because he cannot accept that Jesus knew all beforehand, or that He was aware His death was so near. The writer of the Fourth Gospel he declares (*New Life of Jesus*, p. 327) omitted the whole story, because it did not suit his Logos Christ who was above all such trials. It may be added here, however, that Hase, one of the weightiest authorities in the more modern school of German criticism, goes so far as to say that in the history of the passion and death of Christ all four gospels go side by side with each other, and exhibit in their variations only the various sides and conceptions of the same occurrence (*Geschichte Jesu*, p. 525). Hilgenfeld also admits that the account of the agony is "of the highest originality, full of historic truth."

as Thou wilt,"[1] and each time the prayer seemed to gather in intensity and sublimity. The second time it took the form, "Abba, Father, all things are possible unto Thee; take away this cup from me: nevertheless, not what I will, but what Thou wilt."[2]. The third time it ran in similar words, "O my Father, if this cup may not pass from me except I drink it, Thy will be done."[3] Luke specially notes that "being in an agony He prayed more earnestly," and that "His sweat was as it were great drops of blood falling down to the ground."[4]

But each time on His return from His sanctuary of sacred anguish and prayer Jesus found His disciples asleep—the three on whom He most relied, and whom He had taken apart that they might specially be with Him. This fact, and all that it implied, had also to enter into the cup of which He must drink. At the time when He needed most their fellowship those who had declared they were ready to die with Him could not even keep awake for His sake. Asleep they were as if His agony did not concern them. Asleep though

---

[1] Matt. xxvi. 39.
[2] Mark xiv. 36.
[3] Matt. xxvi. 42.
[4] Luke xxii. 44.

they had heard but a short time before that His soul was exceeding sorrowful even unto death! Asleep in spite of His earnest loving entreaty to watch and be in waiting for His return! Could anything be more touching than those gentle words of expostulation which He addressed to them, "What, could ye not watch with me one hour? Watch and pray, lest ye enter into temptation."[1]

Are we to understand that the Saviour's solitary agony and supplication lasted an hour each time, and that this was the time He was absent from His disciples? If so, an incidental light is thrown upon the Gethsemane agony which reveals still more of its greatness. It was not a momentary spasm. It was a terribly extreme tension of body and soul protracted over some two or three hours. The disciples watched while Jesus was with them and engaged them in converse; it was while He was away, and had special need for their watching unto prayer, that they failed. Thrice the same drowsiness overtook them, and each time it came upon them as Jesus was wrestling in prayer with the Father. The third time it was effectually driven away by the tumult and the fear connected with their Master's apprehension.

---

[1] Matt. xxvi. 40.

"The spirit indeed is willing, but the flesh is weak,"[1] adds the Saviour with a fine considerateness, softening what might otherwise sound harsh and severe. Three times that day the disciples had travelled with Jesus the road between Jerusalem and Bethany, and now it was far into the night. They were suffering from fatigue of body, the wearing out excitement of sorrow and other intense feelings. They were sleeping for sorrow, sleeping soundly like tired children who have cried themselves to sleep. Our Lord's rebuke was thus of the gentlest; and it bore in itself a note of tenderest sympathy with those to whom it was addressed.

It might have been expected that the Master would not have needed to repeat His gentle chiding. But on His returning the second and even the third time it had to be spoken anew. And He spoke it with increasing earnestness, yet without impatience—a striking example of the forbearance and importunity He uses so graciously towards His people. Disappointed in His three chosen disciples a first and then a second time, He might have given over appealing to them. Coming from agonizing sorrow again and again to find those His heart most clung to, parted from

---

[1] Matt. xxvi. 41.

Him in feeling by so enormous a gulf that they were asleep, He might have ceased to ask for a fellowship which, even when it was given, could for Him be so little of a fellowship. But Jesus would still hold them by the cords of love, and would patiently wait till the day when the feeble spark should become a flame, and the men sleeping in Gethsemane men full of noblest life, interest, and devotion even unto death in the service of His Gospel. Thus Jesus rebukes, warns, entreats still with a generous importunity, and with a charity and longsuffering all His own. Where any other would despair He continues His gracious work. When it seems as if we were asleep or dead to what stirs Himself most, He comes again and again to wake us to spiritual life. And who can tell the temptations and dangers assailing us when we are asleep from which we are delivered just because He is watching and interceding for us in the sanctuary, removed more than a stone's cast from us—the sanctuary above that is all His own?

The reason why the tenderest expostulations and entreaties failed is not far to seek. The disciples could not grasp, as they needed to do, the thought that their Master's hour had come. They were in Gethsemane that night just as they had been before. Not even the discourse in the Upper Room, nor the broken bread and outpoured wine—memorials of the coming cross—could bring them to realise fully or clearly that that cross was really at hand. We may spare our wonder or our blame. It is easy to say after an event has happened that it is all so clear. Nations might never have committed the blunders and the crimes they have done had they possessed at the time the moral vision which even their history seems now to give. Are there not multitudes even yet who are strangers to the cross and who stumble at it, though it has had the plainest setting of history? The disciples did not know the cause of their beloved Master's agony, and they could not sympathise with it. This along with their false sense of security is why their willing spirit was not striving as it ought to have been doing against the weak flesh, and why they succumbed so readily to sleep in presence of the greatest crisis that ever overtook them or the world.

How different it was with Jesus. His flesh was also weak. So far as the flesh was concerned He was not superhuman, He was even as other men. The fatigue of the day, the strain of the supper table, and the hours of agony and intercession must have made Him weary indeed. For Him slumber even for an hour would have been a relief and a solace. But in the supreme crisis of His life His spirit was not only willing but all-commanding. His spirit was so intensely stirred, so agonized, that sleep was impossible for Him. The world, when it called for Him as the victim of its sin and malice, did not come upon Him unawares. It found Him keenly alive to all the shame and suffering its sin had prepared for Him, and to all that the Father might require of Him as the divine sacrifice to take it away. And nothing can keep us alive and alert in the hour of trial, and clothe us with power to meet the danger and the conflict, like a living faith in the Cross.

When Jesus came the third time to His sleeping disciples, the victory of the spirit over the weak and shrinking flesh had in His case been won. He was ready for His approaching foes. He had taken the cup into His hands. In spirit He had emptied it with all the coming woes it contained. With the whole strength and intensity of His soul He had said, and three times He had said it, "Father, Thy will be done"; and in the utterance of these words, in view of all He knew to be before Him, He had triumphed. In those hours of His Gethsemane agony He had in spirit encountered His coming cross and all the storm of wrath and woe it could mean for Him as the bearer of the world's sin; He had felt wave after wave of suffering and anguish passing over His soul; but He had risen superior to all and shown Himself more than conqueror in that utterance of sublimest resignation. So far as His spirit was concerned He had already offered His great sacrifice of Himself, and He had achieved His triumph. He had conquered the world with all the evil it could do Him, conquered sin and death and hell, and conquered Satan with all the power to tempt, wound and bruise which might be permitted him. Hence we understand His words as He rouses His disciples from their slumbers the third time, " Sleep on now and take your rest; behold the hour is at hand, and the Son of Man is betrayed into the hands of sinners. Rise, let us be going; behold he is at hand that doth betray me."[1] They are the expression of His perfect self-surrender, and of the settled triumphant peace and resignation with which He went forth to meet His cross.

At that moment, as Jesus spoke, the band was seen approaching. The tramp of their feet could be distinctly heard. The light of their burning

---

[1] Matt. xxvi. 45.

lanterns and torches flashed and flickered in the darkness. They had already crossed the Kedron, and were approaching the entrance to Gethsemane where the eight disciples were resting. Now there was no need for Jesus to say to them, or to the three immediately about Him, "Watch and pray." The danger was at hand, and in presence of it none of them could be neglectful of the warning.

But how much better they should now sleep and take their rest, if only they could! If only they could, they would spare themselves bitter memories and humiliations. Better far asleep than awake only to desert their Master, or basely to deny Him. "Sleep on now," He says, feeling deeply for His loved ones, "Sleep on, if you can, and so be spared the sorrow of seeing your Master fall into the hands that will buffet Him, scourge Him, and crucify Him. Sleep on, if you can, through the hours of your greatest temptations, sorrows, and dangers. My prayer is that I only may be seized and led away, and that you may be untouched. Would that you could sleep till I come again to you in my resurrection glory!"

But it could not be. Those who could not keep awake while watchfulness was needed, were unable to take their rest when sleep would have been their greatest blessing. Jesus' loved disciples were still carnal. The stir and tumult of a band of armed men apprehending their Master and threatening themselves, could effectually rouse them from slumber, while His own sore agony failed entirely to do this. Fear for their own lives made them wakeful and watchful enough: their Master could be sorrowful even unto death, and in His agony be even staining His raiment with His bloody sweat, and they could not watch with Him one hour.

We know how all this was changed afterwards, how the return of Jesus from the grave and the coming of the Holy Ghost awoke them at length and for ever from their spiritual slumber. When they had got their new and true vision of Jesus and His cross, they counted not their lives dear unto them, but rejoiced to suffer for His sake, and to proclaim everywhere salvation through His blood. Till we are awakened, we too are concerned for ourselves rather than for our Master's cause. Things outward touch us more keenly than things spiritual. The world with its changes and its commotions can at any time break our repose, and even fill us with a fear and alarm betokening how little faith we have in God. It is otherwise when Jesus quickens and stirs us into life by His sorrows and His sufferings on our behalf. Then we cannot sleep, as the world does, while He is agonizing. We must needs watch with Him, with a sympathetic interest and anxiety, keenly alive to all that touches His honour and His glory. We must also be ready to rise and go forth with Him, bearing His reproach, and sharing in all His holy conflict.

THE DIVINE MYSTERY OF THE AGONY.

There are three things that impress us with reverent awe as we meditate upon the agony of our Lord in Gethsemane. The first is its peculiar greatness and intensity, the second its cause, and the third the spirit in which it was endured.

The evangelist Luke tells us that "being in an agony our Lord prayed the more earnestly, and his sweat was as it were great drops of blood falling down to the ground." This world has been the scene of bitter griefs. It has had, and still has, its agony and passion, its Gethsemane, in countless lives. Literature and art have endeavoured to explore the mystery of it, and to set forth its pathos and its tragedy. History and experience tell of anguish and tears, and broken hearts, and lives pining away in sorrows worse to be endured than death. Man's inhumanity to man, the breaking of hopes and confidences, the sense of wrong or of wrongdoing, the burden and agony felt from conscious guilt—these and the like fruits of sin, from which no human heart has ever been altogether free, have brought men into their Gethsemane to agonize and to cry unto their God. The physical effects of what they have there endured have been sometimes very striking and even tragical.[1] But in this respect, as in every other, the Gethsemane of our fallen humanity, awful as it is, is surpassed by that of the Son of Man. We cannot conceive adequately of a sorrow so infinite as that suggested by the evangelist's words. The internal conflict and anguish were so severe and intense that there oozed forth from the body, sharing them with the soul, not sweat but blood. The whole bodily system was so strained that the blood started through the pores, and did this so profusely that it fell in great drops to the ground.[2] Those drops were an earnest of the stream that was to flow when the Divine Sufferer should hang upon the cross.[3]

---

[1] Stroud (*Physical Causes of the Death of Christ*, p. 380) cites at least a dozen well authenticated cases on record in ancient and modern times of this sweating of blood—the feelings and passions being touched to such a pitch of intensity that the blood has been forced through the skin of the body. Among these is that of Charles IX., who might well suffer in this way, haunted as he must have been by the horrors of St. Bartholomew. Another is that of a young officer who was betrayed into the hands of a besieging enemy, and who, in view of the tortures and death they were preparing for him, was thrown into something like a bath of blood.

[2] Ellicott's *Life of Our Lord*, p. 329.

[3] In Carlo Dolce's picture the drops as they fall are represented as kindling into heavenly light.

But if the physical effects told thus impressively of the intensity of His sufferings, our Lord's own words are even a more striking and more pathetic testimony on the subject. "My soul," said He, "is exceeding sorrowful even unto death."[1] That *He* should have spoken of His sorrow is deeply significant. Through life He was the Man of Sorrows. But where, except in Gethsemane, do we ever hear of Him breathing a word, we shall not say, of repining and complaint—for that was ever far from Him—but of reference even to the grief and the ills which He endured? Even when on the following day He was buffeted, spit upon, scourged, and made to bear His heavy cross, He never once let fall a word as to the bitter pain and shame men were thus inflicting upon Him. Meekness and patience never had such a triumph. The triumph was divine.

Why then did He speak of His sorrow now? Was this the one moment of His life when He seemed to display some measure of human weakness?[2] Even were it so, we might say that the

---

[1] Matt. xxvi. 38.

[2] Keim (*Jesus of Nazara*, vol VI., 22) holds that Jesus showed here human weakness and opposing desires, and that this was an incipient though not perfected sin. He adds, however, that in His second and third prayer Jesus victoriously left the sinful frontier!

weakness was human, and it was sinless. We can add, too, that it has afforded comfort to many a sufferer, assuring him that in Jesus he had a High Priest touched with the feeling of our infirmities. But we believe that what led Jesus to tell His three loved disciples and the world through them of His unutterable sorrow was that men might know that His soul as well as His body shared in the sacrifice He was making for their sins, and that the sacrifice in either case, the price paid in the agonies of the soul as well as in the pains of the body, was immeasurably great. It was needful that He should make Himself the revealer and the interpreter of His own divine sorrow, the knowledge of which is so necessary to our fellowship with Him in His sufferings and to our trust in Him for our salvation. Had He not thus revealed and interpreted His own Passion how could we ever have known it, and not knowing it, how could it ever have benefited us? In the outburst of His grief, in His deeply touching words, He has therefore given us a glimpse of what was in His very heart, as He was bowed down and agonized under the load of our sins and sorrows which was laid upon Him, that we might see and know what a Saviour we have.

There is another striking circumstance to show the infinite greatness of the agony. "There appeared an angel from heaven strengthening him.'"[1] Thus heaven itself was manifestly moved by the scene in Gethsemane. Men failed Him in His hour of trial, but the hosts above were ready to supply the lack. Loved disciples could not watch with Him one hour, but those whose greatest service and joy it had been to minister to Him above were looking down upon the mystery of His Passion with intensest interest and adoring wonder. Alone He seemed in His sanctuary of sorrow; yet not alone for there was this one of the angelic host to assure Him that all heaven was with Him. This angel's presence, with all that it meant of heaven's interest and God's love, brought to Him more comfort and strength than any sympathy human hearts could offer. And we are thankful for it in the record to lighten up the darkness in our Lord's darkest hour, when He was about to go forth to die, just as we are for the radiance and the entrancing music which the multitude of the heavenly host gave to the midnight sky over the plains of Bethlehem when He was born. But it serves to show incidentally how great the agony must have been that heaven should be so stirred by it, that one must needs leave its blissful seats

---

[1] Luke xxii. 43.

to sustain the Divine Sufferer and to bear Him company. That a world where no sorrow is should sympathise with our Saviour's greatest sorrow in this world certainly adds to the mystery of Gethsemane, but it affords one of the most comforting revelations of the glorious possibilities of heaven's ministering love among sorrowing and suffering men.

But we pass to the all-important question, What was the cause of Jesus' Gethsemane agony? Could it possibly be a timid apprehension of death? Could it be that the mere physical pain of dying on the cross, now foreseen by Him, wrought Him into such an intensity of mental and bodily suffering? If so, we must admit that Jesus has been surpassed by some of His own followers. Not a few of the martyrs in His cause have gone bravely and even joyously to the torturing rack, stake, or scaffold. From a very early period the agony and shrinking from apprehended suffering which Jesus experienced in Gethsemane were laid hold of by adversaries as a reflection upon His character. Celsus and Julian the Apostate contrasted Jesus, sorrowing and trembling in the garden, with Socrates, the hero of the poison cup, and with other heroes of antiquity, greatly, of course, to the disadvantage of the former. "Why, then," said Celsus, scornfully alluding to Jesus' conflict in the garden, "does He supplicate help, and bewail Himself and pray for escape from the fear of death, expressing Himself in terms like these, 'O Father, if it be possible, let this cup pass from me'?"[1] The Emperor Julian, quoted by Theodore of Mopsuestia, uses, if possible, still more scornful language: "Jesus presents such petitions as a wretched mortal would offer when unable to bear a calamity with serenity, and although divine, He is strengthened by an angel." To these heathen philosophers Jesus trembling and agonized in Gethsemane seemed to come far short of the great men of classic antiquity.

But the secret of the Gethsemane woe must be sought in something else than the mere bodily torture awaiting Him, or indeed all the outward ills, sorrows, and reproaches with which an evil world might afflict Him. To one with the pure, keenly sensitive, divinely strung soul of Jesus, what He had already suffered at the hands of His foes through their hatred and unbelief, their deplorable unresponsiveness to all the truth He taught and all the good He did, and their bitter scorn and calumny, must have been far more than any physical pain they could inflict upon Him. To

---

[1] Origen, II. 24. See also Origen, VII. 52.

reach the true secret of the agony we must go beyond the outward and the physical. Jesus Himself has taught His people to rise above the sufferings which afflict the body, or which merely touch the outward earthly lot. Over these He had won the perfect triumph in His own soul. But there was His relation to what lay at the root of all these sufferings, and what was incomparably more terrible in itself than the worst of them. There was His relation to the world's sin, to that without which these sufferings would not have been, and that without which there could have been for Himself no sorrows, no tortures, no cross.[1]

If we leave this out of view, it is simply impossible to understand how Jesus could have been so agonized in the prospect of His cross. His moral excellences, which even the adversaries of the Christian faith in our days are so willing to attribute to Him, should have made His suffering in the circumstances less instead of greater. Suffering is bereft of its sharpest sting when it falls upon one

---

[1] Ellicott (*Life of our Lord*, p. 329) says the Gethsemane agony is only to be explained "by the vivid clearness of the Saviour's knowledge of the awful affinity between death, sin and the powers of darkness." Weiss (*Life of Christ*, vol. III. 323) admits that Jesus made the sin of His people His own, and that it was the fact He was now to endure its awful burden which wrought for Him His woe in the garden.

conscious of his own integrity; he can meet it tranquilly, and even with some feeling of triumph over it, when he knows it is undeserved, or that it is only the penalty of virtue and of devotion in a good cause. But as a matter of fact the agony of the faultless Man of Nazareth surpasses that of the greatest transgressors, when in the hour of their penitence they have been racked and tortured by the vivid apprehension of their crimes. It becomes intelligible only when we accept His own explanation of all His suffering and woe, that He had come to give His life a ransom for many,[1] and to shed His blood for the remission of their sins.[2] In other words, He had come to make the sins of others His own, and to suffer and die as if He had committed them, and as if the guilt and the penalty of them were His.

How Jesus could assume and have this personal relation to sins not His own is the real mystery here. It must ever be, like much else in His divine human being, largely beyond our finite thought. It goes so far to explain it that He was the Son of Man, and that in this unique character He could be for men what no other could possibly be. As the God-man He stood related to humanity,

---

[1] Matt. xx. 28.
[2] Matt. xxvi. 28.

to its burden and its destiny, as no other could be. He was its head and representative. As such He could, while sinless Himself, make the sin, the agony, and the conflict of our fallen race His own. The suffering and the death which this involved He as the second Adam underwent, not for His own sake, but for the sake of humanity, that all might issue in salvation. Thus far the Incarnation throws light upon Gethsemane and Calvary. It did not merely add another to the number of our race, but it gave a new divine centre or head to it, and one in whose personal history the agony and conflict of humanity because of sin might be endured and brought to the victory of redemption.[1]

But considerations such as these seem at once to increase and to enhance the mystery of Christ's vicarious sorrow and suffering. They help to show how He might come to be most closely related to our sin and curse, but the relation itself remains a divine mystery. The mystery, however, is relieved for us, and we are led to rejoice in it, when we see that it is radiant with the glory of self-sacrificing love. It so meets our need crying under the burden of our sins that we feel it must be true. It gives us a new hope for humanity

---

[1] See discussion of the whole subject in Dorner, *Person of Christ*, Division II., vol. III., p. 232-248.

that Jesus thus offers Himself for its help as the Son of Man, and that He rejoices in the name. It affords us, also, a new revelation of God, showing Him in the glory of His grace. We can understand charity and self-denying beneficence meeting the results of evil in this world—the poverty, misery, and suffering it has caused—with their bounty and all the services and forms of self-sacrifice possible to them; but here is philanthropy on the Son of Man's part, going so far as to deal with the evil itself and all its demerit and guiltiness, its relations to the moral order of the universe, and to the claims and glory of God. For divine love to relate itself to human need and suffering, and to multiply its offices of charity in relieving them is a great thing; but for divine love to clothe itself with the shame and guilt of the sufferers and make their cause its own, is another and an infinitely greater thing. For God's Son to come into the midst of suffering men that He might share their ills and sorrows, and provide them with comforts and abatements, would reveal a beautiful compassion and beneficence. But for Him to descend from His divine throne, step into the sinner's place, and suffer Himself to be numbered with the transgressors, bearing their burden and blame—this is grace beyond all we can conceive of grace.

True it is that with God alone such things are possible, but who of our fallen race should not be willing to believe that not only such grace, but that also such power is in God? Surely of all God's creatures, fallen and stained as we are, we ought to be the very last even to wish to deny that such grace and power might be in our Divine Maker and Lord. If the mystery be great, it is glorious; it is altogether worthy of God, it is the teaching of His holy word, and it opens the one way of hope for our ruined humanity.

To quote from the masterly review of theories of the atonement in Professor Orr's recent work, "The Christian View of God and the World," no theory can possibly be adequate or satisfactory which does not recognise as elements in the case "that Christ did enter, as far as a sinless being could, into the penal evils of our state, and finally submitted to death—the doom which sin has brought on our humanity; that He did this with a perfect consciousness and realisation of the relation of these evils to sin; that He experienced the full bitterness of these evils, and, especially in His last hours, was permitted to endure them without even the alleviations and spiritual comforts which many of His own people enjoy; that there were mysterious elements in His sufferings, which outward causes do not seem adequate to explain (*e.g.* the agony in Gethsemane, the awful darkness of His soul on Calvary) which appear related to His position as our Sin-bearer; finally that in all this mortal sorrow He still retained unbroken His relation to the Father, and so transacted with God for men that His death may fitly be regarded as the Redemption of the world."[1]

To consider sin in its effect not on man's character merely, but on man's relation to God, and how Christ relates Himself to this and meets this is, as Denney says, "the ulterior question which really goes to the root of the matter, and on which the whole of Biblical teaching emerges."[2] Christ related Himself to man's sin as it touched his relations to God by taking it upon Himself. He made the burden of God's condemnation of it His own. He took over the responsibilities of our sin as arising out of our relations to God upon Himself, and He discharged them by suffering and dying in our stead. It is this which yields the only satisfactory explanation of the agony or the crucifixion. To quote further the same author (p. 123), "It is hard to believe, hard even to

---

[1] Orr's *Christian View of God and the World*, pp. 382, 383.
[2] Denney's *Studies in Theology*, p. 102.

impossibility, that it was simply the anticipation of pain which so overcame Him. It was the condemnation in the cross which made Him cry, 'O my Father, if it be possible, let this cup pass from me.' It was the anticipation of that experience, in which all sinless as He was, the Father would put into His hand the cup our sins had mingled. . . The cross is the place at which the sinless One dies the death of the sinful, the place at which God's condemnation is borne by the Innocent, that for those who commit themselves to Him 'there may be condemnation no more.'" We have the fullest sympathy with Dr. Denney when he here adds, "I cannot read the New Testament in any other sense."

Bearing in mind then Jesus' voluntarily assumed relation to the world's sin, we can understand somewhat, as we cannot otherwise do, the sorrow that weighed upon Him all through life, and which rose to the height of a divine agony on the eve of His crucifixion. What humiliation and pain it must have been to the sinless Jesus to come into contact and close neighbourhood with the sin of our race! Is it any wonder that when the accursed thing was laid upon Him, it wrought Him into the greatest possible anguish of soul? This was the cup which in Gethsemane He held in His hands.

THE DIVINE MYSTERY OF THE AGONY

Is it any wonder that He shrank from drinking it, and that He prayed it might pass from Him?

It is to be noted that the evangelists offer no explanation of the expression "the cup," used in our Lord's Gethsemane prayer. To them it did not seem to need any for those for whom they were writing. Matthew and Mark, however, by speaking of it as "the hour" as well as "the cup," put the matter beyond all reasonable doubt.[1] Our Lord had so often spoken and meditated in regard to His final sufferings and death, that the time of their occurrence did not need to be otherwise indicated than as "the hour," and clearly these made up the cup which it was the Father's will He should drain to the bitter dregs. He knew He had come to be a sacrifice for sin. The great altar was being prepared on which the sacrifice was to be offered up. The fires, however, which were to burn on that altar, and by which He was to be consumed, were to be so awful that He was stirred in His agony to pray that if it were possible He might be spared them.

What sufferings, what woes indeed must have been in His cup! Who can tell what the cross was which His soul endured, of which that of

---

[1] Matt. xxvi. 45 ; Mark xiv. 41.

Calvary was only the outward symbol and expression? We are fallen creatures, but we know what a cross a burning sense of wrongdoing is to bear, and to what depths of anguish through shame and remorse men may be brought. But to a perfectly pure soul such as that of Jesus, what agony the bearing of the world's sin must have meant! If a sense of guilt makes men hang down their heads among their fellowmen in a world where all have sinned, what shame Jesus bearing our sins must have felt in the sight of God and of heaven! If men with their dulled and limited susceptibilities suffer the most poignant distress as they realise their own share of the world's sin, what anguish Jesus must have suffered when the great Gethsemane agony of the world became His own, and became His in a more awful form than ever the world had known it, when "the Lord laid upon Him the iniquity of us all!"[1] And if, even in the view of men, there is guilt such that no punishment at the hands of men is adequate to it, what shall we say of that cross more awful than the mere material one men saw on Calvary which Jesus must have endured, while in God's hands He was being "wounded for our transgressions and bruised for our iniquities!"

---

[1] Isaiah liii. 6.

THE DIVINE MYSTERY OF THE AGONY

One thing more demands our reverent thought before the mystery of Gethsemane, and that is the spirit in which the agony was endured. Here also we see something which lifts Jesus above all other men, and gives Him a matchless preeminence. The more we meditate on what His coming cross involved, and what the anguish of His soul was in prospect of it, we are the more profoundly touched by the sublime willinghood and resignation which He breathes. "Nevertheless not my will, but thine be done." It was His meat and drink, as He Himself has told us, to do His Father's will and to finish His work.[1] We can understand Him doing the will of His Father with gladness when, in accordance with it, He had miracles to perform, divine blessings to spread abroad, and His own perfectly pure and good life to live. We can also understand Him bravely doing it when, with His soul which loathed evil and every kind of wrong, He bore up unflinchingly against the wrongs and the evils with which He was Himself assailed. But Jesus' subjection went far beyond this when He took the cross from His Father's hand, and meekly said as He did so in Gethsemane, "Not what I will but what Thou wilt."[2]

---

[1] John iv. 34.
[2] Mark xiv. 36.

This was bidding welcome to suffering from which nature shrank. It was taking up the load of others' sins, with all their shame and guilt, at which His own spotless soul could not but be filled with horror. It was also submitting to the wrath and the accursed death due to Him who should be the bearer of the world's sin, and enduring all at the hands of a God whose love and fellowship had been life and bliss to Him through eternal ages. Self-subjection reached its divine climax when Jesus accepted the lot of shame and woe which were appointed Him, and went forth in the spirit not only of resignation but of thanksgiving to meet all that justice could decree, or wicked men and the powers of darkness could inflict.

Here we have an example that appeals to us with the most pathetic force. It strikes at the root of our selfishness. It touches us where perhaps we are weakest—that is, in respect of our wills. It tells us of that being done under the most trying circumstances which, under the most favourable, men can with difficulty be induced to do—that is, to give up their will or way even when it can plainly be shown to be evil and ruinous. It tells us also of an infinite love, ready to suffer and die that even wrongdoers against itself might be blessed and saved. And it tells us of an absolutely limitless confidence in God, ready to go forth to meet any storm of evil and suffering at His call, relying on His faithfulness and power, and impelled by an immeasurable love for Him and desire for His glory.

What a mighty uplifting and transforming power lies in this sublime Gethsemane utterance, "Thy will be done"! Even as He uttered the words ere ever the cross was laid upon His shoulders, Jesus had already overcome the sin and woe from which He came to deliver us. All the shame, torture, agony which followed became but the glorious scars of the conflict and the adornments of His triumph as our Redeemer. The cruel blows and insults showered upon Him, the mock purple robes, the crown of thorns, the cross itself became radiant with an eternal glory. That He met them all as they came as the Father's will for Him, and met them with an unmurmuring acquiescence, made Him the most glorious of God's servants, and turned them all into everlasting honours for Himself and everlasting blessings for His people. And so soon as we are brought to say in any trials which have come from God's hand, "Father, Thy will be done," as our Lord did in the garden, we too become in these more than conquerors. Those trials, which otherwise might crush us beneath their weight, become transformed into angels of God, whom we entertain unawares, and who are sent to raise us to honour and blessing with Jesus. What the world wants to make it a new and a redeemed world is just the Gethsemane spirit of Jesus—His sublime resignation, His willing obedience, His perfect trust.

> "Gethsemane! Joy hath not flowers so sweet
> As those which cluster on thine olive slope:
> Beneath the crimson sheen of Jesus' feet
> Springs up the blossom of a deathless hope.
>
> Oh, not as I, but as thou wilt, my Lord!
> I will not put aside Thy cup of pain;
> Sorrow is turned to gladness at Thy word,
> And life's Gethsemane becomes a gain." [1]

---

[1] Brodrick's *Gethsemane* in Baynes' *Sacred Poems*.

THE APPREHENSION IN THE GARDEN.

It might have been supposed that the priests on that Passover night were engrossed in its religious services, and that nothing would be farther from their minds than to stain the memory of so sacred a season by the holding of courts or the shedding of blood. But Annas and Caiaphas were intent upon the plot which was to end the career of the Man of Nazareth. This had come to possess an intense personal interest for them far beyond the formal or official interest they might have in any religious observance. They had said as to their laying hands on Jesus, "Not on the feast day, lest there be an uproar among the people."[1] But it was to be on the feast day. Their own ordinances had prescribed that the court of the Sanhedrim should not be held on the day preceding a holy festival or a Sabbath.[2] But it was in the earliest

---
[1] Mark xiv. 2.
[2] Talmud, Sanhedrin iv. 7.

hours of such a day that that court was to meet, and with frantic haste to send forth the Christ of God with the brand of a malefactor.

Events in God's providence had so brought it about. To the chief priests the traitor came that night fresh from the fellowship of the Upper Room. It was an unexpected joy. They had given a command that if any of the people knew where Jesus was they should show it, that they might take Him.[1] It was creditable to the people that they gave so little heed to the command, and that the betrayer was not to be found among them. It was what no one, friend or foe, could have looked for, that the traitor should come from the ranks of the disciples. The chief priests lost no time in concluding the bargain with him for his services. "They covenanted with him for thirty pieces of silver."[2]

To get a band which might be sufficient for the arrest, and which Judas might lead, was their next care. The temple police were always at their service, those whose duty it was to maintain order in the sacred courts, and it was not long before a considerable body of them was brought together. But it seemed to be doubted whether a band,

---

[1] John xi. 57.
[2] Matt. xxvi. 15.

armed as they were only with clubs or staves, would be sufficient.¹ Jesus was feared. They did not know what force He might put forth in His own defence. He had done so many extraordinary deeds. Besides, there were eleven resolute and deeply-attached disciples with Him. Judas himself had heard them declare that they were ready to die with Him. So the Roman governor was approached, and he was induced to send a strong detachment, armed not with clubs, but with swords, from the Roman garrison at Antonia to help in the capture.²

Thus a great multitude was, in the early hours of the morning, gathered together. Along with those temple guards and Roman soldiers there were chief priests and elders whose hot zeal against Jesus made them so far forget themselves, servants

---

[1] Baring Gould (*Passion of Jesus*, p. 85) thinks it possible but not probable that the captain of the temple guard asked the assistance of Roman soldiers. But how are we to account for the swords with which some of the band were armed? The temple guards carried only clubs or staves, and to secure a more formidable force recourse was had necessarily to the Roman governor (Geikie, *Life and Words of Jesus*, p. 675). Westcott thinks that the priests would not have taken the step of apprehending Jesus without some understanding with Pilate, that Romans were associated with Jews in that act, and that it is likely a whole cohort (600) was engaged (Westcott, *Gospel of St. John*, p. 252).

[2] According to Keim, there would be about 500 soldiers from Antonia, besides servants of the high priest and of the Pharisees (*Jesus of Nazara*, vol. VI., 25). Weiss thinks that a regiment was kept in readiness in case of need, but that only a detachment of it was sent (*Life of Christ*, vol. III., 328).

of the high priest, eager to see their masters' scheme succeed, stragglers abroad in the streets attracted as the band passed along, and many others drawn by curiosity or interest. Anticipating a stout resistance and the possibilities of escape, they were provided not only with swords and staves but with lanterns and torches.[1] Probably by the same route as Jesus and the eleven had taken, some three hours before, through the eastern gate over the Kedron, and then up the slopes of Olivet they went till they reached the garden to which, as Judas knew, Jesus often resorted. Quickly and quietly they hastened on, hoping to come upon Jesus unawares, and to render escape or concealment impossible. They very likely counted on Jesus and His disciples being at this early hour asleep under the shadow of the olive trees. But when His hour was come He was to be found ready.

Agreeably to the plan which had been arranged Judas, when they were approaching the entrance to Gethsemane, put himself at their head. He went some little distance in advance to seek for his Master amid the recesses of the garden. He

---

[1] Hackett (*Illustrations of Scripture*, p. 140) says "They would need lanterns and torches, even on a clear night and under a brilliant moon, because the western side of Olivet abounds in deserted tombs and caves."

was to single Him out and salute Him; then the guards were to rush forward and seize Him. Thus separating himself from the band, he might make it appear as if he were not really one of them. It might seem to the disciples that he had only returned from doing what he had been understood by them to leave the Upper Room to do, and that the coming of the multitude was a matter for which he was not at all responsible.

But Judas was speedily to be undeceived. His Master who knew what was in man, and had read the traitor's heart to himself, if he could only have profited in time by the lesson, was not to be imposed upon. He was in readiness for him and the formidable band he led. He was not taken unawares. Nor did He act at all as the traitor had expected. He showed no trace of agitation or fear. He manifested no desire or design to put forth His miraculous power on His own behalf. He did not attempt to flee. On the contrary, to his utter dismay and remorse, Judas saw Him put Himself into His captors' hands and allow Himself to be led away as a lamb to the slaughter. It was a charge Celsus made that Jesus was taken while trying to hide Himself and to escape in the most disgraceful way.[1] It would

---

[1] Origen. II. 9

seem as if the charge were met by anticipation, when the evangelist John writes that "Judas also, which betrayed Him, knew the place; for Jesus ofttimes resorted thither with His disciples."[1]

Judas' conceptions of his Master must have been low indeed if he thought He would seek safety in flight, appalled by the force come to apprehend Him. He could have learned little from what he had seen of his Master's ministry. Possibly he thought that when it should come to the worst his Master might, by some exercise of His supernatural power, extricate Himself from the toils of His enemies. But Jesus had never been known to work miracles for Himself, though He had wrought many for others.

Judas is indeed an inscrutable mystery. Unquestionably he filled his cup of iniquity to the brim that night when he violated the sanctities of affection and confidence, and with the kiss of love and discipleship acted the traitor's part. "Whomsoever I shall kiss" said he, "that same is He: hold Him fast."[2] Going forward in advance, he found Jesus where he had expected. "Friend," said Jesus to him, "wherefore art thou come?"[3]

---

[1] John xviii. 2
[2] Matt. xxvi. 48. Mark xiv. 44.
[3] Matt. xxvi. 50.

Unabashed with the touching and searching question, he saluted Him with his "Hail Master," and he dared to throw himself upon His neck and to kiss Him.

Never was there a greater outrage upon love, never a more wicked profanation of its most tender and sacred forms of expression. "Betrayest thou the Son of Man with a kiss?"[1] said Jesus, dealing still more closely with the traitor's soul, every word so expressive and so fitted to touch the conscience of Judas if anything could have done it. The act received its fitting name, and was put in all its blackness before the doer. What aggravated it immeasurably was that it was being done against the Son of Man, and done by the sacred symbol of friendship and trust. It would have been one of the foulest crimes to use any man in that way, but so to use the Son of Man and the Master he had known so long, could one possibly exaggerate such guiltiness?

There is reason to believe that Jesus felt this treason more than almost anything else He suffered at the hands of men. The injustice and wrong done Him at the bar of Caiaphas or Pilate were by men known to be either hostile or indifferent. The buffeting and scourging and indignities He endured

---

[1] Luke xxii. 48.

later on came from hirelings, Jewish and Roman, of whom little else was to be expected. But this came from a professed disciple. Even the humiliating weight of the cross He had to carry, or the physical pain of it He had to bear, could hardly of themselves touch Him so keenly as this wounding in the house of His friends. The Psalmist's words He could make His own, "It was not an enemy that reproached me, then I could have borne it . . . . . but it was thou, a man mine equal, my guide, and mine acquaintance."[1]

Shaking Himself free from the embrace of the traitor Jesus went calmly to meet the band who were now rushing forward to seize Him. The action so unexpected, and so unlike all that officers of the law were accustomed to, at once disconcerted them. They had expected to surprise Him in His hiding place. They were themselves surprised. "Whom seek ye?" This simple question, followed up by the avowal that He was the Jesus of Nazareth they were seeking for, startled them. Nay it seemed as if the words were the stroke of some mysterious divine power, for instantly they reeled and fell backward to the ground. There may have been something in Christ's aspect and in the tone of

---

[1] Psalm lv. 12.

voice in which He spake. There were times when even bad men were awed by His presence. The unhallowed traffickers in the temple courts fled in terror before Him as He moved about with His whip of small cords. While they were in the very act of making Him a prisoner there was a mysterious something to remind the armed band how infinitely little against Him all their arms and their numbers availed, how they were much more in His hands than He could be in theirs, and how entirely voluntary His surrender of Himself was.[1] When they rose from the ground and again advanced to Him, it was the same question as before that He put to them, "Whom seek ye?"[2] adding as He looked round on His loved disciples, " If therefore ye seek me, let these go their way."[3] His disciples' safety concerned Him. He would spare them every trial He could. In this hour of danger He would shield them. Like the Good Shepherd He was, He would interpose His own person between His flock and the peril that

---

[1] Ellicott (*Life of our Lord*, p. 327) holds that there was a miraculous power attending the " I am he." Keim's naturalistic principles fail him here. He admits the falling down of the band to be entirely involuntary and purely physical, but he cannot account for it otherwise than as connected with the mysterious personal influence of Jesus (*Jesus of Nazara*, vol. VI., 34.).

[2] John xviii. 7.

[3] John xviii. 8.

threatened them. Upon Himself He would concentrate the hostile attentions of the band, and draw them off as much as He could from those He so deeply loved.

All the more He sought their safety that He knew how ill prepared they were for the crisis. They had not the strength which comes from watching and prayer. They could not watch with Him in His agony, nor understand His coming cross. So they were to be spared while He went to suffer and die. The cruel and violent hands that should be laid upon Him should not be laid upon them. Alone indeed He should go forth to take up and bear His cross. Not a single disciple He had should share in its shame and suffering.

What an honour to humanity it would have been had Peter and John been seized at the same time with their Master, and had Jesus died on Calvary between two disciples instead of dying between two thieves! But humanity was not to have that honour. It is humbling to think that it did not possess virtue enough, as appears from the history, to deserve it. Not even a disciple could be found to travel the way to Calvary with Jesus. He had to "tread the wine press alone." And such was His boundless consideration, generosity and love, that He willed that it should be so, and that the shield should be thrown over all others so that none but Himself should suffer while He wrought out the world's salvation.

The Master's words, and His calm and dignified demeanour before His captors, appear to have had the effect of rallying the disciples for a little. Dismayed and filled with fear on the first appearance of the great multitude in the garden, they seemed now to gather some courage by the way in which He was meeting them. Their impulse now was to use what weapons they had, and fight in their own and their Master's defence. "Lord, shall we smite with the sword?"[1] said Peter, ever foremost to speak or to act. Without waiting for a reply, he drew his sword, and with it smote off the ear of one in the band. His name was Malchus. Most probably he had been showing himself particularly forward and offensive in his conduct on the occasion. He was a servant of the high priest; and we may well believe that he shared his master's hatred of the Nazarene, and that among those engaged in the arrest he was well to the front.[2]

That sword-stroke was a blundering one. Peter

---

[1] Luke xxii. 49.
[2] Ewald makes Malchus leader of the Jewish section of the band (*Life of Christ*, p. 310).

was not accustomed to arms, and he was too excited. The stroke might have had disastrous consequences. Malchus all but lost his life, and Peter had endangered his own and the lives of his fellow disciples. They had come forth prepared, and probably expecting to capture the whole band of them as well as their Master. Could they possibly stop short of that now when one of them had drawn the sword with such a result? The first blood between them had been spilt, and a disciple had shed it. Was it not to be avenged? If it should be, was not more and more blood likely to flow?

But the Master was equal to the emergency. Promptly He threw His shield over His followers, and with infinite tact, tenderness and power He healed the wound of strife that had been opened. "Suffer ye thus far,"[1] said He to the smitten Malchus as He touched his bleeding ear and healed him.[2]

It was His last miracle, and it was done to an

---

[1] Luke xxii. 51.

[2] In Duccio's picture of the arrest, Jesus is seen in the centre, Judas is beside Him in the act of kissing, the armed men are behind Him. Peter has just struck off the ear of Malchus; his fellow disciples to the right of their Master are in the act of flight, while He Himself is looking in the direction of Malchus, and has His hand raised in benediction and healing (Jameson's *History of our Lord in Works of Art*, vol. II. p. 39).

enemy. It brought healing to one who came to bring to Himself death. It came of the love that was going to die for sinners, and that even amidst the agonies of Calvary moved Him to pray for His murderers. And it revealed, in the very hour when He was giving Himself up as a prisoner into their hands, that He was possessed of a power nothing less than divine. The power that could heal a foe could also destroy him. There was not a man of them indeed who did not owe his life to the infinite forbearance of Him whom they were about to bind with shameful cords.

Jesus, after doing this wonderful healing act, had a word, first for His rash and impulsive disciple, and then for the multitude. "Put up thy sword," said He to Peter, "into his place: for all they that take the sword shall perish with the sword. Thinkest thou that I cannot now pray to my Father, and He shall presently give me more than twelve legions of angels? But how then shall the Scriptures be fulfilled, that thus it must be?"[1] "The cup which my Father hath given me, to drink shall I not drink it?"[2] Jesus at once and for ever disclaims the use of all such weapons in

---

[1] Matt. xxvi. 52, 53.
[2] John xviii. 11.

His cause.[1] *Ecclesia non sitit sanguinem* (the Church does not thirst for blood). But how often has the secular arm been invoked to promote a perverted Christianity? The sword in the service of the Church has had a most melancholy and tragic history. Christ's true people have suffered more from the persecutions of those who have called themselves Christians than they have done from His open foes. Popes and Romanists have added far more to the martyr's roll of His church than pagan Roman emperors such as Nero or Diocletian. Christ trusts for the spread and triumph of His cause and kingdom only to the power inherent in His truth, and to the Spirit of God, commanding freely with His truth the hearts and lives of men.

> " O for a two-edged sword, my God,
>   That I may swiftly slay
> Each foe of Thine—that I may speed
>   Thy universal sway ! "
> " Put up thy sword within its sheath :
> My gift is life ; would'st thou deal death ? "
>
> " Oh for the fire from heaven, my God,
>   That it may fiercely burn
> All those who following not with me
>   To other masters turn."
> With scorching flame would'st Thou reprove,
> But I must win by fire of love.

---

[1] Renan believes that Jesus thought at first to repel force by force, but that He abandoned the plan when He saw the visible fear of His disciples (*Life of Jesus*, p. 403).

> "My son, art thou above thy Lord,
>   A greater one than He?
> When called I for fire or sword?
>   Thou hast not learnt of me.
> Make truth thy sword, and love thy flame,
> Then battle in thy Master's name." [2]

Peter did not share the vision which his Master had. He did not see the legions that were at His command. He saw only His defenceless state, and as he recalled what He had been, and what He had done in the world, Peter would have drawn a hundred swords for Him if he had had them. The cross should be far from his Lord. That was still his mood. He did not yet understand the Scriptures that it behoved Christ to suffer, and then to enter into His glory. But the Master saw all clearly—the divine plan He had come to fulfil, the cross on which He was to be crowned as Redeemer, the future of suffering and struggle for His cause, and the legions also that would be given for His support, and for protection and victory to His cause in the end. And He gave Himself up in the fullest consciousness of His divine freedom and power.

Observing some of the chief priests and elders among the multitude, Jesus addressed some words to them well-fitted to stir their consciences. "Are

---

[2] W. Chatterton Dix: *The Master and the Disciple.*

ye come out as against a thief, with swords and staves, for to take me? I was daily with you in the temple teaching, and ye took me not. But the Scriptures must be fulfilled."[1] It was not the manner of thieves and evildoers to move about openly in the world as Jesus had done. He had lived and wrought in the broad daylight. He had taught and healed in public. He had been a familiar figure in the temple courts. Trusting solely to the armour of truth and righteousness which He constantly wore, He had faced the multitude day after day. And these men knew well how He had spoken, so as again and again to rebuke them, and put them to shame. But they had laid no hands upon Him. Their thoughts and purposed deeds being evil, they had not dared to carry them out openly and in the day. What need had they for clubs and swords as if it were some notorious bandit they had come to seize? Why should they select the midnight hour when they had Him within reach times without number in the full light of day? And why should they invade His private retreat to come upon Him unarmed, and, if possible, asleep, when they had the opportunity of seizing Him at any time as He was teaching the people?

---

[1] Mark xiv. 48; Matt. xxvi. 55; Luke xxii. 52, 53.

But it was their hour and the power of darkness—the deed, the time, and the manner of it all corresponded. It was *their* hour—the time appointed for their doing what God had determined beforehand they should do. And it was *His* hour to put Himself without a murmur into their hands. How ridiculous all their preparations, their swords and staves, their blazing torches and lanterns, their great numbers! He freely gave Himself up, offering His hands to be bound, and entering willingly upon the way to Calvary.

They bound Him with the cords they had brought for the purpose.[1] It was a needless precaution for His captors in the circumstances. It was a humiliation which He might have been spared. But He was dealt with, notwithstanding all that He had said and done, as if He had been the leader of some robber band, caught after a desperate struggle. The fact is, they were afraid. Never man had acted in the circumstances like this Man, and yet they could not believe that He would not resist. Judas even, who had known Him so long yet had so fatally failed to understand Him, evidently expected that they would have the greatest difficulty in securing Him. "Take Him," said he in

---

[1] John xviii. 12.

his abject terror—the dread and remorse now beginning to agitate him which issued so tragically—" take Him and lead Him away safely."[1] Safely (ἀσφαλῶς—well secured), for, as Judas would whisper in their ears, they had no ordinary prisoner to deal with. There was no telling what He might do. So the cords were at once brought, and fastened with cruel care upon His hands; and the whole band gathered around Him, every man making sure that he had his club or his sword in readiness—all of them very resolute and greatly excited.

Behold Him now in their midst bound, and yet the freest among them; having power to lay down His life and power to take it up again; shamefully treated, and yet revealing His divine patience and glory through all His speech and demeanour; calm and resigned, and ready to go onward to complete His work as a Saviour, while all around are excited, and His disciples are panic-stricken.

The sight of their Master in the hands of His foes, fettered, apparently helpless, appears to have been too much for the disciples. It took all the courage out of them, and made them fear for themselves. It seemed as if in that awful moment all their bright hopes had been blotted out, and

---

[1] Mark xiv. 44.

all their past enthusiasm had perished. "They all forsook Him and fled."[1] Even Peter who, a little before was so valiant with his sword, caught the contagion of panic, and sought safety in flight.

But they might have done worse. Their conduct was unheroic enough. It was sadly out of keeping with their brave professions a few hours before when, around the supper table, and on the way to the garden they had declared that though they should die with Him they would not deny or forsake Him. But it might have been more shameful than it was. It was base of them to desert their Master in His hour of trial; but they did not make themselves baser still like Judas by betraying Him and selling Him to His foes. It was to their shame that not one of them offered to stand by Him, or to speak for Him when He should appear before His judges; but not one of them was willing to be found among His foes, or to be associated with them in inflicting the slightest wrong or pain upon his Master. Even Peter's denial, heinous as it was, came far short of the guilt of deliberately assisting to bring upon Him His sufferings and death. It was inexcusable enough that he should declare that he did not know Jesus, and that he

---

[1] Matt. xxvi. 56. Mark xiv. 50.

was not one of His disciples; but he would have descended to a lower depth of infamy had he used his lips to defame and fling taunts at his Master, or had he joined with those who made cruel sport of Him. Doubtless it was the pitying look of Jesus, bringing immediate repentance, that saved him from that depth.

Two at least of the eleven did recover so far from their alarm and fit of cowardice as to follow the company of Jesus' captors at some distance. Peter was one of them, the other was John.[1] For the moment, like the rest, he and John rushed away for hiding into the dark recesses of the garden. But they gathered courage after a little to come forth, and to venture into the city in the rear of the multitude to see what should become of their beloved Master. They could not keep away from Him; and their heartfelt attachment was to survive the crisis, and to save them in the end. John knew some people in the high priest's palace,[2] and so he obtained admission into the place, and he used his influence to get the gate opened for Peter as well. The situation was a perilous one for them both. How Peter comported himself in it, and fell before the trial which awaited him, we shall afterwards see.

---

[1] Luke xxii. 54.   [2] John xviii. 15.

JESUS BEFORE HIS ECCLESIASTICAL JUDGES.

Jesus was now a captive in the hands of His foes. Bound with cords as if He had been a prisoner secured only after a stout resistance, they led Him away. The arrest had not occupied them long. Though they knew it not, when His hour was come He was ready to meet it, and He who could have summoned more than twelve legions of angels for His protection suffered Himself to be led away by probably less than the twelfth of a legion of men. Soon the garden was left to its wonted quiet and solitude, and the motley, excited, clamorous band were on their way back to the city.

In the midst of this band Jesus walked, with not a friend or follower bearing Him company. His disciples had sought safety in flight. Two of them, as we have seen, Peter and John, apparently more daring than the rest, kept following the multitude at some safe distance. They became part, afterwards, of the company round the fire in the court of the high priest's house. We read, also, of a certain young man following, supposed to be Mark. The incident is recorded only in Mark's Gospel, and the probability is that the unnamed youth was no other than the evangelist himself.[1] But, whoever he was, his courage soon gave out. When they attempted to lay hands upon him he fled, leaving the linen garment with which he had hastily clothed himself in their hands. "I looked and there was none to help, and I wondered that there was none to uphold."[2]

To the house of Annas they conducted their prisoner. Annas was an old man of seventy, but the most powerful still in ecclesiastical circles in Jerusalem. Twenty years before he had been compelled to lay down the priesthood, but though not nominally, yet really the office seemed still to be in his hands. Five of his sons had occupied it, and Caiaphas, who at this time held it, was his son-in-law. Then he was wealthy, and all

---

[1] So Weiss (*Life of Christ*, vol. III., p. 332) who is also of opinion that he had just come from his father's house, and that the Supper had taken place there. Others suppose him to be Lazarus, others John.

[2] Isaiah lxiii. 5.

the Sadducean party looked upon him as their leader.[1]

It is remarkable that that party is seen taking the lead in bringing about the condemnation and death of Jesus. Archbishop Whately thought that if only atheism had the power it would be quite as intolerant and persecuting as Romanism.[2] It is, indeed, hard to say whether Christ and His cause have more to fear from the Sadducee or from the Pharisee. There is not much to choose between the Sadducean philosopher of the French Revolution type, who could be terribly passionate and could shed blood freely for the triumph of his faction and his theories, and the bigoted inquisitor who looked upon the tortures and deaths he inflicted as so much pious service to God and the faith. It would be difficult to say which is more to be dreaded.[3]

It was to the Sadducean Annas, at any rate, that the band of conspirators against Jesus at this time looked as their inspiring head. His was the evil genius that formed the plot, and saw to the means for its execution. He probably was the chief party

---

[1] Josephus, *Antiq.*, XVIII., III., 6.
[2] Whately's *Errors of Romanism*, ch. v. 9.
[3] Josephus (*Antiq* XX. IX. I.) says that "the Sadducees were very rigid in judging offenders above all the rest of the Jews."

to the bargain with the traitor. The band that made the arrest in Gethsemane had been gathered together by his direction. Doubtless he was eagerly awaiting their return. Sleep had not concerned him that night. It was the Passover night. He was fresh from its holy celebration. But the feast had been a mere formality with him. It had far less interest for him than the success of the infamous plot in which he was engaged. To his malicious joy, in the early hours of the morning, the Nazarene was at last delivered into his hands. It is said that Annas and the chief priests had a personal grudge against Jesus. That unholy traffic in the temple, to which Jesus with His whip of small cords had summarily put an end, had been, it appears, a special source of revenue to them. Whatever their wrath otherwise against Him, this increased it, and they resolved to terminate His career.[1]

The examination of Jesus before Annas seems to have been of a general and informal character. It was probably not otherwise meant than to take up the time during those early hours of the morning until the Sanhedrim could be brought together. While it was going on, messengers would

---

[1] Edersheim, *Life and Times of Jesus the Messiah*, vol. II. 547.

JESUS BEFORE HIS ECCLESIASTICAL JUDGES

be swiftly traversing the streets of the city to arouse the members from their slumbers, and to summon them at once to a meeting. The purpose of Annas and his party was evidently that Jesus should that morning go forth from their hands, and appear before the multitude with the brand of the condemned criminal upon Him, as one unanimously found guilty by the highest Jewish tribunal. The effect of this, it was expected, would be to withdraw from Jesus any lingering popular feeling there might be in His favour, and to secure the necessary amount of popular prejudice and hostility for accomplishing His final condemnation and death. They were successful beyond their highest hopes.

This examination before Annas being over, the procession was re-formed, and Jesus was led away still bound, to the palace of Caiaphas.[1] There the Sanhedrim was to meet.[2] Entering through a gateway, the crowd soon filled the court within. Through the court the guards conducted their Prisoner up some marble stairs to a large hall above. This hall occupied one side of the court,

---

[1] John xviii. 24.
[2] The usual place of meeting for the Sanhedrim was the Gazith, a hall on the south side of the temple (Friedlieb's *Archäologie*, p. 10). Josephus, however, tells us it was not uncommon in the days of Annas and his party for courts to be held in the high priest's own house.

from which it was separated by a row of pillars. There Jesus had to wait in the custody of His rude guards till the members of the Sanhedrim had had time to assemble. It was while He waited, and also while the trial was going on, that those scenes occurred around the fire in the court and at the gate, when Peter thrice denied his Lord. Lighted up in the interior as it must have been, what took place in that hall above could easily be seen by those outside. Peter could not help casting many an anxious and deeply interested glance at the Prisoner there, so that the bystanders were soon led to question him whether he was not one of this Man's disciples.

At length the council hall became filled with the Jewish fathers.[1] According to the Talmud, a full Sanhedrim of seventy-one was required for so important a trial as that of a false prophet or a high priest.[4] This makes the illegality and injustice of the packed court in the case of Jesus only the more glaring. The seventy, as they are called, would not all be present. It is not likely that members such as Nicodemus, who were in favour

---

[1] A couple of hours are supposed to have elapsed between the two trials—that is, between the first hurried meeting in the morning, and the more formal one after dawn. (Gould's *Trials of Jesus*, p. 17.)

[2] Sanh. I. 5.

of Jesus, would be disturbed in their slumbers that morning and summoned to the meeting by servants of the high priest. The fact is, it was not a regular or legal meeting, but an extemporised one, such as many a revolutionary tribunal has been, when the head of it has had only those around him acting as judges who were of the same faction with himself.[1] It was an instance of what, according to Josephus, was common enough in the later days of Jerusalem, when, to quote his own words, "fictitious tribunals and judicatures were set up, and men called together to act as judges, though they had no real authority, when it was desired to secure the death of an opponent."[2]

We are not left without some knowledge of the men composing this extemporised council who took it upon them to try and condemn Jesus, the Son of God. Annas has already been noticed, a man old in priestly craft and intrigue, and Caiaphas, his son-in-law, of whom as a heartless and unprincipled opportunist we have a sufficient indication in those cold-blooded words of his which the evangelists have

---

[1] About a third—that is, twenty-three members—formed a quorum of the Sanhedrim (Talmud, *Sanhedrin*, I., 6). Jost says it was only the Caiaphas faction of the Sanhedrim which formed the court which condemned Jesus (*Geschichte des Judenthums*, p. 408).

[2] Josephus, *B.I.*, IV., V., 4.

preserved for us, "It is expedient for us that one man should die for the people."[1] There were those five sons of Annas also referred to, so like their father and so Sadducean that some have thought that they were hinted at in the parable of Dives and his five brothers.[2] There was one Alexander, and one John, who stood next in dignity to Caiaphas and Annas, of the latter of whom we read in the Acts of the Apostles.[3] There were the two brothers, Joazer and Eleazar, whose sister Mariamne, the greatest beauty of her time, so fascinated King Herod that he married her. There was also Simon the Quarrelsome, as he was called, who put to death James, the brother of John; and Ishmael Ben Phabi, the handsomest and best dressed man of his time; and Issachar of Kefar Barkai, who must have his silk gloves on when he was offering up sacrifices; and Johanan Ben Nebedai, who did what he could to make a martyr of the Apostle Paul.[4] Such are the men known to have been the leading spirits of the Sadducean party of that time. Their record, as appears from Jewish history, is disreputable

---

[1] John xi. 50.
[2] Geikie, *Life and Words*, p. 671.
[3] Acts iv. 6.
[4] Acts xxiii. 2.

JESUS BEFORE HIS ECCLESIASTICAL JUDGES

enough. The rest of the council were doubtless like unto them.[1]

In their procedure as a court, as in their religious observances, those chief priests and elders were zealous for forms, while otherwise they were most unscrupulous.[2] Looking in upon that gathering of judges in Caiaphas' palace, one might have seen at the outset that it had at least all the appearance, while it claimed the character, of a meeting of the Sanhedrim. Here at one end of the hall would be the members of the council, sitting on cushions, cross-legged and unsandalled, in a semi-circle. Caiaphas, the presiding judge, would be in the centre of this half circle, with Annas and other

---

[1] Geikie, p. 672.

Dante, as might be expected, has a special place for Caiaphas and his friends in his *Inferno*. Caiaphas is the " one crucified with three stakes on the ground," and thus he is described :—

> The transfixed one whom thou seest,
> Counselled the Pharisees that it was meet
> To put one man to torture for the people.
> Crosswise and naked is he on the path,
> As thou perceivest ; and he needs must feel
> Whoever passes, first how much he weighs ;
> And in like mode his father-in-law is punished
> Within this moat, and the others of the council,
> Which for the Jews was a malignant seed.
> —*Inferno*, Canto XXIII.

[2] The Sanhedrim had an upper and a lower house. The former consisted of the high priests, or those who had filled that office, and the heads of the twenty-four priestly colleges, while the elders and rabbis of note formed the latter. In this instance the two houses were united. Hence the expression which occurs so often, " the chief priests and elders." (Gould's *Passion of Jesus*, p. 13.)

notables to the right and left of him, according to office or age. In front of His judges, facing the president, would be the Prisoner, with the guards on one side of Him, and a place for the witnesses that were to be heard on the other. On either side of the semi-circle of grave fathers would be a scribe taking a record of the trial.[1]

But if the old and traditional formalities of this Jewish court were religiously observed, law and justice were otherwise flagrantly violated. To begin with, the Prisoner stood guarded and fettered as if He were a dangerous and already a convicted criminal.[2] The law required that persons accused should be treated with the utmost humanity.[3] It was with barbarity Jesus was treated. The judges were enjoined to favour acquittal, and only to give their voices for condemnation when the evidence compelled them.[4] Jesus' judges came together with

---

[1] The arrangements of the court are described in the Talmud, *Sanhedrin*, ch. iv. 9. The principal authorities to consult as to the Talmud are—Ugolinus, who devotes to it fully a third of his thirty huge volumes, in which the Hebrew text (unpointed) and a Latin translation are placed in parallel columns; Schwab, who has translated into French both the Jerusalem and the Babylonian portions of it; and Wünsche, who has given a German translation of the Babylonian only. It is singular that we should have as yet no corresponding translation of the Talmud into English. We have only brief extracts or selections. The information about the Sanhedrim is in Ugolinus, vol. XXV.; in Schwab, vol. X.; and in Wünsche, vol. III.

[2] Geikie, *Life and Words of Christ*, p. 680. John xviii. 24.

[3] Lightfoot, *Horæ Heb.* in Ev. Johannis, p. 217.

[4] *Sanhedrin*, V. 5.

a foregone conclusion that He was worthy of death, and used the basest means and the most indecent haste to reach it. Any who were known enemies to an accused person were thereby disqualified from acting as judges, or even as witnesses in his case.[1] There does not appear to have been even one in that court who, under that rule, should not have been obliged to vacate his seat. A case involving capital punishment could not be judged on the eve of the Sabbath or on the eve of a feast day.[2] Jesus was tried and found worthy of death on the great feast day itself—the feast of the Passover. A midnight meeting of the Sanhedrim was unlawful.[3] Its members on this occasion knew this. Hence their second meeting after daybreak at which they but confirmed, and very hastily, what had already been done. It was an express rule that the accused should, be allowed to employ one to plead his cause, and that his judges should not also be witnesses or accusers.[4] Jesus was permitted no advocate, and none was forthcoming; and as for the accusations, they were manufactured and hurled at Him by His judges, Caiaphas, the president, being the chief

---

[1] *Sanhedrin*, III. 8.
[2] *Sanhedrin*, IV. 7.
[3] *Sanhedrin*, IV. 1.
[4] *Sanhedrin*, III. 6.

offender, while the witnesses were all on one side, no room or opportunity being given for witnesses for the defence. And still further to crown the iniquities and illegalities of this trial, another wise and humane arrangement was flagrantly set aside— it was this, that in any serious case involving the punishment of death the sentence should not be pronounced on the same day as the trial, and that the execution of it should not take place till at the earliest a day after the sentence.[1] But the sun was not more than three hours in the sky that same morning when Jesus was seen hanging on the cross of Calvary.[2] So keenly, we are told, is the judicial murder, as it may truly be called, of Jesus Christ by the Jewish nation felt by its representatives in modern times that they have invented the view that there was some law existing, according to which, if any one set up as a false Messiah, he might be tried and condemned forthwith on the same day, or even in the night. But Moses had given them no such laws for dealing with a pretender to Messiahship, and the Old Testament prophets had not anticipated such a case. They had foretold, however, pretty plainly that the

---

[1] *Sanhedrin*, IV. 6.
[2] The trial and its illegalities are fully treated by **Keim**, *Jesus of Nazara*, vol. VI., pp. 41-45 also 63, 64.

true Messiah would have just such sufferings as they were about to meteced out to Jesus.

Jost, a Jewish and non-Christian writer of our day, admits that the rabbis of later times have been able to allege nothing against Jesus but that He sought to turn away the people from the religion of their fathers. He goes so far as to say that Jesus' death was a private murder on the part of Caiaphas and his Sadducean party, and that Gamaliel and others of the most important members of the Sanhedrim were not at the council which condemned Him. He declares with warmth that it was not the Jewish people who crucified Jesus, but only a number of arrogant and determined foes, and that the people and the rabbis gave little heed to the event till its consequences came to be of the gravest character for Israel.[1]

Speaking of the condemnation of Socrates, and what he describes "as the event which took place on Calvary rather more than eighteen hundred years ago," the late John Stuart Mill expresses the opinion that the feelings with which mankind now regard these lamentable transactions, especially the latter of the two, render them extremely unjust in their judgment of the unhappy actors. "These,"

---

[1] Jost, *Geschichte des Judenthums*, p. 408.

he adds," were to all appearance not bad men, not worse than men commonly are, but rather the contrary, men who possessed in a full, or somewhat more than a full measure the religious, moral and patriotic feelings of their time and people: the very kind of men who in all times, our own included, have every chance of passing through life blameless and respected."[1] It is enough to say that the judgment of the Christian world which has uniformly and in all ages been different is only too well sustained, and that it has its ample justification in the simple unvarnished account of the trial which the evangelists have given us.

At the very outset it could be seen that justice was not to be hoped for, and that the Prisoner's condemnation had already been determined upon. It was attempted to entrap Him into self-accusation. Usually, a prisoner is told what he is charged with, and he is allowed to prepare some defence and engage some one to plead his cause. But Jesus was invited to accuse and bear witness against Himself. The high priest asked Him about His disciples and His doctrine. Jesus answered him: "I spake openly to the world; I ever taught in the synagogue, and in the temple whither the Jews

---

[1] Mill *On Liberty*, ch. II., p. 14.

always resort, and in secret have I said nothing. Why askest thou me? Ask them which heard me, what I said unto them; behold, they know what I said." If charges were to be brought against Him for anything He had said or done—all had been in public as they well knew—it was only reasonable and dutiful on their part that they should produce their witnesses from the multitude who had heard and seen Him. We are reminded of the noble words, so like those of Jesus here, used by Socrates when he stood also before his accusers and judges: "I have always spoken openly. Let them say if I have taught anything evil instead of good. I know that futurity will bear witness that I did wrong to no man, made no man the worse, but ever laboured to make my friends better."[1]

But we read that when Jesus had thus spoken, one of the officers who stood by struck Him with the palm of his hand saying, "Answerest thou the high priest so?"[2] It was the first of many blows which were to fall upon Jesus. It showed the spirit of the court. It passed unrebuked, most probably causing only a gleam of wicked satisfaction to the assembled fathers, and preparing the guards

---

[1] Xenophon, *Memor.* IV., 8, 10.
[2] John xviii. 22

for the brutal sport in which they so freely indulged so soon as the trial was over.

For such shameful acts of indignity as the chief priests and elders permitted without rebuke to be done in their presence to Jesus their own law, which they were there to administer, required the heaviest fines to be exacted.[1] But the prophet's words were verified, "He was despised, and we esteemed Him not."[2]

The reply of Jesus to that disgraceful blow was fitted, if anything could have done it, to recall the court to a sense of its duty before God and man, and of the wrong and outrage to which it was making itself a party. It was altogether worthy of His meekness and wisdom. "If I have spoken evil, bear witness of the evil; but if well, why smitest thou me?"[3] Until they had established their charges, and by evidence that might reasonably be received, it was only decent that they should withhold their blows and their penalties. But neither the offending officer nor the court ventured upon a reply. Witnesses were now, however, called for. They were forthcoming even at that early hour of the morning. Jerusalem had been searched

---

[1] Gould's *Trials of Jesus*. p. 22.
[2] Isaiah liii. 3.
[3] John xviii. 23.

for those whose evidence might be helpful to secure the ends of the priests. One by one they were brought in, but no two of them could be got to agree. It seemed as if the case were to break down. In the crowd in the palace-yard below, could not some be found ready to give the testimony needful? Some of the fathers went out to find them.[1]

At length two were brought in who declared they had heard Him say, "I am able to destroy this temple of God, and to build it in three days."[2] These were not quite the words He had spoken, and a meaning was put upon them which they were never intended to bear. He had said, "Destroy this temple," meaning the temple of His body, "and in three days I will raise it up."[3] This saying, which was meant as a prophecy of His death and resurrection, was twisted into a sacrilegious attack upon the temple. We can understand how it would be regarded by men to whom the temple and its outward formalities were nearly all the religion they had or knew. It was one of the popular expectations with regard to the Messiah that when He came He should erect a

---

[1] Matt. xxvi. 59, 60.
[2] Matt. xxvi. 64.
[3] John ii. 19.

more glorious temple than that of Herod or of Solomon, and there was an ancient Rabbinical tradition to the same effect.[1]

While these witnesses played their part in this solemn mockery, Jesus remained silent. The accusations answered each other. It needed no word of His to bring out how hollow and false they were. "As a sheep before her shearers is dumb, so He opened not His mouth."[2] His silence is an example and fruitful lesson for ourselves. It rebuked error and wrong more than speech could have done. Caiaphas and the assembled fathers found it more than they could bear. The high priest rose from his seat in a passion and exclaimed, "Answerest Thou nothing? What is it which these witness against Thee?"[3] He pretended to be terribly impressed with the evidence that had been led. The fact, however, was, that he saw the necessity of interposing with what simulated gravity and indignation he could command, to prevent the case from utterly breaking down.

Jesus held His peace. The kind of witnessing to which the high priest had been listening was

---

[1] *Sanhedrin*, I. 5; *Mishna*, VIII. 2.
[2] Isaiah liii. 7.
[3] Matt. xxvi. 62; Mark xiv. 60. The scene here is well described in Keim (*Jesus of Nazara*, vol. VI., 328).

JESUS BEFORE HIS ECCLESIASTICAL JUDGES

a sufficient answer to his question. He did not need to be told what evidence they had been giving against Jesus. But he despaired of founding upon anything that had fallen from their lips a charge of guilt. So, as a last resource, he sprang to his feet again in feigned indignation. "I adjure Thee by the living God," said he, "that Thou tell us whether Thou be the Christ, the Son of God."[1]

Then He who stood silent, while false and hireling witnesses were refuting and contradicting one another, spoke out calmly and fearlessly when the claims of truth demanded it. Had He been a mere man He could not have resisted the temptation to speak and to exult over the utter failure of the witnesses against Him. Had He been merely a pretender to divine honours He would have been silent when the avowal of His claims to them could not but be at the peril of His life.[2] At this supreme moment all eyes were on Him, all ears were intent for His answer. And the answer came without the slightest ring of dubiety or

---

[1] Matt. xxvi. 63.
[2] Renan (*Life of Jesus*, p. 273) attaches so much importance to this that he cannot believe but that Jesus was silent to Caiaphas' question here. Strauss however refrains from attacking the truth of the account given by the evangelists here, and is willing to admit it. (Strauss, *New Life of Jesus*, p. 391.)

hesitancy about it—an answer meant not for the Sanhedrim merely, but for the great audience chamber of the universe and the ages, "Thou hast said, I am the Christ, the Son of God. Hereafter shall ye see the Son of Man sitting on the right hand of power, and coming in the clouds of heaven."[1]

Thus Jesus dared to tell that court that He was the Messiah of whom the law and the prophets had spoken, and that the day should come when He should be His judges' Judge. Caiaphas and those around Him were not slow in apprehending His meaning. It gave them a malicious joy that Jesus should so deliver Himself into their hands. They had otherwise failed to find anything worthy of death in Him. Their witnesses had disagreed, and their charges had not been sustained. But the Prisoner to their amazement and delight had opened His lips against Himself. "He hath spoken blasphemy," exclaimed the high priest. The whole court caught up the words, and one repeated them to another with ever increasing vehemence.

As He spoke the words, Caiaphas seizing His fine linen robes with both hands, rent them in twain[2]

---
[1] Matt. xxvi. 64; Mark xiv. 62; Luke xxii. 67-71.
[2] The high priest tore his garments from bottom to top—the ordinary priests from top to bottom. To mark the sin as unpardonable the rent garments must never be sewn again. Maimonides, I. 1. See also *Sanhedrin*, VII. 10.

—a theatrical way of expressing his feigned horror of the supposed blasphemy, and thereby of rousing abhorrence and creating prejudice against the Accused. " What further need have we of witnesses ? Behold now ye have heard His blasphemy. What think ye ? " The response was as he expected. They answered and said, " He is guilty of death."[1] An incidental proof we have here, not to be overlooked, of the accuracy of the evangelists. In trials for minor offences the president or the oldest of the judges was called upon, according to the law, to give his opinion first : in capital cases, however, the ordinary members of the court were first asked what their judgment was, and when all others had spoken the presiding judge summed up and pronounced the final decision of the court.[2]

Thus Jesus on His claim to be divine was ultimately condemned. Undoubtedly He made the claim, and He made it in circumstances which put the sincerity of His conviction in the matter beyond all doubt. It could not be refuted by clamour and torture and the cross. These have served rather to establish it. We can ask no better proof of it than His conduct before His judges, and the manner in which He endured His cross. And those who

---

[1] Matt. xxvi. 65, 66. Mark xiv. 64.
[2] Schwab's *Talmud*, vol. x. 262.

realise that they owe to His sufferings their salvation, must ever feel that there is no place short of the highest that will do for Him, and that no love, no devotion, no honours are too great to be lavished upon Him. He is God, and He cannot have a rival or a superior.

This midnight council now broke up. True, its proceedings were all irregular and illegal, but it was a successful rehearsal of the play which was to be finished when the council should meet again after daybreak. The end had been gained. The condemnation of Jesus had been secured. From the fathers' point of view, Caiaphas had done splendidly, and that last stroke of his had been a magnificent one. It had entrapped the Prisoner, as they thought, into using words which rendered all further accusing and witnessing against Him needless. They could now retire to rest, and snatch an hour or two's sleep before their next formal meeting.

They left Jesus with His guards. It is not difficult to understand the scene that followed. Jesus, amid a shower of blows and insulting outcries, was brought down from the council hall to the palace-yard below. There, and on the way thither, the sport was renewed. The officer who had struck one blow would doubtless feel that his opportunity had come for many more. But the smiting was not all. One grieves for our poor humanity as it shows itself in its most passionate and brutalised moods. Jesus had to endure shame and spitting—the greatest indignity that any man, but especially an Oriental, could be subjected to. They made sport of Him, covering His face and then smiting Him, and asking tauntingly, "Prophesy unto us, thou Christ, who is he that smote Thee" It was thus the Christ was treated. Thus His holiest offices were turned to ridicule. He who could claim to be divine was used in a way in which it would be an inhumanity to use even the vilest of our fellow-creatures. This scene, which was repeated by the Roman soldiers in Pilate's judgment hall, throws a lurid light upon the terrible possibilities of evil in man. Contact with Christ is seen to be a wonderful revealer of character. The best in His friends and the worst in His foes are the more fully laid bare the nearer they are brought to Him.

After daybreak the fathers again assembled. It was now their lawful meeting, lawful so far that the night was now past, and that the recognised time for the holding of courts had come—but unlawful still as being a packed and irregularly summoned assembly and strangely incongruous as occurring in the most sacred week of all the year. Jesus was again placed at their bar, bearing now the marks of the cruel and disgraceful treatment He had in the interval received, His face and raiment already stained with blood and spitting. The proceedings were purely formal. There was no desire to hear witnesses over again. The high priest rehearsed what had previously taken place, and called for a formal vote of those who were present. With a feeling of malicious satisfaction and triumph the sentence of condemnation was renewed. There was no note of dissent, no Nicodemus to urge even a modest plea in bar of judgment. With a unanimity such as had seldom been witnessed in the Sanhedrim "they all condemned Him to be guilty of death."[1]

But it was "not lawful for them to put any man to death."[2] Caesar had taken from them the power of life and death. Only minor penalties they were at liberty to inflict.[3] What remained, therefore, for the Jewish fathers to do was to approach the Roman governor, and to induce him to carry out the death sentence they had pronounced.[4]

---

[1] Mark xiv. 64.
[2] John xviii. 31.
[3] Josephus, *Antiq.* XVIII. I. 1.
[4] The Sanhedrim could not meet on the feast, but it appears that the execution of criminals was often deferred to the feast day that

JESUS BEFORE HIS ECCLESIASTICAL JUDGES

Three things strike us particularly in Jesus' trial before His ecclesiastical judges. The first is His silence when lying tongues were busy bearing witness against Him. It is only Divine Innocence that could have maintained it. It is like the silence He has often kept since when error, unbelief, and calumny have been clamorous, and He has vouchsafed no answer but that of His own pure life, and His self-sacrificing work and death, and the divine witness men may discover for themselves as to His whole saving work.

The second thing is Jesus' vision of His coming glory even in the hour of His humiliation. That council hall in Caiaphas' house seemed the strangest place for such a vision. There the fettered Prisoner dared to predict the time when He as the Son of Man should be on the right hand of power; and in the very hour when His humiliation seemed the greatest and His doom was at hand, He could speak of His return as Judge of all, attended by every circumstances of heavenly majesty and glory.

---

the people might be deterred from wrongdoing by the sight of its punishment (*Mishna*, 4, 7). We may add here that the only direct reference we can find in the Talmud to Jesus is in *Sanhedrin*, folio 43, where it is stated He was crucified on the preparation day of the Passover, and that a herald went before Him for forty days calling, and calling in vain, for witnesses in His favour, and declaring that He should be stoned because He had used sorcery to draw away the people from the religion of their fathers.

We observe also as deeply significant that His rejection is accompanied by an outflow of the worst passions, of the inhumanity as well as iniquity of man. Something like this seems to mark His rejection always. Those who deny Him as their Lord and Saviour cannot let Him alone. They must needs in their own way and measure renew the story of His shame and suffering. They cannot put an end to Him within themselves but the awful deed must be accompanied with insult and wrong. The Jewish fathers grew the more passionate against the Prisoner the greater the difficulty became of finding any fault in Him. So the very excellence of the religion of Jesus, its heavenly purity and truth, are its condemnation in the eyes of worldly Sadducean men. Their dislike and opposition to it grow while they feel that they cannot answer it, and that it is constantly proclaiming their own condemnation. And the blow struck and unrepented of calls for other and more violent blows. The man who puts Christ to shame in any way, or does Him a wrong or an injustice, feels impelled either to seek Him in contrite confession, or to go onward in his fatal pathway, adding iniquity to iniquity and wrong to wrong. When one does a wrong to another he must either speedily become very contrite, or he will have his antipathy and desire to strike and injure greatly increased. Unrepentant men are impelled to hate more and more those they have wronged. Unrepentant Sadducees and Pharisees could not stop short of crucifying Jesus. They were not likely to leave any means untried of accomplishing that end.

PETER'S DENIAL.

Two at least of the disciples of Jesus—Peter and John—were witnesses of His trial before Caiaphas. Probably Judas also was present, his soul distracted and tortured with his guilty thoughts, and watching with a sinking, despairing feeling the issue of his traitorous deed. But of him we learn nothing at this stage. John was known unto the high priest,[1] and he went with Jesus and the band that had seized Him into the high priest's palace. It is not unlikely that he was even present in the council hall, and watched the proceedings there. The fact that we find him afterwards standing by the cross shows us that throughout all the events of this momentous day the disciple whom Jesus loved was never far from his Master.

Only one glimpse we get of Peter between the arrest and the morning of the third day, when

---

[1] John xviii. 16. Ewald (*Hist. of Israel*, VI. 186) hazards the view that John was of priestly descent. Edersheim also inclines to think that he was a priest. Vol. II., p. 487.

he comes early to the empty grave of his Master, startled by the news that He is risen. It is not a favourable one, but it is full of needed instruction and warning. It is one the world could not have expected to be placed on record by the friends of the apostles, or by the apostles themselves. But there it is in their immortal pages, set forth without apology and without extenuation, showing what manner of absolutely true and unworldly men those were whom Christ made and gathered to Himself. Peter is presented as one of the throng around the fire in the court of the high priest's palace. Naturally when he is observed he is challenged as to his connection with the Accused. He fears in such company to avow himself. He seeks a miserable refuge for himself in denial, and in an attempt, happily for him proving a failure in the end, to make it appear that he is not a disciple of the Nazarene, but only one of the casual crowd that has gathered to witness His trial. In the end he hastens from the scene of his sin and shame a humbled and penitent man. Such in brief is the story the evangelists tells us of his fall.

To understand the situation, we must bear in mind the arrangements of an Oriental house such as that of the high priest would be. It consists usually of a group of buildings varying in their size and architecture, forming a great square in the centre. Often it has a wall shutting it in from the street. In that case there is a forecourt between the front gate at the wall and the main doorway of the house. Then there is the larger court within, around which the different apartments, offices, halls are gathered, and by which they freely communicate with one another. Viewed from the street, the great palatial building presents nothing usually but dead walls; it is only from within that its architectural grandeur is seen. Around the inner court are the porticos and galleries, where the cool shade is enjoyed, and there are the chambers for guests and entertainments. Sometimes the court is paved, and sometimes it is planted with trees and covered with grass, and there is a fountain of cool sparkling water playing in the centre.[1]

The inner court of Caiaphas' palace was a scene of great stir and tumult on the night of the arrest.[2]

---

[1] For an interesting description of an Oriental house such as that of Caiaphas would be, see Robinson's *Harmony of the Gospels*, p. 225.

[2] John xviii. 18. The question has been raised whether it was in the court of Annas' house or that of Caiaphas that the denial of Peter took place. John seems definitely to indicate the former. Matthew definitely and Mark indefinitely the latter. Weiss (*Life*, III. 335) thinks that it was in the former, as strangers would not likely be admitted to the palace of the high priest. He admits, however, that

As soon as they had got their Prisoner within the gate they closed it, and saw to its being well guarded.[1] They seemed to think they had need still for every precaution. They had still their fears that a rescue might be attempted. John had entered with the multitude; Peter was without, whether because he had not reached the gate in time, or because he had not the courage to venture in as one of the band, we cannot say. John used what influence he had, and the maid who kept the door was induced to open it for his friend.

In the centre of the court within which Peter now found himself, a fire was blazing, for it was a chilly April night.[2] Around this fire gathered a strangely mixed company—Roman soldiers still on duty along with the Jews who had been engaged in

---

the oldest tradition, which he believes we have in Mark, represents the court of Caiaphas' house as the place of the denial. Pressensé's view is that the first denial may have taken place in Annas' house and the last in Caiaphas'. Caspari (*Life*, p. 223) offers a solution of the difficulty by supposing that Annas, as father-in-law of the high priest, occupied a wing of the high priest's palace so that his dwelling and that of Caiaphas looked into the same court. Ellicott agrees with Caspari in supposing that Annas and Caiaphas occupied a common official residence; and further, he inclines to think that the three denials took place while the examination in Annas' house was going on, and that it was when Jesus was being led across the court to the council hall in Caiaphas' house that He gave Peter that look which brought to him repentance (Ellicott's *Life*, p. 334). The same views are held by Lange, Steinmeyer, Keim, and others.

[1] John xviii. 16.
[2] John xviii. 18.

the arrest; servants, male and female about the high priest's house; priests and elders with crafty and cold Sadducean looks eagerly watching their prey. Peter perhaps was for a while content with the shaded side of the archway, where he could see and not be seen, and where he could above all observe what might be going on in the council hall yonder. But by and by the cheery blazing fire attracted him, and he found himself among the bitterest foes of his Master.

Peter was sitting by the fire,[1] or as another evangelist puts it, was standing and warming himself.[2] He was listening to the conversation of those around, which doubtless all turned upon the events of that morning, and upon the Prisoner they had taken. We may be sure that the feelings, the bad passions of the grave fathers and priests in the council hall above would be reproduced in the coarsest form by their underlings and followers in the court below. Peter's ears would be assailed by the most abusive language regarding his Master.

Only two courses were open to Peter. He could not be indifferent or neutral in such circumstances where his Master's honour and life were so deeply concerned. Of the two, however, that of confessing

---

[1] Luke xxii. 55.
[2] John xviii. 18.

Christ was fraught with great danger; the other, that of concealing his discipleship for the time seemed to him to give the only promise of safety. And what did it matter though he should impose on the rough company round about him? What would his poor avowal avail against the apparently resistless mass of opposition; or his one small voice for his Master against the multitude of voices on the other side, and all the storm of abuse, malicious taunts and revilings which they were raising? Was it not wiser for him to appear as if he had no more to do with the Prisoner than any other there? Why should he offer his testimony to truth when it would only be scorned, and when he himself would be endangered? Why? the world still asks, and it counts every martyr a fool, a man who gives his testimony where it is not wanted, and gives it so as to excite those who are opposed to him to get rid of him altogether. The world should be very tender towards Peter, for he only yielded, under the strongest temptation, to its spirit, forgetful of the grand example of his Master only a few yards from where he was, who could not be withheld from bearing witness to the truth of His divine claims and His divine mission by all the exasperation of His judges, and by all their threatenings.

But in vain did the disciple try to be like those around him. In vain he disguised himself for the time. He found even the disguise of an unconcerned onlooker uncomfortable. He could not wear it well, and those around him were not to be deceived by it. His uneasy manner, his look of anxiety, his evident deep concern for the Prisoner under trial, his changing countenance as the trial went on, as words of biting insult or ridicule were uttered about his beloved Master, and rewarded by the horrid laughter of the company—all these things betrayed the disciple, and drew down upon him the very attention which he feared and sought to avert.

The world is quicker than is sometimes thought in discerning the differences between itself and Christ's people. It has a special satisfaction in seeing professing Christians imitating its own manners and habits, but it has a cruel way of rewarding them for their attempts. It delights to point out their inconsistency, to taunt them about their Christianity, and to bring to the light their shame and humiliation.

Peter's case is a marked instance of this kind. The maid who kept the door and had let him in at John's request seems to have fixed her eyes on him and watched his movements. After some time she dared to leave her post at the gate for a little, and came over to the centre of the court where Peter was standing and warming himself with many others. Looking closely into his face, lighted up as it was by the glare of the fire, she put the question directly to him, "Art not thou also one of this man's disciples?"[1]

"Thou also!" There was that other on whose entreaty she had opened the gate to Peter. She knew he was a disciple. He appears to have been at no pains either to conceal the fact, or to let it be known. But no one, so far as we learn, assailed him. He could even stand by the cross afterwards, and no hand was laid upon him. A mysterious shield was over him. It was the shield of the Master's prayers which had ensured the safety of the eleven in the garden, and which was to ensure their safety all through. If Peter had only known and trusted it as he ought, he would have found that divine shield sufficient for the protection of himself, as well as John, within the walls of Caiaphas' palace, and even in the midst of the reviling multitude on Calvary. How much better and nobler it would have been for Peter if he had had the courage and honesty at once to say, "It is true, I also am one of this

---

[1] John xviii. 17.

man's disciples!" Is not the avowed disciple as a rule safer among Christ's foes than the concealed or wavering one?

Peter under the fatal impulse of the moment chose a different course. He was confused and put out by the abrupt question of the girl. At first he sought to evade the questioner and her question by seeming to take no notice of either. But the maid was not to be put off or ignored. She promptly renewed the attack on him. "Thou also wast with Jesus of Galilee,"[1] and then turning to those about him she said, "Certainly this man also was with Him."[2] Then Peter, filled with a mortal dread that he was discovered, answered with an angry outburst, "Woman, I do not know Him, I neither know nor understand what thou sayest."[3]

Peter chose the most open manner of denying the charge made against him. He denied before them all,[4] we are told. It was a lie which like most bold ones of its kind overstepped the occasion and furnished its own refutation. Every one there knew quite well what the maid

---

[1] Mark xiv. 67.
[2] Luke xxii. 56.
[3] Luke xxii. 57; Mark xiv. 68.
[4] Matt. xxvi. 70.

meant by her accusation. Every one there knew Jesus of Galilee. There was perhaps no part of the country to which His name and fame had not spread. It was a pitiable thing to feign indifference or ignorance in regard to Him, but on the part of a disciple it was inexcusable. And to speak of Him contemptuously, as if He were only some common criminal who had fallen into the hands of the Sanhedrim, and who was too insignificant for the notice and interest of such a man as Peter, was indeed a shameful transgression.

It had come to this that Peter so regarded, or pretended to regard his Master whom he professed only a few hours before to be dearer to him than life. He pretended not to know that it was Jesus of Galilee about whom all the stir was being made at that early hour of the morning. Jesus of Galilee who is He? what about Him? I know Him not,[1] I know not what you are speaking about![2] Who could have believed that Peter would have come to this? How his words must have pierced the Master's heart! His disciples had forsaken Him. But this was worse than being forsaken, that the foremost of them should affect to treat Him with the contempt of indifference. Yet to

---

[1] Luke xxii. 57.
[2] Mark xiv. 68.

this depth Peter is brought at the first onset of a woman's tongue. By the words of a female slave, bent probably on mischievous amusement, this disciple, who was to have been a pillar that should have stood erect though the world had fallen, was in a moment overthrown.

As the wrangle between the maid and the disciple was coming to a close a shrill sound broke upon the chilly morning air, and could be heard distinctly above the din of human voices. It was the crowing of a cock.[1] What a significance it had for Peter, if he could only at that moment have perceived it! It was the monitor the Master had appointed to warn him when he should be approaching the abyss. If only he had remembered the words of the Lord the night before, then at this first cockcrowing he might have recovered himself at once, and he might have been spared the deeper shame and guilt into which he was to fall.

Thus a first denial was made, and a second and a third followed. The company around the fire became uncomfortable for Peter. To the porch, or the space under the archway at the gate, he retired to be free from his tormentors, and to get his agitated feelings after the first terrible disavowal calmed down. But no place is easy or safe for

---

[1] Mark xiv. 68.

one with an uneasy conscience, and the court of the high priest's palace that morning was the most dangerous of all places for a disciple. In the porch Peter found troublesome questioners as he had done around the fire. There another maid saw him. She, with the one at the gate who had admitted Peter and had gone over to the fire to challenge him, had doubtless been talking about him, and she said in the hearing of others around her, "This fellow was also with Jesus of Nazareth"[1] He evaded her words and her presence as much as he could. But, like the other maid, she was not to be shaken off. She repeated her assertion to the bystanders, "This is one of them;"[2] and one of the men among them making common cause with her, turned directly upon Peter and said, "Thou art also of them."[3] With a passionate emphasis he replied to him, "Man, I am not,"[4] while the maid's persistent taunts as to his being a disciple drew forth from him the fierce denial, backed by an oath, "I do not know the Man"[5]

It is significant that Peter again overstepped

---

[1] Matt. xxvi. 71.
[2] Mark xiv. 69.
[3] Luke xxii. 58.
[4] Luke xxii. 58.
[5] Matt. xxii. 72.

the bounds of the necessities of the case. There was no need for the oath. He might have been content with the simple statement. But it is to be remarked, that while truth can walk abroad in the simplest raiment, falsehood must put on the gaudiest, and must use the strongest colours. The simplest terms will do, and are indeed the best for the purposes of the former, but the latter presses the strongest and the most sacred into its service, and lays its defiling hand equally upon the things of heaven and the things of earth. To the man who is carried away by passion or self-interest so as to maintain a lie, nothing is sacred, and nothing is unclean. The moral sense discriminating between things sacred and things common or even degrading seems for the time to be paralysed within him, and God and heaven have to lend themselves to the basest uses.

If Peter imagined he could purchase peace and safety in that company with denials and with oaths, he was soon to find that he was greatly mistaken. It was not to allay their suspicions and to ward off their attacks and accusations that he should adopt for the time their style and language. It could in that company be for a very short time that the makeshift of the oath would avail. They were only too well accustomed to that device, and were ready rather to laugh at those who trusted to it, and to disbelieve them all the more. Peter drew to himself a greater amount of prying suspicious attention than ever. He was more closely and critically watched. He seems to have moved restlessly about. Now he might be standing under the archway at the door, again, crossing the court and stealthily taking his place once more among those around the fire; at one time he might be on this side of the court, at another he might be seeking a place of quiet on the other.

A brief respite, however, seems now to have been given him. It was an hour, we are told, before the attacks on him were renewed.[1] Probably he owed that hour's respite, less to his oath with which he had meant to secure it, than to the attention of the company being drawn away to his Master in the council hall. Probably between the second and the third denial there was the stir connected with the assembling of the Jewish fathers; there was the momentous trial going on; there were the charges so passionately made by the accusers, and the Accused's silence and dignity so exasperating to His judges; there was the intense excitement as a point seemed to be made or lost,

[1] Luke xxii. 59.

and the fortunes of the trial were followed, and as one father and another came down those marble stairs from the judgment hall to find this one or that one from among the throng in the court, who could remember anything he had ever heard or seen that might be told against the Prisoner. The disciple would be lost sight of in the immensely greater interest gathering round the Master.

But the disciple could not long be overlooked. The interest he had in that trial must sooner or later have betrayed him. For the third time he was attacked. He was again beside the fire of coals.[1] Probably it was a trifling circumstance that brought back the attention to him. He was assailed on all sides. One confidently affirmed, saying, "Of a truth this fellow also was with Him, for he is a Galilean."[2] Then another, who was a kinsman of that Malchus whose ear Peter cut off, annoyed and indignant evidently at the denial given, said sharply to him, "Did not I see thee in the garden with Him?"[3] It was a cruel reminder calling up action on Peter's part which, at that moment and in that company, he must have wished to be utterly unknown. Then a number gathered round

---

[1] John xviii. 25.
[2] Luke xxii. 59.
[3] John xviii. 26.

and declared with one voice that they were sure there must be truth in the charges the two were bringing against him, for he spoke just as might be expected of one of the Galilean followers of Jesus. "Surely thou art one of them, for thy speech bewrayeth thee."[1] "Thou art a Galilean, and thy speech agreeth thereto."[2] Among the Jews the Galilean could be singled out by his dialect, just as the unlettered Cockney or Aberdonian might be among ourselves. The Galileans, according to the Talmud, had great difficulty with their aspirates and vowels. Some instances of their peculiar use of these are given by that authority.[3] And what Galilean was likely to be interesting himself in the trial of the Nazarene, and to be found in the high priest's palace at such an hour of the morning, unless he were a disciple?

The singular thing is that Malchus' kinsman should content himself with asserting that he saw Peter at the time of the arrest, and should say nothing about the armed champion of the Man of Nazareth and the blundering stroke of his sword. Was Malchus not among the servants of the high priest in that court? Why was he silent? Or

---

[1] Matt. xxvi. 73.
[2] Mark xiv. 70.
[3] Wünsche, *Babylonische Talmud, Erubin*, fol. 53, p. 189.

was he employed in waiting upon the Prisoner before the council? He could not readily be mistaken in identifying the man who had dealt him his wound. One would imagine that the glimpse he had of Peter and also of his divine Healer could never have faded from his memory. But that act of healing was evidently to save Peter as well. Malchus does not even appear upon the scene seeking the revenge so easily within his power. How easy for him, or even for his kinsman it would have been, to have brought it about, that Peter should stand side by side with his Master to share in the same condemnation and in the same death! But this surpassing honour was not to be his.

Peter's case was becoming a desperate one. He was surrounded with vexatious questioners. It was difficult for him to gainsay those who had been face to face with him in the garden. And whatever else he might change or conceal, he could not rid himself of his accent. Attacked and tortured on all sides, like a wild beast in the arena, he was goaded to madness, and began to lose all control of himself. "Then began he to curse and to swear saying, I know not the man."[1]

---

[1] Matt. xxvi. 74.

To such a depth of moral debasement this specially favoured disciple was brought!

Peter could hardly have taken to any course more effectually to prove that he was none of Christ's than by polluting his lips with oaths and curses, and exhibiting some of the worst passions and vices of the ungodly. There is a sense of fitness and propriety possessed in a fair measure by men generally. Peter was making violent and passionate appeal to it, when he thus tried to demonstrate to them how he could not be one of this man's disciples, because he could be as coarse and profane as any of the rough throng about him. The world still knows that the man who is touched with the spirit of Christ cannot indulge in its profanity or its vice, and that the man who does so is not to be taken for a disciple of His. And had not Peter been so touched? Could he have been so long with Jesus, and yet not have felt the power of His spirit? And if he had felt it, how are we to account for this dreadful outpouring of oaths and curses? What came to the lips, one would be inclined to say, must have been in the heart. It may have been the revival of old bad habits which had for long been laid aside, but might break out under sufficiently strong provocation, and still awaited the destroying touch of Christ's cross. It betokened at any rate a well of evil and profanity from which there was now a fearful overflow.

When Peter had exhausted himself in this outburst, amidst the comparative quiet that for a brief space prevailed, the crowing of a cock was again distinctly heard.[1] At that very time probably there was some movement in the council hall. Probably the first trial was over, and the Prisoner was being brought down to the courtyard, where he was for a couple of hours or so to be subjected to the roughest and most insulting treatment. Jesus may have been coming down the stairs, or passing through the court. At any rate the eyes of the Master and the disciple met; "the Lord looked on Peter."[4] It was a look of pitying love, a look that touched and broke Peter's heart, and filled him with a deeper penitence than ever he had known. In a moment the reaction of feeling came

---

[1] Mark xiv. 72.

It is singular that there should be controversy as to the cock crowing, whether it actually took place or whether it was only the mode of expression they used for indicating the time of the morning. It is even alleged that there was a Rabbinical law forbidding fowls to be kept in Jerusalem. Edersheim (*Life*, vol. II, 537) doubts this, and certainly no absurd law of this kind would affect the Roman garrison not so far off. It may be true, as is alleged by the author of "Rabbi Jeshua," that there was a temple official called the cock because he cried the hours; but it is more likely that our Lord was referring to the ordinary cock crowing, as marking the hours of the morning, than to the services of any such official.

in resistless flood. Peter could not speak. Never did His Master seem so divinely beautiful, or himself so utterly vile. He was utterly crushed under a sense of shame and contrition. The past came up so vividly, and the warning words that had fallen on his ear so heedlessly. The place, the company became now intolerable to him. "He remembered the words of the Lord, and he went out and wept bitterly."[1] There is a tradition that the remembrance of what he had been and done that night so clung to him ever afterwards that, morning by morning, he was wont to awake at the hour when the cock crew and the Lord turned upon him His look so pitiful and so heart-searching, and to ask anew for pardon.[2]

Who is not tempted in this rough and evil world at times to deny the Lord that bought him, and who may not fall? Our strength is only in Himself. The secret of fidelity is in not "following afar off," but keeping ever near, and letting our life and our actions, whatever be the company in which we must mingle, tell unmistakably whose we are. And the hope of recovery when we have fallen is all, as in Peter's case, in the grace of our Lord, and in His divine look of pitying and

---

[1] Luke xxii. 62.
[2] Geikie, *Life and Words*, p. 668.

forgiving love meeting our look of penitence and shame. The well known prayer of Augustine may well be ours every day. "Gracious Jesus, look on me with those eyes of mercy with which Thou didst look on Peter in the hall; on the sinful woman at the feast; on the thief upon the cross; and grant me to weep with Peter, to love Thee with the woman that was a sinner, and with the penitent thief to see Thee in paradise."

The narratives of the three denials of Peter as given by the four evangelists have always, in view of the differences they present, offered to candid and sceptical critics of the Bible too tempting a field of criticism to be overlooked by them. These differences have been again and again pointed out, especially as to their bearing on the claims of inspiration and the inerrancy of Scripture. But the more closely they are looked at they are found to strengthen rather than to weaken those claims. They are strong incidental proofs of the independence and trustworthiness of the narratives; nor can we doubt that as Alford[1] says, "If we could be put in complete possession of all the details as they happened, each account would find its justification, and the reasons of the variations would appear." If Paulus sneeringly remarks that there were eight denials and not three, is it not a fair and reasonable reply to say that there may have been quite a number of denials on each of the three distinct occasions on which Peter was challenged as being a disciple, and that it is intelligible that each of the evangelists chose those three for his narrative which seemed to him the most striking and significant?[2] A close examination of the alleged variations and discrepancies strongly suggests that they are but supplementary details belonging to the same incidents. Thus as to the first denial we are told that Peter was sitting in the hall without (Matthew), that he was warming himself in the hall below (Mark), that he was sitting by the fire (Luke), that he was accosted by the maid that kept the door (John). Why should not all these statements be true, and do they not afford just the kind of independent testimony bearing upon the same incident

---

[1] Alford's *Greek Testament*, vol. 1, p. 283.

[2] See on this and other points Da Costa's *Four Witnesses*, p. 383; also Andrew's *Life of our Lord*, p. 491: and Westcott's *Gospel of St. John*, pp. 263-266.

which, for the very reason that it is not mere reiteration, is felt to be peculiarly strong? In the second denial, Peter has gone out into the porch (Matthew), he is standing and warming himself (John), and it is another maid who assails him (Matthew), it is a male servant (Luke), it is the bystanders (John). At this second onset may not Peter have moved from the porch to the fire, and have been attacked first by one, then by another, then by several? Then if in the third denial bystanders rally Peter on his accent (Matthew, Mark, and Luke), while one of them, the kinsman of Malchus, amazed at his audacity in denial, asks him whether he had not with his own eyes seen him in the garden with Jesus, does not this conjoint evidence only give us a more vivid presentation of the scene, and a more vivid sense of its reality? The cock crowing and the repentance of Peter are reported with the same refreshing variety.

JESUS BEFORE PILATE.

It was still very early, but much had to be done that day. It was indeed destined to be a day more crowded with the most momentous events than any that had ever dawned upon the world. The Jewish Sabbath followed it, and it was the Sabbath of the Passover week, to which a special sacredness attached. If Jesus was not brought before Pilate that day ere the sun set, it would be a week before the opportunity could recur. What might not happen in a week? The chief priests and elders had their intended victim in their hands now. They had unanimously voted Him worthy of death. If they had had the power they would have carried out their own sentence forthwith, but under Roman rule "it was not lawful for them to put any man to death."[1] To Caesar or his representative therefore

---

[1] Josephus, *Antiq.*, XVIII., I. 1. The Romans claimed the power also of preventing meetings of Sanhedrim being held without their consent (Tacitus, *Annals*, XII. 54; Joseph., *Ant.*, XX., IX. 1.)

they must go to secure the execution of their sentence; but if haste, rancorous zeal, pertinacity and importunity could bring it about, these were not to be wanting on their part.

The Jewish rulers after pronouncing their sentence hastened forth with their prisoner from the council hall to the palace of Pilate. The first streaks of morning were just falling upon the city. We should think it unusually early for a judge to be expected to take his place upon the bench, and to enter upon an important trial. But we must remember that life and business begin early in the East, while the Oriental must needs rest during the hours when we are busiest. They did not doubt that Pilate would be in readiness to receive them.

The procession, as it moved on, doubtless gathered to itself an increasing crowd. It must have been a very unusual sight to see the leaders of the Jewish people hurrying off, in this public way, to the hated Roman governor with one of their own race, that they might give him up to punishment. They knew well that any death a Jew might die in Roman hands would be an accursed one. They knew before they set out, that the death they went to ask for their prisoner at Pilate's hands could be none other than crucifixion—the most painful and shameful of all, especially for any one of Abraham's race. And yet those abroad in the streets at this early hour could see the grave fathers and priests of their nation personally attending one as a prisoner, bound and safeguarded in the hands of their servants, whom many of them must have known well as the Man of Nazareth, and moving with quick steps and agitated looks towards the Praetorium—the headquarters of the Roman governor—to deliver Him up there to the Gentiles!

How the news must have spread through the city, and drawn multitudes from every quarter in the greatest excitement! Who could have believed that such a sight should ever have been witnessed in Jerusalem? It would have been an extraordinary thing had it been even a Barabbas whom the Jewish priests and elders were taking the trouble of putting in this way into the hands of their Roman rulers. But it was their own Messiah they were thus giving up to ignominy and death; and it was not a Jewish mob in an hour of madness that was doing it, but the responsible rulers and representatives of the Jewish people. It was Israel through them playing the part of Judas Iscariot, betraying her divine Master into the hands of the uncircumcised. Thus indeed the apostles ever afterwards regarded the act. Everywhere they went they sought to bring home to the hearts of their fellow-countrymen, that they had been the betrayers as well as murderers of the Just One, and that it had been the basest deed in all their nation's history that they had delivered up the Christ to the Gentiles.[1]

The Praetorium, to which this extraordinary procession made its way, merits some attention in passing. Here Pilate resided when he was in Jerusalem; but this was only at the time of the feasts, as he hated the place and the people, and preferred to live at the Romanized city of Cæsarea. It was a vast palatial building on Mount Zion, erected by Herod the Great.[2] It consisted of two great wings with a central building connecting them. It contained magnificent apartments for the governor and his household, and accommodation for the various government offices, and also for a large garrison. Within its spacious enclosure almost an army, it is said, could be

---

[1] Acts iii. 13, 14. Acts vii. 52.

[2] Caspari thinks there are grounds for believing the Praetorium was the fortified garrison of Antonia on the north-west side of the Temple Mountain. The Gabbatha or Pavement referred to is supposed to be the paved surface of the Temple Mountain which Josephus mentions as being all paved with variegated mosaic work (Caspari's *Life*, p. 225). Edersheim believes it far more likely that Pilate occupied "the truly royal abode of Herod, and not the fortified barracks of Antonia" (Edersheim, vol. II., 566). This is also the opinion of Ewald (*History of Israel*, vol. VI., 39), and of most others on the subject.

gathered together. It thus served the double purpose of a government house and a strong fortification. In the central part was the hall of judgment, where so much occurred in connection with the trial of Jesus. In front of it, and connected by a doorway, was a raised platform called in the Hebrew Gabbatha or the Pavement. There, as on the present occasion, the curule chair was sometimes placed for the governor, and he dispensed justice in the open air.[1] Its tesselated floor was of costly marble, and adorned with stones of various colours. It was spacious enough to accommodate the accusers and accused, and those who attended on the governor's person, or assisted him in judgment.

The Praetorium and the Temple were the chief glories of Jerusalem. Referring to the former Josephus says, "The kinds of stone used in its construction were countless. Whatever was rare abounded in it. The roofs astonished every one by the length of their beams, and the beauty of their adornment. Vessels mostly of gold and silver, rich in chasing, shone on every side. The

---

[1] Josephus, *B. I.* II. IX. 3. Roman governors, it is said, attached so much importance to the tesselated pavement, on which their *bema* might be placed, that they had a portable one which they could use whenever they might be dispensing justice. So says Suetonius of Julius Caesar in his life of him. Suet. *Jul. Caes.*, 46.

great dining hall had been constructed to supply table couches for three hundred guests. Others opened in all directions, each with a different style of pillar. The open space before the palace was laid out in broad walks, planted with long avenues of different trees, and bordered by broad deep canals and great ponds, flowing with cool clear water, and set off along the banks with innumerable works of art."[1]

To this great building, then, the impressive monument and headquarters of the alien government under which they lived, the Jewish fathers brought Jesus. It was the first and last time He was to enter a king's palace, and it was as a prisoner. With Him those fathers, after traversing some steep and winding streets, and then the open space to which Josephus refers, ascended the steps leading to the Pavement. They would not accompany Him further lest they should be defiled. The Talmud says, "Let the court of the stranger be to you as the stable of oxen."[2] Roman buildings, even the most useful of them, were, according to the same authority, objects of antipathy to the Jews.[3] They sent word to the procurator, very likely by some

---

[1] Josephus, *Antiq.* V., IV. 4.
[2] Bab. Talmud, *Erubin*, fol. 62.
[3] Bab. Talmud, *Shabbath*, 33 b.

of the guards or officers whom they found about the Praetorium, that they desired to see him, and that they had a prisoner with them whom they adjudged worthy to be handed over to him. So scrupulous about ceremonial defilement even while they were in the way of committing the greatest crimes! So careful to keep the outside of the cup and the platter clean, while they were allowing the cup within to be filled with the pollution of iniquity and malice![1]

---

[1] If the priests were careful lest they should be defiled because they had the Passover to eat, then it would appear the paschal lamb had not yet been eaten when Jesus was on His trial. Here differences of view emerge. Edersheim (*Life and Times*, vol. II., 487) holds that the paschal lamb was eaten on the previous evening, the night of the Lord's Supper; he even speaks of Peter and John (the latter according to his view being a priest) bringing the lamb, after it had been slain and dressed as the law required, to the house of Mark, where he considers it likely that the supper took place. Caspari (*Life*, p. 204) on the other hand is of opinion that it was not the paschal lamb, but only the paschal meal which was partaken of by our Lord and His disciples on the night before the Crucifixion, when the supper was instituted. The paschal meal, he says, was kept on the day of the preparation—the 14th Nisan—and Judas was understood when he left the Upper Room to be going forth to buy the things—that is the lamb, &c.—necessary for the feast, the real Passover observance on the next day, the 15th. Ewald (*Life*, p. 299) shares this view, and goes so far as to say that if it had been the paschal lamb, and not this paschal meal which had been eaten on the night of the supper, it would have been flesh and not bread Jesus would have used as the symbol of His body. But proof appears to be lacking of the existence of this paschal meal in the time of our Lord. After the destruction of Jerusalem a sort of memorial Passover without the paschal lamb (there being no temple in which it could be slain) was observed, but in our Lord's case there was no necessity for that.

There seems to be no escape in this way from the old Passover controversy. The Synoptists say that Jesus and His disciples ate the Passover on the night before His death. John appears

Pilate knew them too well to contend or parley with them on a point of religious etiquette. Wearing his white robe with its broad purple border, the mark of his rank and authority as a Roman procurator, he came forth at their request, and the trial began. A singular scene, indeed, that open-air court must have presented—the Roman governor as judge in his ivory chair of state, his Roman attendants and assessors about him, the

---

to indicate that the Passover remained to be eaten on the day He died. It is extremely unlikely that Jesus observed it a day before the Jews in general, or that latitude was allowed of observing it on one or other of two days. The only feasible way out of the difficulty appears to be that John applies the term Passover to the whole feast, while the Synoptists use it in the more restricted sense of the paschal lamb. The feast lasted seven days. On each of those days, there was the Passover to be observed or eaten. John uses the expression "to eat the Passover" in the wide sense that it applies to each of the celebrations of the paschal week. On the second day there was the *chagigah*, the offerings of the flock and herd, first to be presented, and then to be partaken of at a festive meal. The *chagigah* also in John's view was the Passover, and the priests would be in the act of slaying the animals at the time Jesus died on the cross. Edersheim says (*Life and Times*, vol. II., p. 568) that no competent Jewish archæologist would care to deny that the term Passover might not apply to the *chagigah*, no less than to the paschal lamb. This second day happened to be the preparation ($\pi\alpha\rho\alpha\sigma\kappa\epsilon\upsilon\eta$), the day before the Sabbath. So also with John it was the preparation of the Passover, that is, the preparation which happened to occur during the paschal week, and therefore unusually important. Jesus ate the Passover on the Thursday evening as the law directed, and as all others did. But there was the Passover to be eaten or observed in other forms and services on the day following, and there is no discrepancy after all between John and the other three evangelists on this point. The whole subject is very ably, concisely, and fully discussed in Andrews' (*Life*, pp. 367-397). It may be added that upon the remark of John, why the members of the Sanhedrim would not enter the Praetorium, Delitzsch has hinged an interesting argument for the Gospels being written in the first, rather than in the second century (*Zeitschrift für Luth. Theol.*, 1874).

Jewish fathers standing at a safe ceremonial distance in front of him, Jesus in the midst, and the Roman soldiers stationed all around the elevated platform on which they were assembled, and with their long spears guarding the place from a multitude growing every moment in numbers and in excitement. Jesus standing between the cultured heathen and the bigoted Jew, the Truth on its trial when He is being tried, and the world looking on and finally uniting in His condemnation! The scene is worthy to be the masterpiece of the greatest artist.[1]

In this trial the character of Pilate, as well as that of others connected with it, is, as it were, held up before the sun. As might be expected from what we learn of him—not from Christian writers who might be supposed to be prejudiced against him, because under him their divine Saviour suffered, but from Roman writers and historians—the trial has only added to his evil reputation, and given him an unenviable immortality. His procuratorship he owed to Sejanus, the infamous favourite of the Emperor Tiberius, and the client was like his patron. He was unprincipled, sensual,

---

[1] It is to be observed that Pilate conducts the examination and trial himself. Had he been a consul or proconsul he would have had his quaestor to conduct it, but being a procurator he had no quaestor. Another incidental proof of the accuracy of the evangelists (Tacitus, *Annals*, XII. 60).

venal, covetous, and pitiless in shedding blood when he could do it with safety and gain to himself, but he was wanting in decision of character and was known to yield under pressure. He could be firm enough when courage cost nothing, but he would vacillate and temporise when the opposition was sufficiently formidable and threatening. He was equal to any injustice and to any deed of blood, and could carry it through without compunction, provided only it should be to his advantage. Morality with him was only a matter of policy and utility, and he could not understand anyone sacrificing himself for either truth or virtue.

Yet Pilate was not worse, in some respects he was better, than some other Roman governors in those degenerate days of the empire, who worked their way to office attracted by the spoils and the wealth which it brought, and who gambled and speculated in a variety of ways for those spoils, bribing, flattering, finessing, and financing, till by some lucky turn in the great imperial lottery, the coveted prize of this or that province should become theirs.[1] Unfortunately for himself, Pilate obtained the government of a people who were the most

---

[1] As Ellicott (*Life*, p. 350) says, Pilate was a thorough and complete type of the later Roman man of the world. We have it on the authority of Eusebius (*Hist. Eccles.* II. 7) that he was recalled, and sent into banishment for his iniquities as a governor, and that he died by his own hand.

intractable and troublesome of all the races that Rome attempted to rule, and the most difficult for a pagan Roman to understand. He had already made himself odious to them; and every movement, especially on the part of their ecclesiastical rulers, he had come to regard with suspicion and distrust. He made no attempt to conceal that repugnance and contempt which he shared with the Romans generally in regard to them, and they repaid him with their sullen submission and their untiring watchfulness for his halting. He carried his pride of Roman authority and power loftily against their pride of race and religion, but in obstinacy and dogged pertinacity he was no match for them. Of this we could hardly have a more striking example than the part we find him playing in the condemnation and death of Jesus.

Reverting now to the Pavement where the court is set up, let us endeavour with the help of the evangelists' brief notes to follow the course of the trial. We may suppose that Caiaphas, like the orator Tertullus when Paul was being tried before another Roman governor,[1] indulged in his opening address in much complimentary language in regard to the procurator, and in much bitter invective against the Prisoner. Concluding, he said, and he said it

---

[1] Acts xxiv. 1, 8.

as if nothing more needed to be said, "If He were not a malefactor we would not have delivered Him up to thee."[1] And Pilate replied forthwith, "A malefactor you say He is. Take Him, therefore, and judge (or punish) Him according to your law." But it was "not lawful for them to put any man to death," and death was the punishment they thought due to this man's offences. The Talmud says that forty years before the destruction of Jerusalem, that is shortly before Jesus was on His trial, the power of pronouncing capital sentences was, by the Romans, taken from the Sanhedrim. We find Rabbi Simon expressing his devout thankfulness at being relieved of the responsiblity.[2] What the priests and elders now desired was that Pilate should affirm their sentence, and command its execution. Would Pilate not abide by their judgment without further inquiry? Would he not be satisfied that they had tried their prisoner and condemned Him? They had found Him guilty of crimes which it was beyond their power to punish. Should not the very fact that they were there with Him that morning be enough to satisfy the governor that His crimes were great?

---

[1] John xviii. 30.
[2] Schwab's *Talmud*, vol. x., p. 228.

But the governor, to his credit be it said, was not to be persuaded so easily. He had a special pleasure in giving the Jewish rulers to feel the weight of his authority and their own dependent and subject state. No mere protestations of the kind which they made could be enough to secure his acquiescence offhand in their sentence, and to gratify their wishes for the Prisoner's death. He would have them justify their sentence before him. What were their charges against the Accused? Were they merely ecclesiastical? He could not allow death to be inflicted for mere differences of religious opinion or practice. It would be a degradation of Rome that her power should be at the disposal of factious Jewish priests, to persecute and punish those they might consider heretics or blasphemers as they pleased. Was it not the case that in their eyes every Roman in the land was worse than a heretic?

This difficulty was foreseen by Jesus' accusers. They had indeed condemned Him for blasphemy, because He had made Himself the Son of God. But before the Roman governor they produced entirely different charges.[1] "We found this fellow,"

---

[1] We may remark here that Strauss (*New Life*, pp. 356, 358) avows his readiness to believe the passage in Tacitus (*Annals*, XV. 44) as to the fact of Christ's death, and also that the Jews trumped up political charges against Him to secure His condemnation; but

said they, "perverting the nation, and forbidding to give tribute to Caesar, saying that He Himself is Christ a king."[1] With what feelings of suspicion and distrust Pilate must have listened to these accusations! The Jewish rulers finding fault with anyone who taught that tribute should not be paid to Caesar! The Jewish rulers now become so loyal and so ardent in Caesar's interest that they give themselves the trouble of laying hands upon a new pretender to a Jewish throne! It was a new *rôle* for them to play that they should appear such friends and watchful defenders of Roman rule. The governor must have at once surmised that there was a great deal behind all this which was being concealed from him, and that their profuse loyalty and disinterestedness were only on the surface.

Those Jewish fathers had heard Jesus calmly and bravely bearing witness at their own bar, knowing well the peril He incurred, that He was the Christ, the Messiah, the Son of God. They had condemned Him on this very ground. And

---

that around these simple facts the evangelists gathered a mass of legendary and traditional lore to suit their purpose, and used it, he allows, in a wonderfully dramatic way. The scene between Pilate and Jesus, he thinks, is admirably theatrical. But as Wace (*Chief Facts in the Life of our Lord*, p. 116) remarks, the Gospel narrative is so marked by the absence of a single false note, that even unbelievers are compelled to acknowledge its truth and reality.

[1] Luke xxiii. 2.

now attaching their own carnal and worldly notions to the Messiahship, and setting Him forth to Pilate as if He aimed at fulfilling them by exciting false hopes among the people, stirring them up against Caesar, and aspiring to be their king, they demanded His condemnation and death. This they did though His whole life and ministry were a refutation of these charges, and though, as they well knew, He had again and again repudiated their carnal ideas of the Christ. Had He consented to be the Messiah they accused Him of being before Pilate, they would never have condemned Him. It was because He would not fulfil their worldly ambitions, and be the Christ after their own hearts, that they rejected Him; and yet while fixing upon Him the character of their own Christ, they asked Pilate on this very ground to put Him to death. Singular perversity and hypocrisy, which it would be difficult to find surpassed!

Pilate doubtless knew something of Jesus' public career. He knew it had been a peaceful one, that Jesus never appealed to force, and that His followers were by no means an armed or warlike band. He had never heard that the multitudes that gathered round the Man of Nazareth had done any violence, or attempted any uprising, or given the smallest trouble to the government. But the accusers had set Him forth as a mover of sedition, a teacher of disloyalty, a claimant of royal honours. They had mentioned Caesar's name, and he dreaded what handle they might make of it against him if he did not show himself zealous for the imperial interest and honour. His interest, if not his perplexity, was aroused. He wished a private examination of the Prisoner. He rose from the judgment seat on the Pavement, retired into the judgment hall that was behind, and gave instructions that the Prisoner should follow him.[1]

There the most remarkable colloquy occurs between them.[2] We see Pilate, with his rough Roman and pagan instincts, making a poor and half sincere attempt to understand Jesus. Not much was there outwardly to prepossess him in His favour. Not much to put him in dread as of a rival potentate, or a disturber of great Caesar's

---

[1] John xviii. 33.

Keim (vol. VI. 85) is amused at Pilate's peripatetic method of conducting his examination and trial of Jesus, his going to and fro between Jesus in the palace and the Jews standing without. But while Roman courts were open, it was natural that the governor who was to be the judge in what he saw from the first was to be a case of peculiar difficulty should wish to see and confer with the Prisoner apart.

[2] The language used between Pilate and Jesus, and indeed throughout the whole of the trial would most probably be Greek. It was the language which Roman governors, who had Eastern provinces to rule, were expected to speak. It was known throughout Judea and Galilee, just as English is throughout Wales or the Highlands of Scotland. Jesus and Pilate therefore needed no interpreter. (Tacitus, *Hist.* V. 8).

empire. A meek and lowly Man, weary and worn with His agony and the trials and buffetings He had already endured—His garments stained plentifully with blood and spitting, His face pale and wan, and yet with something of heaven resting upon it! A King indeed with a greater and more awful sovereignty than that of any Caesar!

"Art thou the King of the Jews?"[1] Pilate asked in beginning his examination. Jesus replied to him, "Sayest thou this thing of thyself, or did others tell it thee of me?"[2] It was answering one question by putting another. Pilate was taken aback. He had probably looked for a complete disavowal of all such pretensions to kingship, especially now that they were removed from those terrible Jewish fathers, and in the judgment hall by themselves. The least disavowal of the kind would most likely have satisfied the Roman governor, now that he was more than suspecting in his own mind that those fathers were but compassing some malicious end of their own, under cover of doing a service for Caesar. But instead of receiving the disavowal he expected he was startled to be asked where he had got his idea of Jesus' kingship, and whether he understood it strictly

---

[1] John xviii. 33.
[2] John xviii. 34.

in his own sense as a Roman, or whether he had learned to attach to it some other meaning. It was a reasonable question, and necessary to be answered if the ground was to be cleared between them. Was "King" to be understood in the Roman, or in the Messianic sense? It was needful at the outset that each should know the language which the other was employing. But it speedily became apparent that Jesus was using a language which to Pilate, as to any other mere man of the world, was utterly foreign and transcendental. Pilate knew of no kingship but that which was after the manner of Caesar's—the idea of any other he left to the dreamers and the philosophers.

The governor appeared to be somewhat nettled at the question addressed to him. "Am I a Jew?"[1] said he. "Your own nation and the chief priests have delivered you unto me. What care I about the dreams of your people about a Messiah? As to this Messiahship they must be the judges and not I. Whatever your claims to it, you are evidently no Messiah in their eyes, for they have given you up into my hands. Tell me what have you done? Your deeds, and not your idle dreams I must be the judge of."

---

[1] John xviii. 35.

Jesus answered with calmness and dignity, "I am a king, but my kingdom is not of this world. If I were a king in your sense, I should have followers and subjects who should bear arms in my cause. They would have fought for me when I was being arrested, and prevented me from being delivered to the Jews. But I forbade them using the sword. I gave myself up of my own will into the hands of my foes, and my followers have made no attempt to rescue me. It should be evident to you that my kingdom is like no earthly one."[1]

"But are you really a king?"[2] asked Pilate again. "If you are not, why do you not deny the accusation they make against you? If you are, what is the kingdom you claim to rule over?"

The answer was at once forthcoming and how sublime it is! "Thou sayest that I am a king. To this end was I born, and for this cause came I into the world that I should bear witness unto the truth. Everyone that is of the truth heareth my voice."[3] A new kingdom indeed to which Pilate with all his knowledge of courts was an utter stranger—the grandest of all however—one

---

[1] John xviii. 36.
[2] John xviii. 37.
[3] John xviii. 37.

whose glorious sovereignty could never be in any but divine hands—a kingdom inward, spiritual, eternal, in which all souls that love the truth find their country and their inheritance for ever. The Prisoner before him dared to claim its divine throne; and nothing, not even the threatened agony and death of the cross, could induce Him to renounce His title to it. He dared also to affirm that the children of the truth everywhere and in all ages were His loyal and devoted subjects, owning His kingship, and hearing His voice.[1]

"What is truth?"[2] contemptuously asked Pilate, when the Prisoner had done trying to make plain to him the kingship which He claimed. Truth, thought he, is a very good thing and a noble study for the schools and the philosophers, but what have Roman courts of law and Roman procurators to do with it? He turned away without waiting for an answer to his own question. We almost feel as if we owed him a grudge that, in so doing, he has withheld from us a reply which would have been of priceless value to the world. Yet Jesus is Himself the answer

---

[1] Yet Renan ventures to remark here that "the great ambiguity of speech which had been the source of Jesus' strength, and which after His death was to establish His kingship, injured Him on this occasion!" *Life of Jesus*, p. 278.

[2] John xviii. 38.

to Pilate's question. He is the Truth; and so every one who is of the truth turns to Him as by the force of an instinct, and responds to Him as He reveals Himself with a holy confidence and joy.

Thus the private interview between Pilate and Jesus ended. The governor returned to the Pavement where the Jewish rulers were still waiting. He had found nothing in Jesus which he could condemn, nothing which Roman law could punish. "I find no fault in this man,"[1] said he to them as he again took his seat as judge in the open-air court. He was disposed at once to set the Prisoner free. Gallio would have come to a like judgment;[2] so would any other Roman procurator. Like Gallio, he did not see that, in any of the things of which Jesus was really accused, there was anything a Roman governor should care for, or could justly punish. He only saw in Jesus a religious enthusiast, a man who talked the merest, but the most harmless transcendentalism about His kingdom and His kingship. What did it all matter to him? What if Pilate had only been possessed of the needful courage and decision, and had played the part of Gallio still farther, driving chief priests and elders,

---

[1] John xviii. 38.
[2] Acts xviii. 12-17.

accusers and Accused, and the people thronging around, all of them from his judgment seat? It would have been the barest justice to the Accused.

The Jewish rulers, however, were not to be got rid of so easily. They were there that morning with a fell purpose, and they would not rest till they had seen it executed. They had laid their hand on Pilate, and they were not the men to relax their hold till he had done as they desired. Pilate's words about the Prisoner's innocence only incensed them the more against Him. Were they to be told that this man was innocent whom they had declared worthy of the last and greatest punishment, and for whom they, in person and very expressly, had come to ask a cross? "They accused Him of many things."[1] In their vehemence and fury one and another, and sometimes several at the same time, could be heard hurling charge after charge against Him.[2]

But in the midst of this pitiless storm, this remorseless outpouring of reproach and calumny, Jesus stood calm and silent. In the majesty of His innocence and sinlessness He left the accusations to answer each other, just as He had done in the council hall before Caiaphas. "When He

---

[1] Mark xv. 13.
[2] Matt. xxvii. 13.

was reviled He reviled not again, when He suffered He threatened not, but committed Himself to Him that judgeth righteously."[1] The governor, we are told, marvelled greatly.[2] He had seen outbreaks of Jewish fanaticism and passion before, but the Jewish fathers seemed on this occasion to surpass themselves. He could not understand the scene. Those Jews, with their Messiah dreams and their religious feuds, were to him the strangest people in the world.

What could the governor do in the circumstances? The silence of Jesus was adding fuel to the flame in the hearts of the accusers, and increasing the clamour of their tongues. It was becoming irksome and perplexing to himself. "Hearest Thou not," said he, "what these witness against Thee?[3] Hast Thou no defence to offer?" But Pilate, who would not stay to hear Jesus, when He would willingly have spoken to him had he been a serious seeker after truth, was not to have any answer from Him now. Jesus left him to answer his own question. He could himself hear what was being charged against the Accused, and he could judge for himself

---

[1] 1 Peter II. 23.
[2] Matt. xxvii. 14.
[3] Matt. xxvii. 13.

whether the charges were such as to call for a reply.

At length a way of escape suggested itself to the governor's mind. Amidst the torrent of accusation and reviling Pilate's ear caught up the word Galilee. Some one had shouted out, "He stirreth up the people, teaching throughout all Jewry, beginning from Galilee unto this place."[1] Jesus then was a Galilean. He belonged therefore to Herod's jurisdiction, and fortunately Herod was in Jerusalem at this very feast. To hand Him over to the lord of Galilee would be an act of diplomatic courtesy which might have many advantages, and it would cost Pilate nothing. It might improve the relations between them which were at that time rather strained and unfriendly. At any rate it promised to rid Pilate of a most unwelcome responsibility, and to deliver him from a position which was every moment becoming more difficult and even dangerous. If Herod should condemn and execute Jesus, as the Jewish rulers desired, it would not trouble Pilate. He would be able to congratulate himself on being done with what was threatening to be a most unpleasant business, and on escaping the toils which the chief priests and elders seemed to be preparing for him.

---

[1] Luke xxiii. 5.

Accordingly Pilate sent Jesus, attended by a strong guard of Roman soldiers, to the tetrarch of Galilee. He himself re-entered the Praetorium, and the court on the Pavement broke up. The place became deserted for the time. The chief priests and grave members of the Sanhedrim now mingled with the rabble, and the whole multitude followed the Prisoner and His guards on their way to the old palace of the Asmoneans, no great distance off, in which Herod Antipas was then living, all eager to witness the next scene in the eventful drama of that day.

JESUS BEFORE HEROD.

The palace to which Jesus was now led was a place of some historic interest and importance. It had been built by one of the Maccabees, and had been the headquarters of the Jewish government in Jerusalem in the days when Judea could boast of some measure of independence. In the struggle with Rome it was the last Jewish stronghold to surrender, and when it was taken by Herod the Great—the father of the Herod Antipas who now inhabited it—the old Maccabean rule came to an end, and the Jews became the subjects of Caesar. When the tetrarch of Galilee came to the capital to observe the feast of the Passover, it was this old palace which he occupied.[1]

It must have been with somewhat mingled feelings that the chief priests and elders accompanied Jesus on His way from Pilate's judgment bar to

---

[1] Josephus, *Antiq.*, XX., VIII. 11.

that of Herod.¹ It could not be pleasing to them to be driven from court to court, and to be compelled to mingle again with the rabble in the streets. But they had this satisfaction at least, that they were going to a judge who claimed to be of their own race and faith, and who as a thoroughgoing Sadducee—though he was not without a dread, strangely enough, of John the Baptist's rising again from the dead²—might be expected to meet their utmost wishes. At the same time they would doubtless have preferred that Pilate had sentenced Jesus as they desired, and that their malicious end had been attained at the Praetorium.

When the chief priests and elders spoke of Galilee, it was with no intention of relieving the Roman governor, and of getting the Prisoner remitted to Herod's jurisdiction. It was rather with the view of furnishing Pilate with another reason for condemning Jesus. Galilee had a bad name as a hotbed of disaffection and rebellion,

---

[1] Renan (*Life of Jesus*, p. 280) regards the narrative of Jesus' appearance before Herod as unhistoric. He thinks it must have been a tradition which had reached Luke, and which he had gathered from a more recent document than the other evangelists had had access to. Strauss allows that it may have happened, but is somewhat distrustful of the account. He thinks that it was put in for a purpose to show that two judges—one a heathen, the other a Jew—pronounced in favour of Jesus' innocence! Otherwise he admits the account contains nothing that might not have really happened as it is told (*New Life*, vol. II. 362).

[2] Matt. xiv. 2.

and it was insinuated that Jesus was only another dangerous demagogue kindling the flame of discontent there with Rome.[1] The tragic action of Pilate in slaughtering a number of Galileans while offering their sacrifices was still fresh in men's minds.[2] Probably in these circumstances the Jewish fathers thought it was enough to say that Jesus was a Galilean stirring up the people to induce the governor to join with them in condemning Him. But somehow the case did not so appeal to his mind. He distrusted those fathers. He decided to send them with their Prisoner to Herod. But if by doing so he gained time and temporary relief, it was only to have them all returning to him, as we shall see, with their feelings of vindictiveness and their relentless persistency in the prosecution of Jesus unto His death increased and intensified by the delay.

Pilate was under no necessity to hand Jesus over to the jurisdiction of Herod. Even though he belonged to another province, the native of a subject state as Jesus was, not being a Roman citizen, might be tried and condemned by the

---

[1] "He stirreth up the people . . . beginning from Galilee" (Luke xxiii. 5). Professor G. A. Smith compares the relations of Judea and Galilee at this time to those existing between England and Scotland soon after the Union (*Historical Geography of the Holy Land*, p. 423).

[2] Luke xiii. 1.

Roman governor within whose province he had been seized, without any claim to extradition other than one *ex gratiâ* of the governor himself. Yet it appears that the principle of *forum delicti commissi*—that is the rule of remitting prisoners to the governor within whose jurisdiction their alleged crimes were committed came to be more and more observed.[1]

It is to be noted that the Jewish fathers entered with the Prisoner and His Roman guard into the court of justice in Herod's palace. They could not enter the Praetorium lest they should be defiled. But this was the dwelling of one who could boast of Jewish descent, and who observed the Passover.[2] They believed therefore they could be in Herod's hall of judgment just as they might be in their own council. Yet when we compare Herod with Pilate we find that whatever difference there is, is in favour of the latter rather than the former. If Herod's professions were Jewish, his practices were heathen. He did more to Romanize the Jews, and make them utterly pagan at heart than any Roman procurator could have done. His capital, Tiberias, which was on the western shore of the sea

---

[1] Rein, *Criminalrecht der Römer*, p. 177.
[2] Josephus (*Antiq.*, XVIII. V. 3) tells us Herod was in the habit of coming up to the feasts.

of Galilee, he aimed at making a Rome in miniature. There he erected theatres and baths, and a palace for himself, for, like his father, he was great in architecture if in nothing else; and there he gathered around him crowds of actors, singers, and jugglers. No Roman could have taken life less seriously, or have given himself more freely to sensuous indulgence and entertainment. Yet those Jewish priests and rabbis feared no contamination by being under the same roof with him, because like themselves he was ceremonially clean, and entitled to eat the Passover! And he was to be the judge of their Messiah!

Into the presence then of this petty king, with so discreditable a record, they brought Jesus to be tried. They struggled to make their way with the throng into his court of justice. The place was not large, and it was soon filled. Herod came and took his seat on the throne of judgment. The courteous message of Pilate was delivered to him handing over the Man of Nazareth to his jurisdiction. Then the Prisoner was set before him. He stood with the marks of the suffering and humiliation He had already borne, wearing the chains they had anew bound upon Him after Pilate had dismissed Him; and Herod, like the chief priests, had no thought of sparing Him the indignity of continuing to endure them.

It was the first time He and Herod had met. Yet it might have been otherwise. Herod was tetrarch of Galilee. In the very country over which He ruled Jesus had been brought up. There He had fulfilled the greater part of His ministry. There He had gathered round Him multitudes of people belonging to all classes, the rich and the poor, the nobleman and the peasant, the learned rabbi and the fisherman, the blameless Pharisee, and the woman that was a sinner. To these multitudes He had addressed His words of truth and life, and on their sick and suffering He had wrought those miracles which had spread His fame far and wide. Of Him Herod could not but have heard, and of His divine ministry and His mighty works he might have been a personal eye and ear witness if he had so chosen.

But he had not so chosen. Religion was not popular in his palace. Neither those who taught it, nor those who lived it were after his liking. A man more void of conscience, of all moral scruple, it would have been difficult to find. He was one of that worst class of men in those degenerate days who, while professing to follow Moses, laid themselves open to all the inroads of Gentile vice and superstition. For just as a merely nominal Christian, who sins against the light which the Gospel has brought him, can surpass even the heathen in his immoralities, and sink to a lower depth, so this nominal worshipper of Jehovah, who was a pagan at heart, outdid many of the heathen in vice and moral callousness. John the Baptist fell somehow into his hands. That prophet of the wilderness and preacher of repentance had the courage, as might be expected, to denounce him to his face for his sin in taking Herodias, his brother Philip's wife. He was requited for his fidelity by being put into prison, where at length his execution was ordered to reward the dancing of the daughter of that shameless and heartless woman.[1]

We are not surprised therefore that such a ruler had never before seen his most illustrious subject. Nor need we wonder at the reception he gave Him. He was glad to see Him, just as he might have been to see any clever conjuror or popular impostor. He had no sense whatever of moral proportions. Moral considerations did not enter for a moment into his conception of the person or character of Jesus. He would have liked to see some miracle done by Him.[2] He desired the Prisoner

---

[1] Matt. xiv. 3-12.
[2] Luke xxiii. 8.

to perform one in his presence, just as if Jesus had been some strolling magician, who would only be too glad to give some exhibition of His conjuring skill before a king, especially when it was likely to purchase a king's favour, and escape from a dreadful death. The miracle would have been to Herod an entertainment, something to wile away a weary hour, and something to talk about to wondering lordly guests on banqueting days to come. But its moral significance would have had not the smallest interest or consequence for him. Like the thorough man of the world he was, he had lost the moral significance of his own life, and his spiritual vision was so blinded that Jesus even could stand before him, and he could see nothing of His exalted character or of His moral excellence.

Pitiful it is indeed, but at the same time deeply instructive to see Herod with Jesus as a prisoner standing before him for examination and judgment. Jesus hears his request for a miracle, and all the response He makes is to fix upon him that steady penetrating look, more telling than any speech. He had been prompt to answer every appeal made by the suffering, even the poorest among them, and to put forth His almighty power in healing and restoring them according to their faith. But for the man, so lost to all reverence for divine things that he could ask the exercise of divine power merely for his entertainment, and without the smallest sense of personal need, and that he could treat Him who was possessed of it as if He were no better than a master of the black art, Jesus could have nothing but a look of infinite pity.

Then we learn that Herod questioned with Him in many words but that He answered him nothing.[1] Herod was not an ignorant man. He could talk about religion, though it had no real or vital place in his heart. With the questions of the day regarding it he was familiar. Very likely he had often discussed them with Sadducee and Pharisee, with priest and with rabbi. He was glad to have the opportunity of showing off, before the learned fathers in his presence, how much he knew of the law and the prophets and of the Christ who was expected. He did what he could to draw Jesus into a discusssion. He propounded question after question, and, being a voluble man, he talked at great length on the points he raised.

We have not a few like him in our own day. A debate about religion is a diversion they enjoy, but

---

[1] Luke xxiii. 9.

religion is by no means a serious business with them. They like to discuss doctrines. They overwhelm you with questions. They start no end of difficulties and objections. But they are not greatly concerned whether they are on the one side or the other. The questions discussed have only a speculative interest for them; they do not touch their consciences or affect their conduct, and any floating impressions they have about them are not such as to induce them to be martyrs for their faith. You would make the greatest mistake possible, were you to imagine that they would be won for the faith by any victory you might obtain over them in argument. You can but leave them to talk on and exhaust themselves, as Jesus did with Herod, now that He stood before him.

Herod is the only one of all His judges before whom Jesus is altogether silent. But what answer could He have for such an utter worldling? What can His gospel signify to one who sets its most glorious mysteries of divine truth and grace at nought, and counts them of far less importance than the last good dinner he ate, or the question of how that absolute trifle of a personal affair is to end next week? Jesus, so ready to open His lips in warning and entreaty where these were needed, and were likely to meet with some fitting response, is silent in presence of the man who, stained with the blood of the last of God's prophets, is hastening on in his career of woe. If the Baptist himself had been there would he have been silent? And was he not in some sense there?[1] Was he not there in that very hour pleading with Herod, through the recollection of his martyred form, to beware of filling his cup of woe to overflowing by imbruing his hands in the blood of Jesus whose forerunner he was?

Jesus would doubtless have spoken had there been the slightest evidence of moral seriousness or of repentance on Herod's part, had there been any readiness to listen and be saved. How hopeless the case of the man to whom Jesus will say nothing! How awful is his case in whom no self-reflection, no enquiry, no remorse can be stirred! Yet such a depth of moral hopelessness appears possible even in this world. It seems to have been reached by Herod, who, however, at one time gave promise of better things. No ice, they say, is so close and hard as that which forms upon the surface after a thaw has been. His heart had once been touched. He had listened gladly at one time to the Baptist, and had done many things because of him.[2] But

---

[1] Matt. xiv. 2.
[2] Mark vi. 20.

heart-hardening had set in after that. Now Jesus can but keep silence before the mystery of evil he has become.

What a sight that is which presents itself in that judgment hall, one fitted to stir the most solemn reflection and the deepest pathos—Herod with all his moral sensibilities weakened or destroyed by long sinning against his better knowledge and better self, sitting on his royal *bema* and babbling about religion—while Jesus standing in his presence is mutely listening to him, and with those tender piercing eyes of His searching His judge through and through, if haply there might be even one moral chord within, which might be responsive to His divine touch, and searching all in vain! What an impressive warning that sight is to listen to the voice of Jesus while we may! That will be the most woeful of days for a man when he hears only the babble of the world, and the attractions and the threatenings of the Gospel alike fail to touch him, and when Jesus can only look upon him in his frivolity and sin with an awful and ominous silence.

But the silence of Jesus unloosed the tongues of His accusers. "The chief priests stood and vehemently accused Him."[1] They had had their

---

[1] Luke xxiii. 10.

own experience already of Jesus' silence. It had been more than they could endure. But they had succeeded in breaking it in their own council, and in moving Jesus to let fall words which they could use for His condemnation.[1] Probably they hoped for a similar result now that they were in Herod's judgment hall. If so, they were to be disappointed. One and another of them uttered their fierce accusations. The hall rang with their vehement outcries. But the Prisoner stood silent in their midst. It was the sublimest self-possession and self-control He thus revealed. It was not after the manner of men thus to be silent when groundless reproaches and calumnies were being hurled against Him, and thus to be patient and unmurmuring amid the storm of abuse and falsehood assailing Him. It was conduct worthy of the divine Man whom He claimed to be.

Herod could not understand the vehemence of the chief priests. He could not see why they should be so furious against this Galilean subject of his. Did they speak of Moses despised, the law violated, blasphemy uttered? What were these things to him? As to these offences alleged, were they not all his own? But he had no keen feeling

---

[3] Matt. xxvi. 63, 64.

or real concern about them. The frivolous, conscience-hardened tetrarch had a delight rather in provoking the vehemence of the priests by his air of proud indifference as to the whole affair. He would not treat Jesus seriously, notwithstanding all their fierce protestations; nor would he give heed to the charges they were bringing against Him. He would not put himself to the trouble even of pronouncing a judgment with regard to Jesus. He had no desire to be burdened with the responsibility of the case. Jesus was Pilate's prisoner, and His accusers were not Galileans but the leading rabbis and priests of Jerusalem. His case therefore seemed one for Jerusalem rather than for Tiberias. Then, like Pilate, he could find no fault in Him; and there was a mysteriousness, an otherworldliness about the Prisoner which was altogether distasteful and incomprehensible to his poor secularized or rather paganized mind.

Herod regarded Jesus even less seriously than the Roman governor had done. If he began in a spirit of irreverence by asking for a miracle as a sort of diversion to himself and his little court, he ended in a spirit equally frivolous and callous. He, with his men of war, as they are called—those who were attending upon him, and were meant to give the court some show of dignity and authority—set Jesus at nought.[1] There was even a touch of malice mingled with the mockery. Very likely he resented the silence of Jesus, and that He would not so much as make answer to his request for an exhibition of His wonder-working power. At any rate Herod went further than Pilate had as yet done. Though he could find in Him nothing worthy of death, he dared to put Him to shame. It was he who first taught Pilate how to turn the kingly claims of Jesus to ridicule. As he sat upon his chair of judgment he looked with undisguised satisfaction upon his soldiers making sport of Jesus, arraying Him in a gorgeous robe—a white robe, we are told, the emblem of Jewish royalty in mockery of His claims to be the heir of David's throne [2]—and indulging in very rude play as pretended subjects before Him.

The attendants and men of war did what they could to amuse their frivolous master. They bowed the knee, and offered their feigned homage to Jesus as a puppet king. They excited the merriment of the crowd by their exaggerated imitations of the ways of courtiers before Him,

---

[1] Luke xxiii. 11

[2] Geikie, *Life and Words of Christ*, p. 696: Josephus, XIX., VIII. 2.

mingling with these no doubt a good deal of rough handling and insulting rudeness. They thus set an example which was copied and carried to a still greater degree by Pilate's soldiers afterwards, when they arrayed Him in a purple robe—the emblem of imperial majesty—and put a crown of thorns on His head, and a reed for a sceptre in His hand. Then when they had grown somewhat weary of their play, Herod bade them attend the Prisoner back to Pilate. Feeling that he could do nothing more with Him, and that there might be some diplomatic gain in returning the Prisoner as courteously as He had been sent, he gave instructions as he quitted the *bema* that this should be done. So with the mock raiment of royalty still on Him,[1] and amid shouts of laughter Jesus was led from the court, and conducted, probably by the way He had come, back to the Praetorium.

Thus Herod did what so many have done with Jesus since. He mocked Him, made light of everything connected with Him, and then dismissed Him from his presence and from any serious thought on his part. Many have followed and are still following his example. In their hearts Jesus

---

[1] It is not said that it was taken off, or that His own raiment was put on again. That is distinctly stated as Jesus goes forth bearing His cross. Mat. xxvii. 31. Mark xv. 20.

is condemned, and there He is continually put to shame. Yet they utter no formal sentence against Him. They are willing that others should provide the cross, and be responsible for the violence, cruelty, and agony under which He dies. Sometimes, to hear them speak, one might think they wished religion well, and that they were as far as possible from desiring to persecute it. But they set it at nought, as if worthy only of their contempt and derision. It is not a matter with which they are seriously concerned. If others assail it, it is no business of theirs to defend it. If it fares badly in the world, is despised and neglected, what is that to them? Like Herod they can even look on and enjoy the spectacle of Jesus being put to shame. They can find entertainment when religion is being turned into ridicule, and the sublimest things into comedy. Yet like Herod also they would rather not have the responsibility of Jesus' death. They would prefer to roll over upon others, if possible, the odium of such a deed. But they consent to His being crucified. They would willingly be rid of Him and His religion altogether. Christianity might perish from the earth, but, so long as their own secular interests and pleasures should be untouched, its loss and destruction would not excite their regret.

The narrative of Jesus' appearance before Herod closes with the significant statement, "And the same day Pilate and Herod were made friends together, for before they were at enmity between themselves."[1] The evangelist says nothing as to how this enmity arose. We are left to infer from history otherwise what was its probable cause. One circumstance that seems to throw some light upon it may be mentioned. Herod Agrippa I. and Herod Agrippa II. had both been treasurers of the Temple; it is probable therefore that Herod Antipas held the same office. In that case we can understand somewhat Herod's estrangement from Pilate after the latter had seized the temple revenues to pay for bringing water into the city.[2]

But two such men could hardly be otherwise than at enmity. They ruled over people of the same race, who would have been better united under one government. There was plenty of scope for jealousy and suspicion between them; nor could long time elapse without something occurring, such as the circumstance referred to, or the slaughter

---

[1] Luke xxiii. 12.

[2] Josephus, *B. I.*, II., IX., 4. There is a letter by the emperor Claudius extant appointing Agrippa II. to be keeper of the pontifical or high priestly vestments. This office carried with it that of manager of the temple and its revenues. When Fadus, the Roman governor, appropriated these offices, the Jews made an uprising in which they were successful (Josephus, XX., I 2).

of the Galileans,[1] to give rise to a rupture. Two such unprincipled, ambitious, self-seeking, and intriguing rulers, within such near neighbourhood of each other as Caesarea and Tiberias, and meeting from time to time in Jerusalem, could hardly be expected to be long without some quarrel. Renan compares the situation not altogether inaptly to that of an arrogant and self-seeking English governor in India in his relations with a native prince in his neighbourhood, who has a kind of independence under the British protectorate, and who might naturally be supposed to be jealously watchful of the few rights and honours which are still left to him. It was strange indeed that between the Roman governor and the petty sovereign, or tetrarch rather, of Galilee, Jesus at this time should have proved the peacemaker.[2]

The temporary agreement and friendship which Jesus brought about between them is deeply significant. It is first of all a striking tribute to the faultlessness of Jesus. Had Jesus been the

---

[1] Luke xiii. 1.

[2] Weiss (*Life of Christ*, III., 351) thinks the reason why Herod would not seriously sit in judgment and pronounce sentence upon Jesus was that he would not allow himself to be surpassed in politeness by Pilate. His right to try his Galilean subject had been admitted, and he was satisfied. He would not exercise the right, but he would show his courtesy and his confidence in Pilate by renouncing what had been so graciously accorded to him.

malefactor He was falsely accused of being, had He been a Barabbas, for example, there would have been no diplomatic courtesies between the two rulers over His case. He would not have been sent from the bar of the one ruler to that of his hated rival. Pilate would have shown himself zealous enough for the vindication of law and order within the bounds of his own government. His pride, his affected zeal for his office as the representative of Caesar, would not have allowed him in such a case to surrender his functions as a judge to another. It was the innocence of Jesus, the impossibility of convicting Him of transgressing any law which perplexed Pilate. It was this that made him desirous of passing the responsibility of dealing with His case to another. It was the same with Herod. He could allow his men of war to mock Jesus and make cruel sport of Him; but regardless of morals though he was, he felt he could not condemn Him.

It is a fact, not without significance, that most of the adversaries of the Christian faith are agreed in paying their tribute of honour to the character of Jesus Christ. They are ready to admit that by no standard of justice or morality can He be condemned, and even that He does not come short of the highest requirements of goodness. Neither His own conduct nor His religion contravenes any law worthy of the name. From the pages of scepticism some of the finest tributes to His matchless excellence might be gathered. He can still look round upon His adversaries and confidently ask, " Which of you convicteth me of sin?"[1] They are constrained to be silent; and it would seem as if the only thing they could do was to pass Him from their own bar of judgment to another, and try to veil their hostility under a cloak of sceptical or cynical indifference.

Further, the friendship of Pilate and Herod indicates another point in which worldly unbelieving men are agreed, and that is in rejecting Jesus. It seems strange that they should be agreed in recognising His guiltlessness, and at the same time in wishing to have nothing to do with Him. His faultlessness should have won them over to His side. It should have impelled them to throw over Him the shield of their authority, and unite in resisting the violence and outrageous demands of the mob, with all the resources of power which as rulers they possessed. But they had no zeal for morals, no eye for true goodness and spiritual

---

[1] John viii. 46.

excellence, and no love for such a character or cause as that of Jesus. It could hardly have been expected that they should.

Would we discover the point of harmony among the enemies of the religion of Jesus, we shall find it here. They are divided among themselves. In nothing are they absolutely at one but in their opposition to Jesus and to His demands upon their consciences and their lives. Like the witnesses against Him when He stood at the bar first of Caiaphas and then of Pilate, those who assail His truth are generally found to answer one another, and to destroy each other's arguments and testimonies. Ask the indifferent and those living without God what fault they have to find with Jesus. Prosecute your inquiries, and you will discover that with them, it is His very faultlessness that is His greatest fault. Through every line and feature of His character they read the condemnation of their own. They see in Jesus one who lives only for righteousness and for God, and as they live for neither, the real voice of their hearts is, "Away with Him." To receive Jesus and to bear His yoke, would, with their unchanged hearts, be an intolerable burden. They are not sighing for any moral deliverance, for any real salvation from sin. What they are desirous of is rather that they should go on following the drift of their worldly desires and ambitions, only with less loss, disappointment and suffering to themselves than the working of sin usually brings. They have no wish to talk with you either about the evils of sin, or about the beauties of holiness. The truth is the crowning difficulty in the way of the acceptance of Christianity is the moral one —the aversion felt to such a character as that of Jesus is, and the want of any real desire, by any saving work whatever, to be brought into conformity with it. How men like Herod can become followers of Jesus is a problem very specially for the conquering grace of God.

What became ultimately of the patched up friendship between Pilate and Herod we are not informed.[1] We know only that it had the effect at the time of strengthening and encouraging each other in their unworthy and alien attitude to Jesus. Pilate's soldiers, as we shall see, surpassed

---

[1] Within less than ten years from this time Herod Antipas came to his downfall. Josephus (*Antiq.*, XVII., VII., 2) tells that after the death of Tiberius in A.D. 38 he went to Rome to obtain for himself the title of king, but that instead he was sent into perpetual banishment at Lyons. Eventually he went to Spain whither he was followed by Herodias—one of the few good things recorded of her— and there he died (Josephus, *B.I.*, II., IX., 6). We may add here the testimony of the same Jewish historian (*Antiq.*, XVIII., V., 3) that within a hundred years almost all the family of Herod the Great, notwithstanding their numerous marriages, were utterly destroyed.

those of Herod in their cruel and insulting treatment of their Prisoner; and doubtless Herod's treatment of Jesus prepared Pilate for breaking through every scruple, and giving up Jesus to the shameful scourge and the still more cruel and shameful cross. Their friendship meant enmity to Jesus; and the humiliation and woe endured upon Calvary reveal how terrible that enmity could be. But the words of the Psalmist, prophetic of their unholy alliance and of its ignominious and woeful result, are applicable to all combinations against Him. "The kings of the earth set themselves, and the rulers take counsel together, against the Lord and against His anointed, saying, 'Let us break their bands asunder, and cast away their cords from us.' He that sitteth in the heavens shall laugh. The Lord shall have them in derision. Then shall He speak to them in His wrath, and vex them in His sore displeasure."[1]

---

[1] Psalm ii. 2-5.

JESUS AGAIN AT PILATE'S JUDGMENT BAR.

From the court of Herod Antipas Jesus was now led back to the Praetorium. The tetrarch of Galilee had not been able to condemn Him; but with his men of war he had set Him at nought and covered Him with ridicule. Jesus, in his view, was not to be taken seriously. He was but a harmless visionary, against whom nothing criminal could be proved, and whose claims to be a king or to be divine were worthy only of being laughed at. He was to be treated as a fool.

This was the shame now put upon Jesus, that through the streets of the city He was compelled to walk wearing the mock raiment of a king in the midst of a jeering crowd.[1] A lamentable spectacle indeed was that hilarious mob, and the Son of God so apparelled, moving on meekly and silently, the object of taunt and insult on every

---

[1] Luke xxiii. 11.

side—a sight to make angels weep. Even had Jesus been a criminal, it was a disgrace to justice and to humanity that He should be so treated for the entertainment of the multitude. It could not but have the effect of preventing the people from considering the claims of Jesus seriously. By this pitiful exhibition before their eyes they were being prepared for their final rejection of Him. Their hilarity now was soon to be changed into bitter reviling. Their jeers and laughter were to lead before long to their frenzied outcries in answer to the appeals of Pilate, "Away with Him, crucify Him." Those who can go so far as to ridicule religion must have a deep and even passionate hatred of it within their hearts. They are on the way to "crucify the Son of God afresh, and to put Him to an open shame" (Heb. vi. 6).

Pilate was doubtless waiting, with some interest and anxiety, the issue of the proceedings in Herod's court of justice. He was in readiness for the company when they returned. He came forth from his palace and took his seat as before on the Gabbatha or Pavement. The scene of the former trial repeated itself. The Prisoner again stood before him. But the raiment which was put on in mockery was taken off, so also were the chains with which He was bound. Fetters and mockery for an accused person were not in harmony with the customs of Roman courts. The accused, however he might be guarded, was unbound till he was condemned. Jesus appeared as before in the garb He was wont to wear as the Man of Nazareth. The chief priests and elders drew near, prepared to renew their accusations; and the crowd gathered again round the open-air tribunal, kept back at a respectful distance by the guard of soldiers in attendance.

Thus the second trial at the Praetorium began. The accusers were not asked to state anew their former charges, though they had the opportunity of bringing fresh accusations, if they were so minded. They were not even called upon to produce witnesses and substantiate their charges.[1] It may seem strange that Pilate did not require this from the very first. But the charges, even if they could have been proved by overwhelming testimony, would not have amounted to guilt in the eye of Roman law. Witnesses, therefore, in support of such charges were unnecessary. Pilate felt this all through the trial. There was nothing which fell from the lips of the fiercest accuser among those fathers which could render Jesus worthy of death, or indeed of any punishment whatever at

---

[1] Luke xxiii. 13-16.

the hands of a Roman judge. The return of Jesus from Herod's bar, uncondemned, confirmed him in this view.

So Pilate summoned courage to address those Jewish fathers with the view of delivering to them the judgment regarding Jesus to which he had come. With an air of great judicial authority and decision he said to them, " Ye have brought this Man unto me as one that perverteth the people, and behold, I, having examined Him before you, have found no fault in this Man touching those things whereof ye accuse Him. No, nor yet Herod, for I sent you to him, and lo, nothing worthy of death is done unto Him."[1]

So far, bravely and justly spoken ; Pilate had stated the facts of the case in true and worthy terms. In declaring that he found no fault in Him, he had done simply what any just Roman judge would have felt compelled to do. What then might have been expected to be his conclusion from premises he had himself laid down so well? It was a halting one. "I will therefore chastise Him, and let Him go."[2] Pilate hoped, as Jeremy Taylor expresses it, that "a lesser draught of blood

---

[1] Luke xxiii. 14-15.
[2] Luke xxiii. 16.

might stop the furies and rabidness of their passion."[1] But he was to find himself disappointed in the end, and that the "leeches would not so let go." There was to be the scourging first, and then liberty for the Prisoner. He was to be chastised, the painful and humiliating scourge was to be laid upon Him; and He uncondemned and guiltless! What a cruel mockery of justice! It was only convicted criminals who were scourged; and Jesus was to be treated as if He were one. But as nothing worthy of death had been proved against Him, He was to be let go. After being thus shamefully handled, visited with the most degrading punishment, He was to have His liberty!

Pilate's proposal was a miserable compromise, a gross paltering with justice and with duty. The chastising was the satisfaction he was willing to give the rabbis and priests who were the accusers. It was the compliment intended for these fathers, the politic acknowledgement that they had not been altogether without grounds for their complaints and accusations. On the other hand, as the offences they alleged were not such as Roman law could punish, the Prisoner should be released.

Pilate was thus compromising matters with the

---

[1] Jeremy Taylor's *Life and Death of Jesus Christ*, vol. III., ch. XV. 27.

Jewish rulers. He had no objection to order the flogging. That was going but a step further than Herod had gone, when he sent the Prisoner back to him covered with ridicule. But he could not yet consent to sentence the Prisoner to death. He was wavering between what was his duty as a judge, and what was his interest or advantage in dealing with his troublesome Jewish subjects. The note of vacillation was distinctly in his deliverance. Its weakness and hollowness were promptly perceived. It was caught up at once, and the utmost advantage was taken of it. It was answered by a perfect storm of dissent. "They cried out all at once."[1] The decision incensed them to the highest pitch. They tightened the grip which they felt they had upon the weak and yielding governor. They increased their efforts to compel him to do as they wished.

Pilate, we are inclined to think, meant the scourging to take the place of crucifixion.[2] Not so the mob. It should only be preliminary. Release should never be. That day should see

---

[1] Luke xxiii. 18. How they could make a clamour Josephus tells us (*Antiq.*, XVIII., III , 2) where he speaks of the Jews boldly casting reproaches upon Pilate till he was so incensed that he caused forthwith a fearful massacre of them.

[2] According to Weiss (*Life of Christ*, III., 355), Pilate meant the scourging as the usual preliminary to crucifixion, but hoped when they saw the result that the people might be moved to rest satisfied with the suffering thus inflicted.

Jesus die. And their fell purpose triumphed. They had the wicked satisfaction of seeing Jesus first scourged, and then crucified. They beheld Him treated worse ultimately than the malefactors who were crucified with Him. He had to endure both the lash and the cross, and these accompanied with barbarities which the others were spared. Pilate after scourging Jesus laboured hard, but in vain, for His release.

But the procurator's attitude of compromise was altogether like him. It was the attitude which was assumed in regard to most things by Roman politicians and governors. They seldom found a straight course to their end. There was always so much to be yielded to those opposed to them, and so much more, if possible, to be secured for themselves. The lines of right and wrong, justice and injustice, morality and vice faded away before the more distinct ones between what seemed practicable and pleasing, and what was not. What was politic and expedient took the place of what was just and dutiful. So here it was not a question with Pilate what was due to his Prisoner, but what could be done in the circumstances with the least trouble and the greatest advantage to himself. It occurred to him as a stroke of statesmanship, and as an admirable solution of the difficulty that there should be scourging inflicted to please the Jewish rulers, and the release afterwards to meet the demands of Roman law and authority.

It was some considerable time, as we find, before the governor was brought to give up the hope of such a solution. He was surprised when it was not accepted at once. He tried the chief priests, and from them he turned to appeal to the people,[1] but all in vain. His miserable compromise was rejected with scorn and indignation by both rulers and people. He was taught ultimately that, whatever else he might do with the Prisoner—make sport of Him, buffet Him, scourge Him, as he pleased— nothing would satisfy them but His death upon the cross. His compromise was destined to end as all compromises of the kind always tend to do.

Pilate's feet were in fact slipping down a steep incline; and there were the forces behind, which he could not resist, bent on pushing him downward till he should touch the bottom, by giving up a Prisoner whom he declared innocent to a death than which a more awful could not be inflicted even upon the guiltiest, and thereby covering himself with infamy. Or, changing the figure, we might say that, allowing himself to drift from the safe guidance of principle and of duty, he was at

---

[1] Matt. xxvii. 20.

once on the way to complete moral shipwreck; and he was all the more swiftly and disastrously borne along that his poor frail bark had such a tempest of popular passion to endure.

The lesson is plain enough, and hardly any is more frequently set before us. The lives of too many are but a series of wretched compromises with righteousness and duty. Both are generally sacrificed in the end. Many are ready to admit that nothing can be said against Jesus or His religion; but they will not confess Him, or honestly act up to their own avowals. It is always in these cases irreligion that wins. Let a man dethrone conscience, and refuse to listen seriously to her voice; let him slight duty, and deny to it its divine character and obligation once and again and again; other powers than justice, truth, and goodness will then get the mastery over him, take all moral strength out of him, and work out his ruin. Away from the rock of principle there is really no firm footing. Any compromise with justice is always a triumph for injustice, any half-hearted dealing with religion is a victory for the world, any trifling with convictions is a defeat for all that is serious and sacred.

There is one striking incident at this stage of the trial, which deserves our special attention, and which shows that Pilate was not without warning before announcing his fatal resolution. As he was about to take his place on the judgment seat, and to open for the second time the proceedings of the court, a messenger hurriedly entered and delivered a message to him. The message was from his own wife.[1] She had evidently heard of the case going on. In some providential way, of which we have no record, she had come to be deeply interested. It is intelligible that she had learned more even than the governor about Jesus and His wonderful ministry in Galilee and Judea. It is possible that, like some other truly noble Roman ladies, she had become acquainted with the Jewish Scriptures, and that she was even a Jewish proselyte.[2] If the wife of one high in Herod's service and household could be reached and touched by the ministry of Jesus,[3] it would not be wonderful if the wife even of the Roman procurator had heard enough of the Prophet of Nazareth to have her sympathies moved towards

---

[1] The law prohibiting governors from taking their wives with them when they went to their provinces was not observed from the time of Tiberius. Another incidental proof is thus given of the accuracy of the Gospel records. In Tacitus (*Annals*, III. 33, 34) we have an interesting report of a discussion in the Senate at Rome on a motion, which was lost, to renew the prohibition.

[2] The Gospel of Nicodemus represents Pilate's wife as a proselyte.

[3] Joanna, the wife of Chusa, Herod's Steward. Luke viii. 3.

Him. And if, on inquiring, her servants told her of His appearance before the governor, of His remarkable air of mingled meekness and divine majesty, of His wonderful silence and self-restraint while so many throats were sending forth the most passionate invectives against Him, of His being remitted to Herod, and then of His return to the Praetorium for His final sentence—if she were informed of these things, it is not difficult to understand why she should be very particularily moved about this case, and should hasten to interpose some warning word before any decisive step should be taken. That night, she had had a dream. It had troubled her greatly.[1] Jesus had been the central figure of it. He had appeared with an awful holiness of character about Him, so that the guilt of doing to Him an injustice could not but be the greatest possible. Her message to her husband ran in these remarkable words: "Have thou nothing to do with that Just One, for I have suffered many things in a dream because of Him?"[2]

Every Christian thanks Claudia Procula (for such, according to tradition, is the name of Pilate's wife) for that message, and admires her for the noble

---
[1] Matt. xxvii. 19.
[2] Matt. xxvii. 19.

testimony she thus gave to Jesus. She has won a place in the heart of a grateful Christendom that she should thus pay her tribute to the purity, the perfect guiltlessness of Jesus. He is the Just One in her eyes,[4] and the guilt of condemning Him appals her, and makes her tremble, lest it should fall upon her husband. We do not wonder that the Greek Church should have canonized her.

It is remarkable that, with a solitary exception, her tribute to Jesus ere He was condemned, and the Roman centurion's who said "Truly this was the Son of God,"[5] as he saw Him die, should be, so far as we learn from the evangelists, the only tributes paid Him throughout all this eventful day. Jesus was passed from bar to bar, and at length led bound to Calvary, and there was only another voice in addition to those two Gentile voices heard speaking on His behalf. It was that of the penitent thief who, amidst the storm of reviling round Calvary, said, as he turned to his divine fellow-sufferer, "Lord, remember me when Thou comest into Thy kingdom."[6] His indeed was a fuller and more striking tribute

---

[1] Her words are Μηδὲν σοὶ καὶ τῷ δικαίῳ ἐκείνῳ. Whether she recognised in Him anything supernatural or divine it might be hazardous to say.

[2] Matt. xxvii. 54.

[3] Luke xxii. 42.

than theirs. It came from him with touching appropriateness as the representative of that large class of the consciously guilt-laden and outcast whose friend and saviour Jesus was, and for whom He had come to die. Two Romans and a robber receiving "the due reward of his deeds"— these the only persons testifying on Jesus' behalf on the day of His trial and woe!

What the dream of Procula was, we are not told. Poets and painters have laid hold of it as a subject, and wrought it up according to their fancies. Gustave Doré's representation of it is well known. Pilate's wife is seen, with eyes still dazed with sleep, descending the steps of a broad staircase. An angel hovers beside her, seeming to rest upon the marble rail of the staircase, and whispering in her ear the story of the vision she has in her dream. Before her, as the central figure of the wonderful scene on which she looks out, is our Saviour on whom a flood of light is falling. Around Him are the rude soldiery who kneel at His feet, and the evil-eyed priests and rulers cowering and muttering their dismay. In the background are long lines of figures, group behind group, representing the various epochs of the Church's history—the apostles, the early Church Fathers, the Crusaders, the martyrs, crowds of worshippers of all lands and languages, witnesses to the development and extension of Christianity down to the latest ages. Encompassing or hovering over all is a radiant host of angels, filling the sky; and above them shines out a starry cross shedding rays of silvery light over the whole scene.

Thus the painter has represented the dreamer as seeing in vision the future triumphs and glories of the Cross. He has supposed that Procula's dream concerned the future of Jesus, the Just One, who had come to inspire her with a holy awe; and he has dared to interpret that dream in the light of the history of Christianity. He has painted what, for us at any rate, is not a dream but a most impressive reality. And whatever there was in Procula's dream fitted to warn Pilate to do nothing against the Just One, the history of the religion of Jesus through these past nineteen centuries ought to make on our minds, and on the minds of the most indifferent or most adverse to the Gospel, a still greater and more lasting impression, not only in the way of warning us to do nothing against Jesus, but in the way of encouraging us to faith and devotion, and to doing all we can for His cause and for His glory.

The subject has fascinated the modern poet

as well as the modern painter. Sir Edwin Arnold introduces it in an interesting way in his "Light of the World." He represents Pilate as spending a night in Nazareth, on his way back to Rome where he was to answer for his faults as governor. The place reminds him of the wonderful Prophet who had so long dwelt there, and who only three years before had suffered death at his hands. As they stand on the balcony of the house where they were lodged, talking together and recalling the events of the crucifixion day, Pilate's wife repeats to her husband the story of her dream. She tells how in her dream she saw "a presence most sweet and most majestical." He wore a crown of thorns, and His hands and feet were pierced. But He looked kingly and even divine; and she stretched out "eager, quick hands of worship unto Him," and fell upon her knees in reverence and wonder. Jesus spoke to her of His coming cross, and of the curse and shame it would bring to Pilate should he yield to the multitude. As she awoke she heard "the angry roars, as if of hungered beasts," from those clamouring that Jesus should be crucified and Barabbas released. Drawing near her latticed window and looking out she saw the divine Man of her vision, and was so impressed with

His bearing before her husband's tribunal that she felt impelled to write him forthwith the message she had sent, warning him not to involve himself in the guilt of this Man's death.[1]

Pilate, no doubt, was troubled by the message that came from his wife. Even the most enlightened Romans believed somewhat in dreams and in omens,[2] and Procula's was no ordinary dream. There was so much in it that accorded with his own vague feelings and impressions in regard to the Prisoner. And why should he not set Jesus at liberty at once to please his wife? If Herod could abandon himself to the injustice and wickedness of executing John the Baptist to please a base woman whom he had brought to take the place of his wife, would it not have been the most gracious and honourable act Pilate ever did had he, at the earnest request of his wife, given life and liberty to Jesus? Alas, as the event shows, Pilate did not dare to be his own master in these matters, otherwise he might have done this at once.

---

[1] Arnold's *Light of the World*, pp. 61—65.

[2] Cicero, *Nat. Deorum*, II., LXV., 163. "Multa cernunt haruspices, multa augures provident, multa oraculis declarantur, multa vaticinationibus, multa somniis, multa portentis, quibus cognitis multae saepe res ex hominum sententia atque utilitate partae, multa etiam pericula depulsa sunt."

JESUS AGAIN AT PILATE'S JUDGMENT BAR

But his wife's message had at least this effect, that it made him the more anxious to secure Jesus' release. When he found the Jewish rulers would not hear of it, he bethought himself of a custom by which Roman governors had been wont to pay a certain tribute of honour to the most sacred of Jewish observances. It was the custom of releasing a prisoner on the Passover day for whom the people might desire this boon.[1] He would take advantage of this custom. Probably he did not think seriously of the imputation of guilt it involved for Jesus. In seeking such a favour for Jesus he should be seeking what was meant only for a notorious criminal. But Pilate was anxious to have done with Jesus' case, and at the same time to be, if possible, guiltless of His blood. He was sanguine the people could be induced to ask for Jesus' release. He turned therefore from the priests and elders before him—" for he knew that for envy they had delivered Him "[2]—to the multitude gathered together in front of the Pavement. Virtually he thereby remitted Jesus from his own bar to that of the Jewish people. At that bar of the populace he

---

[1] Matt. xxvii. 15.
[2] Matt. xxvii. 18.

who was the judge abnegated his office and became advocate. He was to find to his humiliation in the end the case decided against him. How he pleaded, and pleaded all in vain, for Him in whom he could find no fault, we shall see plainly enough from the sequel.

JESUS AT THE BAR OF THE PEOPLE.

It had been the desire and the strategy of the Jewish rulers that Jesus should be tried and condemned that morning, before the multitude had had time in any considerable numbers to gather. Hence their own hurried procedure, the eager haste with which they went to Pilate, and the clamorous urgency they used to induce him to acquiesce in their sentence. In fact they were afraid of the multitude. They remembered the hosannas with which, a few days before, the temple courts had rung. They could not trust those who had raised them. Nor could they tell how widely feelings in favour of Jesus might be spread. They would rather have avoided an appeal to the popular judgment, being uncertain as to how it might issue.[1] Their hope was that, before the multitude had had time to act, the condemnation of Jesus might be secured at the hands both of

---

[1] Matt. xxvi. 5. Luke xxii. 2.

Pilate and of the Sanhedrim, and that His going forth with this double brand of being a malefactor might turn any tide of popular feeling which there might be in His favour. But it was the multitude after all who had the final decision to give in the case of Jesus. They, in the end, were the judges at whose bar Jesus stood, and from which He was dismissed with the sentence passionately shouted out by thousands, "Let Him be crucified."

Before this popular tribunal, then, took place the final trial of our Lord. The priests had delivered Him to the governor, and the governor remitted Him to the judgment of the populace. Priests and people, rulers and ruled, were all to be involved in the guilt of His death. It was not to be said that His death was merely a judicial blunder, a gross miscarriage of justice. It was to be the crime of the Jewish nation; nay more, it was to be the crime of the world. Christianity is not an affair merely for official recognition and judgment, whether ecclesiastical or civil. It makes its appeal to every man. Not only so, but the question, "What think ye of Christ?" is one that must be settled ultimately, not in courts and councils, nor by count of heads and the voices of the mob, but in the judgment hall of every man's heart.

Recall, then, the scene and circumstances of this

trial. Pilate is sitting in his chair of state on the Pavement in front of the Praetorium. Jesus is before him, clothed in the homely garb of a Galilean peasant. His accusers, the members of the Sanhedrim who had that morning already condemned Him, are around Him. The governor can find no fault in Him, and this he has publicly declared. He is anxious to release, but he is morally weak and irresolute. He is willing to do justice, but only if it should cost him nothing. His wife's dream troubles him, and he is all the more desirous to be rid of his Prisoner on the easiest terms. But those priests and elders before him are not to be easily put off. Nothing but the death of Jesus on the cross will content them. Pilate offers to scourge Him. It is not enough for them. So in his perplexity he turns to the people.

Round the Pavement the people are crowding. They have been increasing in numbers and in excitement as the news of the trial has spread. They are looking on with intensest interest. They are with difficulty kept back by the Roman spears. As Pilate is soon to learn, they share the mood of their priests and rabbis. As the latter grow more fierce in their accusations, their followers in the crowd become more excited and unrestrained in their outcries. The outburst of passionate dissent with which the Jewish fathers receive Pilate's sentence, "I will chastise Him and let Him go," is caught up, and repeated in greater volume by the multitude.

For the moment Pilate misinterprets their shouting. He imagines it may have come from friends of the Prisoner, and that it is in His favour. He will take advantage of it, and make his appeal to the multitude. He recollects also that this is the Passover morning, and that his Jewish subjects are expecting to be gratified as usual by the release of a prisoner. "Ye have a custom," he says as he rises from his chair of judgment, and addresses himself to the throng surging in front of him and on either side, "that I should release unto you one at the Passover. Will ye therefore that I release unto you the king of the Jews?"[1] Thus begins the trial of Jesus by the people, in which, before the mob as determining judge, Pilate plays the part, as we shall see, of the half sincere, half-hearted advocate for the Accused, while the Jewish rulers are the insidious, unfaltering, and weighty counsel on the other side.

The custom to which Pilate refers it is somewhat difficult to trace. "General acts of pardon

---
[1] John xviii. 39.

and release," says Rein, "were not seldom granted by the emperors on their accession, ecclesiastical festivals (as for example, the Passover), birthdays, and other joyous occasions."[1] But the authority he quotes for this statement is the Theodosian Code which belongs to the first half of the fifth century. It had, however, been the custom for the Romans on Caesar's birthday, or on some other festive occasion, to grant to people of subject provinces such as Judea a gratification of the kind referred to. The Passover was a commemoration of deliverance from bondage. Roman governors had deemed it fitting and politic, it would appear, by the release of a prisoner whom the people might choose, to pay their tribute to the great Jewish festival. It is a custom which has been often observed in more modern times, as when a new ruler like the Czar of Russia ascends the throne, and he chooses to give a proof of his benignity by opening the prison doors to a certain number who have been confined within them. In an enlightened and well ordered country where the law is, as it ought to be, placed beyond the arbitrary handling of the sovereign such a custom is hardly to be expected. The ruler has no more title to open the prison doors

---

[1] Rein, *Criminalrecht der Römer*, p. 272.

to anyone, unless in exceptional circumstances where the prerogative of mercy may be called for, than the humblest subject of his realm. He is on the throne to execute the law, not to annul it at his pleasure. Moses certainly had never contemplated such a custom, least of all that a man guilty of sedition and murder should get the benefit of it.[1]

At the same time one can understand how in a conquered country like Judea, suffering under the oppression of a foreign tyranny, such a custom might sometimes be a real boon. Seldom would the prisons of Jerusalem be without Jews whose greatest fault was that they dared to denounce and to resist the tyranny of Rome. It was some satisfaction that the people had it in their power, even once a year, to demand the liberty of one such political offender. The custom would have been honoured, as it never had been, had the people on this occasion demanded the release of Jesus.[2]

---

[1] Baring Gould (*Trials of Jesus*, p. 71) says that at the Passover the Jews were wont, during the Maccabean period, to bring criminals out of prison, some to be executed, others released. But his authority (*Pesachim*, XCI., 1) has a doubtful reading, and we have failed to find anything in the Talmud to justify the statement.

[2] Winer (*Realwörterbuch*, vol. II. 202) says that the practice originated with the early procurators of Judea adopting a pagan custom, and applying it to the festivities of the Jewish Passover. There is, however, some difficulty in tracing this custom. It was not Mosaic in its origin. Livy (V. 14) refers to a time of great

Yet, whether Pilate knew it or not, he was insulting Jesus by proposing that He should have the benefit of such a custom. It was for condemned criminals. It was no favour for the governor to release innocent men—it was an act of justice. To propose that Jesus should be released in accordance with the custom of the feast was really to imply that He was guilty. It was to put on Him the brand of the transgressor, and then to let Him go free. Then Pilate proposed to do this to one in whom he declared he could find no fault. It was an outrage upon justice and consistency. And to ask the mob that he might be allowed to release Him, as if He were some deeply-dyed, blood-stained criminal whose fate, notwithstanding His crimes, might call forth their compassion, was for the governor to exhibit his own weakness, to degrade his office, and to put his prisoner to open shame.

But the proposal was of a piece with that other which Pilate had before made to the Jewish rulers, "I will chastise Him and let Him go."[1] It was

---

distress when, among other things done to appease the anger of the gods, prisoners were freed from their chains. Josephus cites one instance (*Antiq.*, XX., IX. 5) when Albinus, a Roman governor of Judea, a successor of Pilate, opened the prison doors to a number of minor offenders, in order to please the Jews. But the fact of the custom as stated by the evangelists there is really no reason for calling in question.

[1] Luke xxiii. 22.

a discreditable compromise, destined like that other to end in failure, and to add rather to the shame and suffering of the Prisoner. Pilate could not treat Jesus as a convicted criminal, plead for His release on that ground before the multitude, and then expect that he could save Him from the cross. Ask the world's indulgence for Jesus, while you allow its aspersions and accusations against Him to pass without answer or rebuke; it will laugh you to scorn, and crucify Him all the same. And if you suffer Jesus to be so treated in your own mind; if you are not concerned about the upholding of His honour, and of His claims on heart and conscience; if you attempt to compromise matters regarding Him, and treat Him as if it were a charity to let Him alone and not to bring positive injury and disgrace upon His cause—if that is your mood and attitude you will find that you have to reckon with forces of evil in yourself which, like the passions of the Jerusalem mob, will carry you farther and farther till there is a Calvary for Jesus within your own soul.

It must be admitted, however, that Pilate meant well by his appeal to the multitude before him. He believed the people would favour Jesus. He knew that for envy the chief priests had delivered Him into his hands.[1] He thought he understood human nature. It seemed to him that the reason why the priests and rabbis were so bitter against Jesus was simply that Jesus had a growing influence among the people of which they were jealous. It seemed to him that they were afraid that, as the popularity of the Prophet of Nazareth increased and spread, their own influence would decline. Nor was Pilate doing them any injustice in attributing to them such feelings and fears. Only a few days before they had been saying one to another, "Perceive ye how ye prevail nothing; behold, the world is gone after him."[2] He had the hope, therefore, that in Jesus' case he might be able to foil the priests by using the people against them. If the people could only be induced to ask for the release of Jesus, he would be able to rid himself of his unpleasant responsibility on easy terms, and have the peculiarly agreeable satisfaction of a triumph over those Jewish rulers with whom indeed he had a standing feud.

This attempt to win the people against the priests was made, as we see, with wonderful adroitness. First the governor speaks the people fair. He begins by offering, before they have

---

[1] Mark xv. 10.
[2] John xii. 19.

asked, the usual Passover favour. He reminds them of their custom. He assures them of his willingness to comply with it. They shall have a prisoner released to them whom they may desire. But he will guide them in their choice. Shall it not be Jesus, the King of the Jews?[1] His words are astutely chosen. He calls Jesus by the name best fitted to touch their patriotic feelings. He is a Roman, and may be presumed to be jealously watchful of Caesar's honour and interests. But he will play the magnanimous part. He will not call in question the kingly claims of Jesus. He will show his regard for their national feelings and hopes. He is willing to do them the pleasure, that he will set this Jesus at liberty; he will let them have their king that they may do with Him as they please.

When was Roman governor so condescending and so gracious towards a Jewish multitude? He believes himself to be doing an act which was a special tribute to Jewish feeling, to Jewish nationality; and even had Jesus been a false Christ it could justly be so construed. Could he imagine that it would not be reciprocated, or that his offer would be rejected with scorn? It would not have been wonderful if he had cherished just a little fear

---

[1] John xviii. 39.

that it would be only too promptly accepted. He might have anticipated that with this Jesus restored to the people, and the people gathering round about Him as, in some sense still mysterious to Pilate, their king, there might be new and unforeseen troubles to the Roman government in the land.

But the shouting that came back in response surprised him.[1] It revealed at once that Jesus and His kingly claims were not in the favour he had supposed. It revealed at once that some skill and tact would be needed to persuade that multitude, if Jesus was to be released. The governor was not wanting in these qualities, and he made all the use of them he could in the circumstances.

Foiled in the direct appeal he made at the outset in favour of Jesus, Pilate forthwith tried another. He suggested an alternative of two names to the people,[2] putting before them that of the most notorious criminal he could at the moment recall along with that of Jesus. The alternative was so cleverly framed that one would have thought there could be no doubt of the choice that would be made. He selected from

---

[1] Luke xxiii. 18.
[2] Matt. xxvii. 17.

those who were then lying in the dungeons of Jerusalem the criminal with the worst record, a man named Barabbas, "who for a certain sedition made in the city, and for murder"[1] had been cast into prison. He gave the people to understand that their choice must lie between this worst of men in Jerusalem and Jesus. Then, with the view of making a deeper impression upon the people, Pilate ordered the man to be brought forth from his cell, and placed side by side with Jesus on the Gabbatha.[2]

There was some delay before the wretched man appeared. The time was diligently employed by the chief priests and elders. They and their following were busy among the people, "persuading them that they should ask Barabbas and destroy Jesus."[3] Their instructive propaganda succeeded only too well. But had not many in that crowd been indulging only a little before in insulting and making sport of Jesus in the streets, as they came back with Him from Herod? And through all the trial, of which they were keenly interested spectators, the multitude had never given a single expression of feeling in favour of the

---

[1] Luke xxiii. 19.

[2] Matt. xxvii. 21. "The twain," so that in all probability the two were side by side.

[3] Matt. xxvii. 20.

Prisoner. Now that they had to choose between following Pilate and following their priests it was only too easy to induce them to do the latter. So by the time Barabbas appeared the people were prepared to give Pilate such an answer as might well have appalled him.[1]

What a sight those two, Barabbas and Jesus standing side by side in presence of the multitude![2] Barabbas is fresh from the dungeon. He still wears his chains. The rags with which he is covered, his lean and haggard looks tell of the misery and neglect in which he has long lain. He bears the marks of crime, and has the air of one who is still defiant under the ban of society. He knows the priests would gather up their garments in proud disdain if he should come near them, and as for the people he cannot imagine that they should ask for his life. He stands in bewilderment before them. Can it be

---

[1] There was a Barabbas who was leader of the insurrection which Pilate caused in Samaria by his attempt to plant the Roman eagles on Mount Gerizim. Whether he is the same with the Barabbas of Gospel history it is impossible to say. To ask for the release of such a fanatical upholder of Judaism, however agreeable it may have been to the Jewish populace, must have been a peculiarly bold action on their part. Had he been the person whose release was desired we would most probably have heard more of the governor's unwillingness to comply, and it is unlikely that the governor would have brought forward his name. (Josephus, *Antiq.*, XVIII., IV.)

[2] Ewald (*Hist. Israel*, VI., 436) says that Barabbas' name was also Jesus, and that he was the son of a rabbi, but Tischendorf rejects this view.

that he has been brought forth only to be cruelly tantalised with the hope of freedom, and then ordered back amidst the jeers and curses of the mob to his dungeon and his deserved doom? And who is this Prisoner to whom it is just possible he may be preferred—one so calm and silent while all around are excited, so dignified and wearing an aspect so unworldly, so divine?

Was there ever such a striking contrast presented? Pilate himself is impressed by it, and believes that it cannot be without effect upon the multitude. For the moment, as he looks upon the spectacle, he congratulates himself upon the happy thought that suggested to his mind the placing of it before them. He cannot imagine any hesitancy in choosing between the two, the deeply-stained, repulsive-looking malefactor and the Prisoner in whom he can find no fault.[1] He rises from his chair, and pointing to the two as they stand side by side before him he asks, "Whom will ye that I release unto you? Barabbas, or Jesus which is called Christ?"[2] But there is no hesitancy, and there is no divided opinion among the multitude. There is a unanimous outcry rending the air, staggering to

---

[1] According to Weizäcker, Pilate proposed the liberation of Jesus that he might not be compelled to free Barabbas. Quoted in Weiss, *Life of Christ*, III., 354.

[2] Matt. xxvii. 17.

Pilate, instructive to all ages, "Away with this man, and release unto us Barabbas."[1]

Pilate can hardly believe his ears. He tries to reason with the multitude. He is but pouring oil upon the blazing fire. "What will ye, then, that I shall do unto Him whom ye call the King of the Jews?"[2] And the answer comes unhesitatingly from the assembled thousands, "Crucify Him."[3] Yet again he reasons and expostulates with them, "Why, what evil hath He done?"[4] If the Roman oppressor could not find guilt in Him, what possible charges could His own countrymen have against Him? But the mob is not there to listen to reason. It is content to make shouting do duty for argument. "Crucify Him" is the reply, and it is delivered with such passionate force that the bewilderment of the governor is greater than ever. And when he asks a second and even a third[5] time, "Will ye that I release unto you the King of the Jews?" and pleads with them to be content with His being chastised—joining in so fierce an outburst as to make any further reasoning vain, they all cry again, "Not this man but Barabbas."[6]

---

[1] Luke xxiii. 18.
[2] Mark xv. 12.
[3] Mark. xv. 13.
[4] Mark xv. 14.
[5] Luke xxiii. 22.
[6] John xviii. 39, 40.

As Luther forcibly expresses it, "They would sooner have asked for the release of the devil than that God's Son should escape."

Thus far Pilate's appeal to the multitude only ends in bringing fresh humiliation upon Jesus. It was humbling that appeals on His behalf, even from such a man as Pilate, should be treated so scornfully. It was humbling that a Barabbas should be preferred to Him, that the people would sooner release the worst criminal in the land than they would release Him, that He should be so unblushingly numbered with transgressors, that scourging even should not be thought enough for Him, and that He should be held so vile as to be given over by the unanimous voice of the multitude to be crucified.

It was as painful as it was humbling. It must have given Him sharper agony than the nails that pierced His hands and His feet on the cross. It had in it that sharpest sting of all, the sting of deep ingratitude. Had not Jesus made Himself one of the people, stooping to their condition and their lot of toil? What a life of singular excellence He had lived! What a glory He had brought on the land, on Bethlehem and Nazareth, on despised Galilee and Judea, on Cana and Jericho, on Nain and Bethany, on

Capernaum and Jerusalem! What miracles He had wrought! Could there be a crowd gathered in Jerusalem in which there were not some He had healed? Where were the lepers He had cleansed? Where was the blind man who had received his sight after washing in the pool of Siloam? Was not Malchus there whose ear He had restored, even in the hour when He was seized in the garden? Was not Bartimaeus, who had followed Him from Jericho, and who could make his voice heard above the din of a multitude?

Then, was it true that the common people heard Him gladly when He preached? Where now were the grateful hearers? How true it was that whenever the spiritual was uppermost and not the temporal, the masses were no longer with Jesus. It was the Gospel of loaves they wanted. Never had there been such a prophet, never such a ministry in Israel; and this was the people's response to it all—"Not this man, but Barabbas!" Ingratitude has written many a shameful page in human history, but never a darker or more disgraceful than this. They tell us, sometimes, that it is a grand principle to trust the people, and that the *vox populi* is the *vox Dei*. But what people, we would ask? A people priest-ridden, and in their hours of unreasoning passion and infatuation, like the multitude that chose Barabbas and designed a cross for Jesus? No, we must trust or follow unquestioningly neither the masses nor the classes, neither democracy as represented in that mob, nor aristocracy and learning as represented in those priests and rabbis; but we must think for ourselves, engage in our own search for truth and principle, and trust only and at all times in God.

Side by side, like Jesus and Barabbas before Pilate and the multitude, are placed for us in this world truth and falsehood, faith and unbelief, innocence and purity, the kingdom of evil and the kingdom of God. What is the choice the multitude are making? Why should it be so much easier to persuade them to unbelief than to the grateful acceptance of the faith? Why so much easier to delude them with errors and falsehoods than to convince them of the truth? Why should men be so ready to believe anything faulty about Jesus Christ and Christianity, and be so credulous about the Barabbas that would rob them of their only hope and Saviour? It is human nature, we admit, but it is fallen and unregenerate human nature. The enmity to Jesus is native to the human heart, and abides till it is slain by His cross. There is small hope of anyone making the right choice, who does not carry the matter away from the distracting cries and misleading influences of the multitude into the presence of God, and the quiet sanctuary of his own mind and heart, and seek very earnestly with divine help to have it determined there.

But let the world choose its Barabbas if it will, it may be assured of this, that though he may have the voices still of the great mass of mankind in his favour he will never be its Saviour. Money, force, sedition, murder, anarchism, not any of these means or disguises which Barabbas may use— neither the compulsion of the law, violent revolution, nor daredevilism of any kind, will ever avail to bring about the world's redemption. Jesus' programme of spiritual reform and salvation by His atoning and regenerating work is the only one that is at once reasonable and ever likely to succeed. Change men's hearts, and set them in new and harmonious relations with God ; thus only can you hope for a redeemed world.

What the feelings of Barabbas were when he was released we do not know. It must have been the greatest and the most agreeable surprise to him. Probably he thought there was not a prisoner in any of the dungeons of Jerusalem who had a smaller chance of life and liberty. Murderers are not popular usually; and Barabbas was one whose hands were terribly stained with blood. Probably the one redeeming feature in his character in the eyes of the Jewish people was that he had been involved in some uprising against the Roman government. But what recommended him most to the mob at this time was that he was the worst and most abandoned criminal they could think of, and that to prefer him to Jesus was to give the greatest sting to the insults they were in the mood to pour forth upon Jesus.

However it may have been, Barabbas owed his life to Jesus. That is a touching fact, not without deep significance. The worst man in Jerusalem owed his life to the best. Jesus received the scourging and the sufferings of the cross which should have fallen upon Barabbas. But for Jesus, Barabbas would have been dragged forth from his prison to the most cruel and ignominious death a criminal could endure; and the people might have rejoiced rather, and have breathed more freely that they were rid of one who was a blot and a terror to society. Instead, however, of coming forth from his prison amid the execrations, he comes forth amid the cheers and the enthusiasm of the mob. He is made to feel, in the wonderful upturn of things, as if he had become in some inexplicable way the hero of the day, instead of being a candidate for the gallows, a victim destined for the cross.

Is there not an acted parable here? Have we not here a striking illustration of our own case as guilty sinners in the sight of God? Jesus has borne the stripes which should have fallen on ourselves. He has endured for us the cross, despising its shame. This makes it possible for the prison door to be opened to us, laden with guilt though we are, worse before the pure eye of God than any Barabbas could be in the eye of the world. The freedom, the favour, the honour and blessedness that belong to innocence are imparted to the guilty trusting in Jesus. And in one important respect their case is better than that of Barabbas, for, through their Lord who died for them, they are delivered, not merely from the punishment their sins deserve, but by His cleansing blood from the power and defilement of the sins themselves.

What Barabbas' future was, we cannot tell. We have nothing further on record regarding him. We should like if we could think of him as having bestowed more than a passing thought on Jesus, whose appearance at Pilate's bar so signally brought about his deliverance. It would be pleasing to know that the death of Jesus had been to him new spiritual life as well as bodily deliverance. We can, so far, sympathise with the modern novelist [1] who makes of him a hero, an interested and sympathetic witness of the sufferings of the divine Man who died for him, one of the first to come to the grave with Mary Magdalene and others on the morning of the third day, an earnest enquirer into the truth as it is in Jesus, and by-and-by a confirmed and ardent believer, going back after a while to his dungeon in Jerusalem because he had been wrongfully delivered, and finding there a way by death into the paradise of his Lord. We are willing enough that these things should be true of the historic Barabbas after his release; but whether they are or not we have no means of knowing. It is for us, however, to see to it that His bearing the cross is a true release and a true salvation to ourselves, and, as those who feel that the greatest deliverance has been brought to them, that we avow our faith, and show our gratitude and devotion to Him by whom it has been so dearly won.

---

[1] Marie Corelli in her popular work of fiction entitled *Barabbas*.

PILATE WASHES HIS HANDS BEFORE THE MULTITUDE.

The governor was in evil case. He had referred his Prisoner to the judgment of the multitude. He had virtually laid down his office as judge and made himself advocate. He had, however, utterly failed in his pleading. Judgment had gone contrary to his wishes and his hopes. And every attempt he made to dispute the judgment, every plea he put forth, every word for Jesus he spoke was received with a fresh burst of contempt and fury on the part of the mob. The priests had indeed persuaded the people. If Pilate talked of release, then anyone might be released, Barabbas or any other vile criminal, but not Jesus. If he appealed to them on behalf of his Prisoner whether on the ground of patriotism or justice or humanity, he was answered only by shouting which grew the more fierce the longer he delayed to do as they required.

Pilate saw that he could prevail nothing.[1] The scene before him probably recalled to him another he had witnessed once in Caesarea soon after he had entered upon his procuratorship. He had dared to allow some Roman legions to enter Jerusalem carrying their heathen military standards with them. It is well known what regard, what ardent devotion soldiers have to their colours. Wherever the regiment marches they are carried. They are in the forefront of every battle. They are the last things a regiment would think of parting with. Many a heroic tale can be told of soldiers preferring to give up their lives rather than their standards. It was the same with Roman soldiers as with our own. And it seemed hard to them that they could not take their colours with them into Jerusalem as well as into the capital of any other province that their own arms had conquered. But the Roman standards consisted of what to a Jew were idolatrous images. It was regarded as a defilement of the holy city to have those Roman eagles and those busts of the emperor, of which the standards consisted, within its sacred walls.[2]

---

[1] Matt. xxvii. 24.

[2] Even in their coins the Jews showed their antipathy to images. Those issued by Herod the Great and Archelaus had none upon them, neither of gods nor men. The Roman procurators succeeding them

The excitement over the matter was intense. A multitude of the citizens went down to Caesarea. For five days and five nights they besieged him in his palace, assailing his ears continually with the same cries that the standards might be removed. On the sixth day he had them all gathered together in the circus. There they made their outcries more loudly and defiantly than ever. The soldiers whom he had in readiness he ordered to enter, with their drawn swords, the arena where the Jews were crowded. Still they continued their shouting. Their law was dearer to them than their lives. They laid bare their throats, and knelt down to receive the strokes of the sword with which they were threatened. Pilate had to make his choice between a wholesale massacre and a humiliating surrender. Dreading what might be the effect of the former, should it come to the ears of Caesar, he preferred the latter. The Roman legions had thereafter to do without their standards when on duty in the holy city.[1]

Now such a scene as that at Caesarea threatened to repeat itself before the Praetorium on this

---

put upon their Judean coins such harmless figures as palms and lilies, and only the name of the reigning Caesar. The ordinary Roman coins had, of course, Caesar's image as well as superscription (Madden's *Jewish Coinage*, pp. 135-153).

[1] Josephus, *B I.*, II., IX., 2.

occasion. Here again Jewish fanaticism was at the boiling point, and behind it the pertinacity which could go to any extreme to gain its ends. What could Pilate do? He had divested himself of his judgeship. He had given over his Prisoner virtually to the disposal of the mob. He had even lent himself so far to the side condemning Jesus as to say that he would chastise Him. The mob were ready to take every advantage and concession he would give them. They were most willing to take his power and office out of his hands, and to use both against his own feeble and half-hearted protests and his infirm purposes. The popular torrent swiftly rose to flood, and threatened to sweep away the irresolute governor. While he was protesting, "Why crucify him? what evil hath He done? I have examined Him and I find no fault in Him," the governor was to be seen pitiably yielding to the mad current of the hour. While they were instant with loud voices requiring that He should be crucified, his own voice became lost in the uproar.[1] It became in vain to speak, and still more so to reason.

Pilate was not the man to brave the flood. With him justice was a very good thing if it

---

[1] Luke xxiii. 23.

could be had for nothing. But here to do right was to face and fight out all that fanatical opposition. Who could tell how many lives that might cost, and what results it might have for the governor himself? Were a hundred lives to be sacrificed for this one? And what was this one life? That of a poor Jew about whom, as it seemed to him, the most diverse opinions were held, and who might be forgotten and dismissed from men's thoughts in a few days after His death. Pilate hated tumults. He had had enough of them already in his procuratorship of Judea.[1] So then, "willing to content the people,[2] he gave sentence that it should be as they required, and he released unto them him that for sedition and murder was cast into prison whom they had desired; but he delivered Jesus to their will."[3]

But while he did so, Pilate made yet another appeal to the people. Not in words was it made but in acted form. Words in the tumult prevailing would have been thrown away. A symbolic act,

---

[1] Josephus (*B.I.*, II., IX. 1, 2, 3) mentions three of these tumults out of which Pilate had on each occasion come badly. Writing of Pilate's conduct in the tumult about the shields, Philo (*Legatio ad Caium*, p. 38) says, "He was afraid that if they should send an embassy they might discuss the many maladministrations of his government, his extortions, his unjust decrees, his inhuman punishments. This reduced him to the utmost perplexity."

[2] Mark xv. 15.

[3] Luke xxiii. 24 25.

however, could speak to the eyes of all; and it was such an act—one which was intelligible alike to Jew and Roman, and one which could not but rivet the attention of all beholders—that Pilate chose now to perform. The act, it is said, is more Jewish than heathen in origin, but there are traces of the custom among the Gentiles as well. If a crime was done, a murder committed, blood-guiltiness incurred, which there was difficulty in discovering, it was a custom among the ancients for those who wished publicly to protest their innocence to take water and wash their hands.[1]

Moses had ordained a similar custom. When a man was found dead in a field, and it was not known who had slain him, then the elders of the nearest city were to meet with the priests and the people; and over the beheaded body of a heifer they were to wash their hands, and to say, "Our hands have not shed this man's blood, neither have our eyes seen it."[2]

Thus the act Pilate chose now to perform appealed alike to Gentile and to Jew. While the storm and tumult that made speech vain were prevailing, the governor, seated on his chair of state, beckoned to one of the officers in

---

[1] Sophocles, *Ajax* 654; Virgil, *Æneid* II. 719.
[2] Deut. xxi. 7.

attendance upon him. The attendant caught up at once the whispered instructions of his master, and left to fulfil them. He returned bearing a vessel, doubtless richly gilt, filled with pure and clear water. The governor, rising from his *bema*, and flinging back his magnificent flowing robes of office, advanced in face of the populace, and put his richly jewelled hands into the basin which the attendant held out to him. The act and movement of the governor struck all beholders. The clamour for the time ceased. Every eye was turned to Pilate. They watched him dipping and washing his hands in the vessel, and then raising them and shaking off the glittering drops of water. Amidst the silence which the action for the time commanded they could hear him saying, by way of interpreting what he had done, "I am innocent of the blood of this just person; see ye to it."[1]

At once the expression, "blood of this man," was caught up. The people seemed to have far less hesitancy and far less fear as to the guilt of shedding Jesus' blood than Pilate himself. They were in fact in a state of frenzy. They were at this time bent upon victory in their cause as against Pilate at whatever cost. Moral scruples did

---

[1] Matt. xxvii 24.

not stand in their way. The passion of the hour was proof against all appeals. Under its influence they were absolutely scornful of all threatenings and of all fears. It was a frightful climax which they reached when they followed up their infatuated outcry, "Let Him be crucified," by daring to challenge heaven to send any issue it pleased for their putting to death this Jesus, this Just One. "We will see to it, Pilate. We will have this man's blood. We will take the consequences for ourselves and for our children coming after us." Then answered all the people and said, "His blood be on us and on our children."[1]

Little did they know what those consequences were to be. They knew not that while they were that day calling for a cross for this Jesus, they were actually decreeing crosses for hundreds of thousands of their children even in the next generation, and preparing the saddest future for their race and nation in their being scattered and despised for ages.[2] His blood is still on them, and

---

[1] Matt. xxvii. 25.

[2] Thus Josephus (*B.I.*, V., XI., 1) writing of the multitude of captives taken at the siege of Jerusalem and of the cruel fate prepared for them says, "They were first whipped and tormented with all sorts of torture, and then crucified before the walls of the city. The soldiers, out of the wrath and hatred they bore the Jews, nailed those they caught one after one way, another after another, to crosses, by way of jest, when their multitude was so great that room was wanting for the crosses, and crosses wanting for the bodies. This miserable procedure made Titus greatly pity them."

will be on them for condemnation and suffering till they see in Him the Christ of their hope, and turn in penitence to find their salvation in the cross they gave Him.

But if Pilate's handwashing before the multitude was a fruitless appeal, it was also an empty and hypocritical formality. Pilate might wash his hands before the multitude, but he could not thus free himself from the responsibility of Jesus' death.[1] The people of Jerusalem and all the world would have known there was reality, and not merely idle form, in Pilate's symbolic act, had he manfully taken up the cause of his Prisoner, and stood between Him and the mob thirsting for His blood; had he ordered his soldiers to be a guard of honour and defence around Jesus; had he given the people to understand that all the power and authority of Rome which might be at his service would be used to prevent them carrying out any sentence against Him. But when Pilate did nothing after washing his hands beyond speaking weak words; when he made his base surrender to the mob; when he

---

[1] The words of Ovid (*Fasti*, II., 45), a poet of his own race, and about his own time, Pilate might have found peculiarly appropriate to himself:—

Ah! nimium faciles, qui tristia crimina caedis
Fluminea tolli posse putetis aquâ.

gave up the just person, the man Christ Jesus, in whom he could find no fault, to be scourged and then crucified; when he even allowed and commanded his soldiers to do the scourging, accompanied as it was with other tortures and insults, and to prepare the cross and to see Him die thereon—when he did these things his washing of his hands became the greatest act of mockery, and the guilt of Jesus' death he made his own so that no waters on earth could ever cleanse the stain of it from his soul. Had there been in Pilate a soul that could have been stirred by a keen sense of sin, he might, on looking upon his hands, have made his own the words put into the mouth of Macbeth after his murderous deed :—

> What hands are here? Ha! they pluck out mine eyes.
> Will all great Neptune's ocean wash this blood
> Clean from my hand? No, this my hand will rather
> The multitudinous seas incarnadine,
> Making the green one red.[1]

The poet represents Pilate saying to his wife some years after as he recalled the events of this momentous day :—

> I could not wash
> My conscience clean. The water, to my eyes,
> Ran foul and grimy to the golden bowl
> From each palm, vainly laved. So did He pass
> To lofty death, and I to life defamed.[2]

---

[1] Macbeth, Act II., Scene II.
[2] Sir Edwin Arnold's *Light of the World*, p. 69.

Here, indeed, is reason for our deepest self-abasement and contrition. The blood of Jesus is on us. The guilt of its being shed is ours. Our sin-laden and condemned state gave Him His burden and condemnation. Our sins brought Him to the tree, and wrought for Him there all His shame and agony. We dare not, and it avails for us nothing to do as Pilate did—wash our hands and declare our innocency. Yet in that very blood that is on us is all our hope. Here is cleansing such as the laver in which Pilate washed his hands could not give. This blood, which would otherwise stain and condemn for ever, faith turns into the thing that cleanses and everlastingly saves every truly penitent soul.

But further, while Pilate's symbolic act might be a fruitless appeal and an empty formality it afforded a very striking testimony to the innocence of Jesus. He was a just person. His death would, in the governor's view, involve blood-guiltiness from which he for his part wished to be free. Yet why should he be so concerned on this point? Every day, probably, cases of persons tried and condemned by the courts of the land were coming before him for review and confirmation. How often such cases were passed with small consideration of whether the accused were guilty or not. And the Prisoner in this case was the lowly Nazarene. There was none to plead His cause. There He was before him and the multitude, in mute dignity seeming to refuse to plead for Himself. If He had friends or followers they were not there to speak for Him. Not a voice seemed lifted up on His behalf. It seemed that Pilate might condemn Him if he chose, and that he ran no risk of offending any party or faction.

But the unique character of his Prisoner impressed Pilate. His whole bearing throughout the trial had an influence over him which he could not have explained, but which he could not throw off. And his soul was constrained to speak out and give such tribute to Jesus as it could. So the heathen judge proclaimed the innocence of Jesus. He deigned for the moment to be the pleader of His cause, and he adopted the most impressive and emphatic form he could think of for publicly testifying on His behalf when he took water and washed his hands before the multitude.[1]

Was there ever more striking testimony given to the character of a prisoner at any human bar? We have the judge giving it, a judge whose interest and prejudice might have been supposed to be all against the Prisoner. We have the judge

---

[1] Matt. xxvii. 24.

giving it in the face of a multitude who were witnesses, and very many of them unfriendly witnesses, of the words and acts of Jesus. The judge's bar was open at that time to any of them. If they could have brought any accusation against Him it would have been welcomed. If they had ever known Him do a wrong act, or teach what any law on earth could have justly condemned; if He had ever done or said anything in the slightest degree calling for censure or condemnation they had their opportunity, and it would have been a positive relief to the troubled conscience of the judge to hear it. But nothing of the kind could they adduce; they could but answer the testimony of a heathen judge and governor like Pilate by unreasoning and passionate outcries.

The great Jewish historian pays Jesus this remarkable tribute:—"He was a wise Man, if at least a Man He may be called. He was a great worker of miracles, and a teacher of those that were curious and desirous to learn the truth, and He had a great many followers, both Jews and Gentiles. This was the Christ that was accused by the princes and great men of our nation. Pilate delivered Him up to the cross, and, all this notwithstanding, those that loved Him at first did not forsake Him. He was seen alive again the third day after His crucifixion, as had been foretold by several prophets, with other wonders that He wrought; and there are a sort of people that to this day bear the name of Christians, as owning Him for their head."[1]

Thus Jesus compels homage even from His foes. And in another spirit than that of Pilate those who know Him declare His infinite purity and excellence. They not only find no fault in Him, but they find in Him every perfection. Tried as He has been in every way, by friends and by foes, put to the proof of experience by those who are His friends, and found to be better than the best they have ever been able to think of Him, they know Him to be worthy of their perfect confidence and also of their reverence and adoration. And if His adversaries will go as far as Pilate even, if they will go so far as to allow that He is the Just One whom to injure or even to asperse were a crime, why, we would ask, do they not believe in Him? Not to believe in Him while admitting the surpassing excellence of His character is to be silent while He is being condemned: it is to cover Him with empty compliments and honours, and at the same time to let Him go on His way to the cross.

[1] Josephus, *Antiq.*, XVIII. IV. 3. Ewald, however, sees in th passage the work of a christian hand in the second century

But if that washing of his hands was the most public testimony Pilate could give to the innocence of Jesus, its being followed up, as it was, by his base surrender to the will and clamour of the multitude made it the severest sentence of condemnation he could have passed upon himself. What did it mean? It meant that Pilate, governor though he was, was less concerned for justice than for his own ease and advantage. It meant that he was a thoroughly time-serving man, one of the last men who might be expected to make sacrifices for righteousness' sake, morally one of the weakest and most unprincipled of mortals. He declared, as plainly as words could have done it, that he was ready to sacrifice a just person rather than risk losing the favour of the people. He had not the courage of his own convictions. Avowing Jesus to be innocent, he gave Him up to be treated as if He had been the greatest of malefactors. What a splendid hero he might have been if he had found himself at the head of a people bent upon doing magnanimous and heroic things! He might have shone as their leader. He might have made grand and impressive orations appealing to virtue and justice and honour. He might have figured as a valiant champion of the good cause, while the people were there to give the applause, and there was no opposition, no foe to fear.

There are so many still who are like him. They praise virtue and righteousness, but drop the practice of them whenever it becomes difficult and costly or involves self-denial. They make fine figures in religious society, and shine there as long as there are only speaking and handwashing and praying to be done. They are the men too to lead popular movements; and while they have the multitude shouting with them their words are bold, their enthusiasm is great, and they seem to be the men to write noble chapters of history. But let the tide turn, and they are turned with it. Let the people wish something else, and they wish something else. Let their surroundings change from being very religious to being very secular, and they are changed with them. Or let the way of uprightness and godliness become rough, and they are off, notwithstanding all their brave professions, to try the smooth and alluring slopes of Bye-path Meadow.

Pilate could hardly have revealed himself in a worse light than when with one breath he declared Jesus to be a just person and entitled to release, and with the next, in deference to the clamour of the mob, he gave orders to his soldiers to carry out their will, and see to Jesus being scourged and then crucified. That act showed him to be one of the weakest and basest of men—a man who preferred himself to truth, justice, everything—a man who was the slave of his selfish fear and ambition—the kind of man who, to-day as in the past, is so particularly dangerous to himself, to society, and to every good cause.

It is the most important and momentous discovery a man can make when he finds that there is something or some one to be preferred to himself; some one whose will should ever command his own, whose interests are ever greater than his own; one for whom he rejoices to live, and for whose sake he would even be ready to lay down his life. That is a place which only Jesus the Prisoner at Pilate's bar can fill. Preferring Him to all else men have taken joyfully the spoiling of their goods, and as martyrs have died. Preferring Him to all else, and regarding His work and His will ever as supreme, they learn to fear neither the commandment of a king, nor the clamour of a mob. They do not merely practise the virtues—are honest, truthful, chaste, and just, when it is convenient and when it pays; but they strive after these virtues continually as men living in the presence of the Holy One, and charged with the honour of His name.

But those who prefer themselves to Him and to all else are ever vacillating and time-serving as Pilate. And they have dark paths to traverse where truth and virtue and God become more and more difficult to be found, and where at last the self, for which all else may have been sacrificed, is overwhelmed with shame and woe.[1]

Pilate, doubtless, had many defenders in his own day. He has found at least one apologist in our own times in Sir J. Fitzjames Stephen. The defence he offers is, if not in form, in substance such, we think, as Marcus Aurelius might have made. Briefly, it is this: Pilate's position was very much like that of one of our lieutenant-governors in India. Before all things he had to maintain the peace and order of the Roman empire, and to do this in the province which was perhaps the most troublesome of all to govern. Jesus did not, and could not be expected to concern him any more

---

[1] In W. Canton's graphic version of the legend of Pilate's suicide on Mount Pilatus (*A Lost Epic*, pp. 211-215), he is seen standing by a torrent and despairing of all its waters to wash his "red hands." Descending to give himself up to the Roman soldiers marching through the valley below, and disappointed that they will not take him and end his wretched existence, he casts his life away that he might never more behold

"Those awful eyes—that thorn-crowned head which fills
   The nights with terror."

than a new Guru arising among the Hindus, or the expected Imâm appearing among the Mohammedans, might interest an Anglo-Indian administrator. It became plain to the Roman governor that to listen to this new Prophet of Galilee and to do Him justice would be to cause the most serious breach of public order, and to incur the suspicion at Rome of acting disloyally and of imperilling imperial interests. In all these circumstances Pilate only did what might have been expected of him, and what the ordinary rules of political expediency would have guided him to do.[1]

It seems to us that such an argument or apology, so saturated with opportunism, needs only to be stated. Then to say that Jesus might be to Pilate what a Hindu or a Mahommedan religious pretender might be to a British governor in India, passes quite too severe a judgment on Pilate's moral discernment, poor as we know it was; and it is not borne out by the facts which the evangelists have given. Time has revealed nothing to abate the judgment Pilate has received at the bar of the Christian world. The poet has hardly overstated it when he says:—

> His action brought him
> The burden of a shame, sinking his soul,
> The burden of a name, intolerable,
> Accurst through all the ages, hated, scorned.[2]

---

[1] Stephen, *Liberty, Equality, Fraternity*, pp. 89-95.
[2] Arnold's *Light of the World*, p. 64.

JESUS SCOURGED AND CROWNED WITH THORNS.

Pilate's act of washing his hands before the multitude was an idle and delusive ceremony. It made but a passing impression. While it was being performed the crowd ceased their tumult and their dreadful outcries, and looked on in wonder. When it flashed upon them what it all meant they became the more urgent that the governor should do as they required. Pilate making such a show of his integrity as a judge, so scrupulous about his hands being unstained—the symbolic act, especially when they remembered what the governor had been, only excited their derision and contempt. They probably interpreted it, and interpreted it rightly, as only the prelude to a complete surrender. It was indeed, as the issue showed, a great historic instance of what is seen not unfrequently in the world, when the loud and ostentatious protestings of men are followed by their doing the very things they have lifted up their hands against in holy abhorrence. It seems as if for their consciences they thus sought a theatrical, for want of the real solace and satisfaction which come only from honest and just action.

Pilate at any rate followed up his ceremonious hand-washing by doing the very thing he had thereby declared to be a crime. He yielded to the torrent which he had not the courage or the moral force to resist. He now released Barabbas to the multitude, and he gave up Jesus to be scourged.[1]

This was a punishment only for slaves and for foreigners, the conquered enemies of Rome. Cicero's well-known words in regard to it may be recalled: "It is a crime to bind a Roman citizen; to scourge him is a wickedness; to put him to death is almost parricide. What shall I say of crucifying him?"[2] It appears, however, that corporal punishment in the form of cudgelling or flogging *(fustigatio vel flagellatio)*, had a place in the military penal code. Probably it was applied chiefly, if not entirely, to

---

[1] John xix. 1.
[2] Cicero, *In Verrem*, V. 66. It was one of the greatest crimes Cicero could allege against Verres that he had scourged Roman citizens. The scourge was the "horribile flagellum" of Horace.

the troops raised in the provinces. But as a civil punishment scourging, being regarded as the most ignominious, was awarded only to slaves.[1] For want of the lictors who usually performed it, the scourging in a province like Judea was done by the soldiers.[2] To them this duty was, as a rule, agreeable. It gave them an opportunity of paying off old scores against the troublesome people they had to keep in order. It afforded them peculiar pleasure to lay the lash upon Jewish offenders who were given over to them for this end.[3]

Nor need we wonder that to those rude Roman soldiers Jesus was nothing more than such an offender. When their superiors judged Him, as it must have seemed to them, worthy of scourging and of death, we could hardly expect that they should have eyes for the excellence and grandeur of His character. Then it is true that it was not usual for Roman soldiers to be in sympathy with a Jewish mob. In ordinary circumstances they would have been specially careful to see that a prisoner against whom

---

[1] Rein, *Criminalrecht der Römer*, pp. 699, 913.

[2] Throughout Josephus' history it is always the soldiers who are seen employed as lictors (Jos., *B.I.*, V., XI. 1).

[3] Several instances of this are to be found in Josephus (*Antiq.*, XIX., 9, 1; *B.I.*, II., 12, 1; and *B.I.*, V., 11, 1).

Jewish wrath might be raging received no unfair treatment; but in this case it was only too easy for them to be carried away by the evil spirit of the hour. For once, at anyrate, they were at one with the mob of Jerusalem. The bitterest enemy Jesus had in the city could not have wished for Him greater indignity and torture than He received at their rough hands.

Now upon the merely physical sufferings of Jesus, whether under the scourge or on the cross, we have no desire to dwell unduly. But, while it is possible to give to them an undue prominence, it is possible also not to dwell sufficiently upon them, and to lose thereby much of their impressiveness and significance. The days have been when every detail was set forth and even exaggerated, and when it was thought to be an act of religion to realise all the dreadful externals of our Lord's passion as fully and vividly as one could.

The modern mood of the Christian world is different. The tendency now is to make too little of the physical sufferings. As a consequence we are apt to lose much of what they reveal of the infinite greatness and love of Him who for us endured them. We believe that to have seen the suffering Saviour as those did, who were eyewitnesses of Him as He went on His *via dolorosa*, could not but have called forth towards Him our deeper reverence and devotion. The Saviour as He was could not possibly be surpassed by the Saviour idealised however beautifully in our minds. The lowly life, the homely garb, the mock royal raiment foully bespattered, the bleeding brow under the crown of thorns, the body bruised and broken by the scourge and then by the cross, and the visage more marred than any man—these things, far from hiding the true glory of Jesus, are the very things that help us the more to realise it while we think of the surpassing meekness, dignity, and grace which He showed through them all.

We would see Him then standing mutely before Pilate's judgment seat. The governor gives the order, "Go, bind His hands and let Him be beaten."[1] He is seized by the soldiers. He is stripped to the waist, and to some post or over some block near at hand He is bound in a stooping posture with His hands tied behind His back.[2] Then upon His bared back is laid the cruel lash, formed of some rough knotted rope or

---

[1] The usual formula (Livy. I. 26).

[2] Painters generally represent Him as bound to the post, some with His back, others with His face to it (Jameson, *History of our Lord in Works of Art*. Vol. II. 71-83).

of plaited leather thongs, with small sharp-pointed bits of bone or bits of lead at the ends. The cruel strokes cut open the flesh, and the blood starts and freely flows. As it is only one destined for the cross with whom, as they suppose, they have to do, the soldiers who relieve one another in the awful work are indifferent where the strokes fall. Scourging being the usual preliminary to crucifixion, they know that the heavier the blows they deal the sooner they will be done with the task of crucifixion. "Under the fury of their countless stripes," says Geikie [1] "The victims sometimes sank amidst screams, convulsive leaps, and distortions into a senseless heap; sometimes died on the spot; sometimes were taken away an unrecognisable mass of bleeding flesh to find deliverance in death from the inflammation and fever, sickness and shame."

In presence of the mob that condemned Him, Jesus was thus scourged and put to open shame. We are unwilling to believe that Pilate stooped so low as to play the part of the judge in cases of this kind, who was wont to stand by while the scourging was being done by the lictors, and to incite them to their duty towards the condemned saying, "Give it him, give it him." But even if

---

[1] Geikie, *Life and Words of Christ*, p. 699.

he did no more than look on, as he sat in his official seat, the people were there to reward with their applause every merciless blow.

When they had grown weary of their dreadful work, the governor, yet with a lingering hope and desire that his Prisoner might in some way eventually be spared, delivered Jesus to the centurion that should have charge of His crucifixion. Then, from the open grounds in front of the Praetorium in which the scourging was done, the soldiers took Him and led Him away to their own quarters. It was their odious privilege to have Him in their power for a while to do with Him what they pleased, short of denying the multitude the satisfaction of seeing Him die upon the cross. Like a hunted creature flung to the dogs before the finishing stroke is given, so was Jesus now among the soldiers. Into the common hall[1] the whole band trooped to share in the brutal entertainment they were to make for

---

[1] Sir Charles Wilson (Art. *Jerusalem* in Smith's *Dict.*) thinks that "the common hall" into which were "gathered the whole band of soldiers" to make sport of Jesus would be at the tower of Antonia. According to him, Jesus was taken first to Herod's palace—the Praetorium in which Pilate resided; after He was condemned the soldiers brought Him to Antonia, which was at once their headquarters and the state prison; and from Antonia He was led forth to be crucified. Sir Charles Warren, who has shared with Sir C. Wilson the work of the Palestine exploration expedition, has recently discovered in a subterranean chamber, on what is believed to be the site of Antonia, a truncated pillar such as that to which Jesus might have been tied in order to be scourged.

themselves. They crowded into the place just as they might have done, had they been in Rome, into the amphitheatre to look on the degrading spectacle of a gladiatorial fight or of a ribald play. From what we learn of their doings we can appreciate the remark of Luther, that "men in those days were treated as brutes are treated now." We might go further and say, that they were treated as even brutes are not treated now. Yet Armenian and other horrors and outrages of our time remind us that inhumanity seems to lose nothing of its repulsiveness and savagery by lapse of ages.

We must remember that Jesus was fresh from the wounds and sores the scourge had left Him. From the whipping post or block, even as He was, the soldiers led Him into their quarters, bent upon adding mockery to torture. In the course of His trial they had heard it said that He claimed to be a king. The higher the dignity claimed, the more easily it lent itself to purposes of ridicule. It occurred to them to make Him a mimic representation of mock royalty in their midst. Over His half-naked body, covered with cruel wounds, they threw an old cast-off military cloak to serve for an imperial robe. They next thrust a reed or cane pole into His hand—common enough in Jewish houses, and put to a variety of uses—as the emblem of His kingly power. For a crown an ingeniously cruel hand snatched some twigs from a thorny bush, growing in the grounds around the Praetorium, and twisted the prickly leaves round His brows, pressing them down till the blood started and trickled down the Sufferer's face.[1] Then the soldiers, following the the example of Herod's men, and even going beyond it, began their courtly play, and turned it into the rudest buffoonery and burlesque. They approached Him with mock obeisance. They offered Him mock homage. Some of them, bolder and more insolent than the rest, took the reed, which they had dashed in their violence from His hand, and smote Him with it on the head. And we blush for our poor humanity that we must add that they covered Him with spitting—the greatest mark of abhorrence or disgrace man can put upon man. Truly there is no cruelty like that of underlings. And one can hardly exaggerate the evil of which men are capable under the dominion of their basest passions.[2]

---

[1] Ellicott thinks the soldiers took what first came to hand, whether likely to inflict pain or not (*Life*, p. 348); Geikie, that they were the tough twigs of the thorny Nubk which they twisted into a cruel crown (*Life and Words*, p. 700).

[2] As to the mockery and buffeting in the common hall, Renan (*Life of Jesus*, p. 279) says, "It is difficult to understand how Roman

Yet Jesus endured all without a murmuring word. The pain of the wounds from the scourge must have been great, the pain from those insults and buffooneries to a nature so sensitive as His, must have been still greater. But there is no word of complaint. To go through all, and to keep silence, to be the same meek, dignified Sufferer, never chargeable with an unworthy look, a vindictive word or act—this proclaims, more eloquently than almost anything else could, His sovereignty over suffering, His absolute divinity. See Him in Gethsemane apparently crushed under His coming load, and praying that it might be spared Him. See Him here in the common hall among the rude mocking soldiery, a King in verity, triumphant over shame and pain, revealing a conquering power and grace truly divine in the silence and composure with which He bears Himself through all. His silence, what is it but His calm and sublime resignation to His Father's will? The victim

---

dignity could stoop to acts so shameful." He thinks they were not really Roman but auxiliary troops, composed of Syrians, &c., and that Romans would not have so degraded themselves. Farrar (*Life of Christ*, p. 677) favours this view, and supposes they were just "the mercenary scum and dregs of the provinces." Philo (*In Flacc*, 980) relates how on one occasion Herod Agrippa I. was publicly insulted at Alexandria in the person of an idiot who, arrayed in pretended royal robes, was treated to mock homage and ridicule as he was led through the streets. Also in Graetz, II., 183.

destined for the cross is already its victor. He who can endure pain and shame, as Jesus did, has truly all things under His feet.

Pilate was an interested spectator of what took place in the common hall. The crowd were not there; they did not witness what would have been so gratifying to their malice and contempt for the Nazarene. But the governor saw the rude jesting, the cruel mockery to which they subjected their Prisoner. He looked on their discreditable conduct, and did nothing to abate it. On the contrary it is more than likely that his presence and presumed patronage encouraged the soldiers to use the wildest licence.

Yet Pilate had mingled feelings. He became more than ever perplexed about his Prisoner. He did not know what to make of Him, so unlike was he to any other that had ever stood before him. His demeanour in the midst of this scene of revelry and insult was to him passing strange. The thought of His innocence grew upon him, and the desire to release Him came back with redoubled force.[1] A certain dread possessed him that it was not safe to have a hand in the death of such a Man. Was there no escape from such an unwelcome responsibility? It occurred to him

---

[1] John xix. 4.

that what was so strangely moving himself might also move the people. As he beheld the pitiable spectacle of Jesus mocked, buffeted, roughly handled, tortured in the midst of his soldiers, he felt somehow that in this there was that which might touch the hearts of the Jewish mob, there before him in front of the Praetorium, clamouring for Jesus' death. A Jew so insulted by Gentiles, so cruelly used by Roman soldiers whom the Jewish people cordially hated at all times! Would not the sight have some effect in stirring up their compassion and causing them to relent? A son of Abraham so shamefully treated by the uncircumcised, however dark His crimes—surely that was enough to rouse resentment against the Roman authorities and pity n favour of the Accused

Pilate therefore brought Him forth in full view of the Jerusalem crowd, wearing the crown of thorns and the purple robe, and with all the marks of the shame and pain He had endured, and exclaimed "Behold the Man."[1] The effect of the sight upon the Jewish multitude was not what he expected. It only roused them to greater fury, to a very frenzy of hatred against Jesus, and the insensate cry "Crucify Him, crucify

---

[1] John xix. 5.

Him'"[1] rent the air. We may well be astonished no less than Pilate seemed to be—astonished that even Jewish patriotism should so forget itself, and should unite with all else to deliver up the Christ to ignominy and death, as if the whole nation had come to execrate Him and to cast Him off.[2]

But what is the effect which the sight of the suffering thorn-crowned Jesus has still upon the world? The very sufferings of Jesus are a stumbling block. His cross is an offence. The world is blind to the glory they reveal. It refuses to identify, with omnipotence, such weakness as men can make sport of, and such endurance or shame and pain even unto death with kingly and divine claims. It refuses also to take or to believe in salvation from the hands of the Crucified.

But on those awaking from the dreams of the world, recovering from the blinding and hardening power of sin the sight of Jesus with His crown of thorns has a totally different effect. It is the most powerful appeal to all that is best,

---

[1] John xix. 6.

[2] When Plato in his *Republic* (p. 360—Jowett's Translation) writes, "The just man will be scourged, racked, bound, have his eyes put out, and will at last be crucified," he seems to utter the most remarkable prophecy of how the world was to treat the sinless Jesus. It is amazing that this forecast or dream of the heathen philosopher should have become history.

tenderest, and most sacred in their hearts. It is love's divine appeal. When it meets with an answering love and faith the divine King in His beauty stands revealed, and His kingdom and salvation have come to our souls. We give our homage to Him as we would not give it to another. The thorns that wreathe His brows become a veritable crown for us—love's grandest crown; and all the wounds He suffered, and the blood He shed are unspeakably dear as love's greatest sacrifice, the price of our pardon, the hope of our salvation. In the beautiful words of St. Ambrose, "the thorns are the sinners of this world, thus woven into a trophy, and worn triumphant upon the bleeding brows of the Redeemer."

Pilate, by thus bringing Jesus forth a spectacle of woe and pity, after all He had suffered from the scourge and at the hands of the soldiers, made then another and most striking appeal to the multitude. The appeal, pathetic though it was, utterly failed. The sense of pity, of humanity, was met and overborne in the priests and people by that religious hatred which is the fiercest of all passions. The sight that might have melted the stoniest heart only called forth anew, and in fiercer accents than before, "Crucify Him;" and it was the chief priests and the officers who led in the cry.

Angry and impatient at this fresh repulse the governor thereupon replied, "Take ye Him and crucify Him; for I find no fault in Him."[1] "Go, find the cross for Him, and let yours be the responsibility of His death. He is one of yourselves. If you will persist thus in your fury against Him, take Him and do with Him what you will. I will be no party to your crime."

But Pilate was not to get off even on these iniquitous terms. He was to find himself compelled in the end to pronounce the sentence of condemnation with his own official lips, and to provide the cross for Jesus and the soldiers also who should see to His dying there.

"We have a law," the Jews answered him, "and by our law He ought to die, because He made Himself the Son of God."[2] In so saying the Jews reminded him of his oath and duty as Roman governor to respect their law. Their customs and laws as a people the Romans had promised to regard and protect.[3] Jesus might

---

[1] John xix. 6.

[2] John xix. 7.

[3] They could plead that Tiberius had expressly promised that their laws and institutions should be respected (Philo, *Legatio ad Caium*).

be faultless so far as Roman law was concerned, but according to Jewish law He, as claiming divine honours, was the greatest of transgressors. Their courts had tried Him on the charge. Was it not for Pilate to uphold their authority, and to confirm their decision?

This opened up a wide and delicate question. It was not one that could be safely discussed between the governor, seated on his official chair on the Gabbatha, and a heated and frenzied mob in the open air. And the expression "Son of God" they had used had, as applied to this Jesus, something ominous about it for Pilate's ears. He rose therefore from his seat of judgment, and bade Jesus for the second time follow him into the hall of the Praetorium behind. When they were there alone he asked Jesus with a troubled air, "Whence art Thou?"[1] Jesus gave him no answer. Why it seems difficult to understand, unless it be that silence was itself the best answer; and that if he had not already found an answer to his question in all that he had seen of Jesus and heard from Him since He came into his hands, nothing that Jesus could say now was likely to enlighten him. With no true sense of the divine in him, God incarnate could stand

[1] John xix. 9.

before Pilate and be unrecognised. In vain we argue for the supernatural and the heavenly with men who do not see and feel the supernatural and the heavenly in the Christ of Gospel history.

The governor was annoyed at the silence. If his question came from the fear that he was after all in the presence of some superior being,[1] the silence only increased it. But with the fear there was his pride of office, and the umbrage he felt that he could not get those lips of Jesus to open just when he would. "Speakest thou not unto me? Knowest thou not that I have power to crucify thee, and have power to release thee?"[2]

Then on these words being uttered, the lips so long sealed amid a storm of accusation and abuse were opened. "Thou couldst have no power at all against me except it were given thee from above; therefore he that delivered me unto thee hath the greater sin."[3] Thus the proud governor was rebuked, while at the same time Jesus, holding in His hands the balance of judgment between Pilate and the priests, extended His charity so far to the former by saying that his sin was the less. Jesus reminded him also and

---

[1] John xix. 8.
[2] John xix. 10.
[3] John xix. 11.

the world that there was One above in whose almighty hands Pilate and all who had to do with His death were but instruments, willing or unwilling; that they were but carrying out His sovereign will to provide in this wonderful way the one great sacrifice for the world's sin.

It did not lessen Pilate's fears that he was thus spoken to, and reminded of his comparative impotence by the Prisoner who seemed so entirely in his power. On the contrary, he was the more afraid. He left his Prisoner in the hall, and returned to his chair of judgment on the Pavement. Again he sought to release Jesus. But to all his pleading the multitude answered in words which had a new terror for him. They contained the threat which had once and again in days past been found effectual with Pilate. If he failed to listen to it he knew there were ample forces of a tumultuary kind in that mob, and diplomatic skill and fanatic zeal enough in those Jewish rulers to make it good. "If thou let this man go, thou art not Caesar's friend; whosoever maketh himself a king speaketh against Caesar."[1] Again we see the same fatal confusion of Messianic kingship and earthly kingship. But Pilate could not discriminate. What he perceived clearly was that

[1] John xix. 12.

if he did not let the Jews have their own way they would report him to his imperial master in Rome. As his record was not good,[1] he could hardly afford to give them occasion for doing that. He could therefore give the multitude no answer.

He returned to the hall of judgment where he had left Jesus, and brought Him a second time before the people. The morning was well advanced. Three hours had gone by since He was placed before him as a prisoner, and it was now the third hour—nine o'clock in the morning.[2]

---

[1] Josephus, *Antiq.*, XVIII., III., 1-2, and *B.I.*, II., IX., 2-4; also Philo, *Legatio ad Caium*, 36.

[2] Mark states it was the third hour when they crucified Jesus (Mark xv. 25). Matthew and Luke do not say when the crucifixion began, but all three mention the darkness as coming on about the sixth hour. The Synoptists also agree that it was the ninth hour when Jesus died, while the fourth Gospel is silent on that point. John, however, marks the hour definitely as the sixth hour (John xix. 14) when Pilate said, "Behold your king," and thereafter delivered Jesus to be crucified. Thus there is an apparent discrepancy between the statements of Mark and John as to when the crucifixion began. To get rid of it some suppose that John reckoned from midnight and Mark from sunrise. But neither Jews nor Romans reckoned from midnight. The latter divided the day into twelve hours from sunrise to sunset, so that in summer the hours were long and in winter short. The Jews in our Lord's day seemed to have followed their example. And to suppose John reckons from midnight only increases the difficulty otherwise. Another offered solution is that John is not referring to the commencement of Jesus' sufferings on Calvary, but to something else—the fact perhaps that the special preparation ($\pi\alpha\rho\alpha\sigma\kappa\epsilon\upsilon\acute{\eta}$) began at noon, the sixth hour according to the usual reckoning, and that Mark's statement has therefore really no statement opposed to it at all. Many authorities think that the true solution of the difficulty is that there has been an error in transcribing the number in the original text, only they are divided,

Pilate was utterly weary of the case and careless how it should end, if only it did not touch himself or his relations with Tiberius. With a gesture of impatience and a tone of contempt he said to the multitude as he placed Jesus again before them, "Behold your king."[1] "Away with him, crucify him,"[2] was the cry again raised in response. "Shall I crucify your king?"[3] said he again, and the tone of irony and contempt was more marked than before. "What patriots you are! And this is your Messiah King! Is it your will that He should be treated as the vilest malefactor?" He was their Messiah, their King, and it was so they willed He should be treated.[4]

In their infatuation denying all their Messianic

---

some being of opinion that τρίτη in Mark should be read ἕκτη, others that ἕκτη in John should be read τρίτη. Caspari (*Life of Christ*, p. 228) adopts the former view, and thinks it would be midday before Jesus was lifted upon the cross, and that the three hours' darkness came on very soon after, and lasted till He died about three in the afternoon. But six hours seem too long for the trial and three too short for the crucifixion. Alford's view (*Comment. in loc.*), which was the view of the early fathers, Eusebius and Theophylact, and that adopted by Farrar (*Life of Christ*, 683), Ellicott, Keim (*Jesus of Nazara*, vol. VI. 122), &c., is that the erratum is likely to be in John, and that τρίτη should be read for ἕκτη so as to harmonise all satisfactorily. The tradition had been very generally, if not universally, accepted that Jesus hung upon the cross six hours, from nine till three in the afternoon, from the third to the ninth hour.

[1] John xix. 14.
[2] John xix. 15.
[3] John xix. 15.
[4] As Renan says "If ever crime was the crime of a nation it was the death of Jesus" (*Life*, p. 282).

hopes, and basely kissing the foreign chains which bound them, they cried out "We have no king but Caesar."[1] The cry carried with it the hint that Caesar should know of it if Pilate by releasing Jesus should show himself unfaithful to his interests.[2]

Pilate yielded. He was baffled and beaten by his own worldly weapons in the end. He was no match for the crafty Jewish priests and elders, or for a Jewish mob inspired and led by them. "Then delivered he Jesus unto them to be crucified." He rose from his judgment seat. He gave orders now finally to his soldiers to see to the crucifixion. Then without daring to

---

[1] John xix. 15.

[2] Philo, writing of Pilate threatened in this way on another occasion, says—"This last sentence exasperated him more, as he feared they might in reality send an embassy to the emperor, and impeach his whole government in respect of his corruption, his acts of insolence, his rapine, his habit of insulting people, his cruelty, his continual murders of people uncondemned, and his never-ending and most grievous inhumanity" (*Legatio ad Caium*, XXXVIII). Trials for treason were conducted in Augustus' time by the Senate, and they were very few as he was a trusted and popular ruler. In his later days Tiberius took those cases involving supposed crimes against himself into his own hands, and so liberally rewarded informers (*delatores*) that they became a numerous class. Tacitus (*Annals*, V. and VI.) gives many examples of the cruel and unjust way in which those accused of *crimen maiestatis* were dealt with, and informs us that very few of them ever escaped. Not a few of them took away their own lives on the first intimation of their being accused (*Annals*, VI., 38, 39, 40). A striking instance we have in the case of Nerva, a favourite of Tiberius, who lived in such dread of delation that he resolved, notwithstanding that emperor's personal entreaties, to starve himself to death before the informer should have even singled him out.

look again into the face of that truly divine King, clothed in mock raiment and crowned with thorns, standing so near to him, he withdrew from the Pavement for the last time, and retired to his palace leaving the multitude to have their will.[1]

The dread of Caesar, the fear of losing the favour of the world and involving himself in trouble had prevailed with Pilate. The innocence of Jesus, the claims of justice, the better voices of the heart—these availed nothing against the interests and inclinations of self and the allurements of the world. But how often this moral tragedy is repeated! Men that might have put wreaths of glory around Jesus have by their lives plaited for Him the crown of thorns, subjected Him to the scourge of their sins, and abandoned Him and their better selves as well.

---

[1] We have reason to believe that Pilate did send some report afterwards to the emperor Tiberius as to what he had done with his remarkable Prisoner. Justin Martyr and Tertullian in their Apologies appeal to official records of the trial and death of Jesus in such a way that they must have been in existence. Eusebius states (*Hist.*, II., 2) on the authority of Tertullian that Tiberius having heard from the "Acts of Pilate" of the miracles and resurrection of Jesus proposed to his senate that he should be placed among the gods. But we have no quotation from these "Acts" either in Christian or pagan writers, and no writer referring to them claims to have seen them. Yet it is not unlikely that Pilate transmitted some official report of our Lord's case to Rome.

THE TRAITOR'S END.

The fate of Judas is recorded by two of the evangelists—Matthew and Luke. Luke's reference to his end is incidental, being contained in the report he gives (Acts i. 16-19) of Peter's words to the assembled brethren in the Upper Room, after our Lord had ascended into heaven, in regard to the election of a successor to the traitor as one of the twelve. Matthew[1] gives details which Peter omits, but the two narratives fit into and supplement each other. The latter was speaking, as may readily be understood, to an audience well acquainted with the manner of Judas' death; and he had to refer to the facts only so far as they were needed to serve the purpose of his address.

Strauss, it may be remarked, regards the whole story, as he does much besides in the gospels, as mythical. The Christian records, according to him, were not to be complete without some calamity or

---

[1] Matt. xxvii. 3, 10.

tragedy befalling the actors concerned in the crucifixion of Jesus. Hence one such tragedy had to be invented. The Christians of those days were the shadiest of people, with a wonderful propensity for inventing useful falsehoods and imposing upon the credulity of the world. They laid hold of Zechariah's prophecy about the thirty pieces of silver and the buying of the Potter's Field; and it was easy for them with the help of the 69th Psalm to fill up the outline, and to put a disciple as traitor and then suicide in the forefront of it all.[1]

It is a striking and instructive fact, however, that Judas is the only one concerned in Jesus' death, the circumstances of whose end are related in the New Testament. We must turn to Josephus, or Tacitus, or to the apocryphal legends for the woful end of Annas and his five sons, of Caiaphas, and of Pilate and Herod—the leading actors in that event.[2] The evangelists simply

---

[1] Strauss, *New Life of Jesus*, vol. II. 350, 355.

[2] Annas and his five sons were, one after the other, deprived of their high priesthood, and so also was Caiaphas (Josephus, *Antiq.*, XVIII., VI. 3). Ananias, the son of Nebedai, was sent bound to Rome (*Antiq.*, XX., VI. 3): his palace was burned to the ground (*B.I.*, II., XVII. 6): he himself was found at last in a sewer and brought forth along with his brother Ezekias and executed (*B.I.*, II., XVII. 9). Ishmael ben Phabi was beheaded in Cyrene (*B.I.*, VI., II. 2): and Jonathan, the son of Ananus, was murdered by the Sicarii (*B.I.*, II., XIII. 3). Herod Antipas seems to have been banished, first to Lyons in Gaul (*Antiq.*, XVIII., VII. 2), and then to Spain

record the part they played in the condemnation and death of Jesus. They refrain from expressing any judgment upon them. They leave their words and deeds to speak for themselves. And they say nothing in regard to their future. It would have been very different had they been the unscrupulous dealers in fiction Strauss seems to think them to be. It was for the sake of the Church of Christ, for its instruction and warning in after times, for our learning and spiritual profiting, they have preserved for us the memory of their fellow disciple's woful end, and we cannot doubt that their record is true.

The evangelist Matthew tells us it was when Judas saw that Jesus was condemned he went on his way of despair. He had been a spectator deeply interested and deeply involved in all the proceedings. We remember his treacherous kiss in the Garden.[1] He is one of the great band who bring his Master after His capture, first to Annas, and then to Caiaphas. He follows the trials by the priests and the Sanhedrim with an agitated

---

where he died (*B.J.*, II., IX. 6). Pilate was ordered by Vitellius to Rome to answer before Caesar the accusations that were exhibited against him and he died in banishment (Josephus, *Antiq.*, XVIII., V. 2). The legend of his suicide on Mount Pilatus, near Lucerne, is well known.

[1] Lightfoot says it was not unusual for a master to kiss his disciple, but it was very exceptional that a disciple kissed his master (Lightfoot, *Horae Heb. in Ev. Matt.*, p. 303).

heart, his hopes or his fears rising at each stage of the procedure. His eye and interest are fixed on Him above all others whom he had been wont to call Master. His whole bearing, the answers He gives he eagerly observes. Very likely he is disappointed, even from the outset, with the turn things are taking. To his carnal worldly mind Jesus seems to offer a poor defence of Himself. He makes no use of His miraculous power to confound His judges and foes. He seems even to deliver Himself over to His enemies by putting forth claims on His behalf which to the court appear blasphemies. And when He is condemned He accepts His sentence meekly, and then submits without a murmur or protest to all the indignities and blows that follow.

Judas' heart sinks as he witnesses all this. It sinks still more as he follows the crowd of priests and elders going to deliver Jesus into Pilate's hands, and as he watches the singular course of events at the Practorium and in Herod's judgment hall. When at length a Barabbas is openly preferred to his Master, and Jesus is handed over to the Roman soldiers to be scourged and then crucified, his feeling of despair grows to an intensity which becomes unbearable. Probably the last sight he sees before rushing upon his tragic end is his Master standing before the mob with the robes put on in mockery, the crown of thorns on His head and the sad traces of the blows He has received.[1]

He cannot bear to witness more.[2] The money he has got for his traitor's service is now an intolerable burden to him. He rushes from the place where he has been a spectator of all he has had so large a hand in bringing upon his Master. He crosses over with hurried steps to a part of the Temple[3] where only consecrated feet may tread, and where some priests are to be seen. For aught we know to the contrary Caiaphas himself is among them. The door is open. Without daring to pass the threshold of a place thus sacred to the priests Judas flings through the open door the thirty pieces of silver they had given him for betraying

---

[1] Matt. xxvii. 3. "When he saw that He was condemned, repented himself, &c."

[2] In a remarkable picture by Thomas, a Belgian painter, Judas is represented as coming suddenly in the course of the night or early morning upon two men fashioning the cross, intended for his Master, by the light of a fire, and as being transfixed with horror by the sight.

[3] See Sepp (*Leben Christi*, VI., 78), Geikie (*Life and Words of Christ*, p. 705) and others. Judas forced his way into the inner portion of the Temple where the priests were preparing for the feast and where also penitents were wont to be in waiting for them, and there he flung down the price of blood.

his Master,[1] and scatters them about their feet over the sacred floor. "I have sinned," he cries in his agony of remorse and despair, "in that I have betrayed the innocent blood."[2]

Those sacred courts had been associated with the greatest joys and the greatest sorrows of men. Many a touching bit of spiritual history had been enacted within them. They had been the scene of many a penitent's confession, but never had been heard there a more remarkable or pathetic than this. Men had come to them to confess great crimes, but never a crime such as Judas now confessed. He acknowledged himself a sinner of the deepest dye—a traitor responsible for bringing to a shameful death the greatest of benefactors and the most perfectly free from all fault or sin.

Multitudes had found relief in those temple courts as they poured forth their hearts in penitential sorrow. So might Judas have done. But it was to the priests there he turned with his remorseful confession, and not to God. Had he only taken it to Jesus Himself, how different the result might have been! To have gone with

---

[1] It is interesting to recall that thirty *minae* was the price which the disciples of Socrates offered to redeem him—the heathen sage thus being reckoned at more than thirty times the value of the divine Teacher of Nazareth (Plato, *Apologia*, par. 38).

[2] Matt. xxvii. 4.

it to Him whom he had so deeply wronged would have been manly and honourable. To have made his touching tribute to the spotlessness of Jesus heard above all the mad cries for His death—to have dared to stand by the side of the condemned Man of Nazareth, and declare that the greatest sin of his life had been to betray Him, and that it was truly God's holy One they were hurrying to His cross—this might have given Judas the place of the greatest of heroes among fallen men, while it might have secured for him that day the glory of sharing martyrdom with his Lord. Had Judas taken his confession to the quarter where it was most of all due, he, no less than the penitent thief, would have been with Jesus that day in paradise; and, instead of a terrible darkness investing his eternal future which we do not seek to penetrate, he would have stood forth to all coming ages the brightest example of the pardoning grace and saving power of his Master.

But Judas went to the priests and not to Jesus. To them he went as a disappointed, despairing man, hoping doubtless by fixing a share of his guilt upon them to relieve his own distressed soul. Well did they perceive, and perceive at once, the drift of his action. Immediately he was to learn that of sympathy or comfort he should have none from them. If his conscience troubled him over what he had done, they were ready to tell him that was his affair, not theirs. "What is that to us?" they said; "see thou to that."[1] He must bear his own burden. They would not trouble themselves to sit in judgment upon his actions. It was no concern of theirs either to praise or to blame him. He had served their purpose, and they did not care now what became of him. So if he had hoped for great things from going over to the service of the priests he was now completely disenchanted.

His money even they were unwilling with their consecrated hands to touch. Hurrying from them in his despair he left it lying on their sacred floor.[2] He found it so easy to rid himself of the reward of his iniquity, but so difficult to be rid of the crime itself. The consciousness of it was as a hot burning in his soul. The burden of it became for him heavier than ever. Those priests he had served too well would not, and could not lighten it for him. They were exulting over the success of their wicked plot, but their success was now his awful failure and distress. In vain he sought pity for himself from his partners in guilt. Abandoned of men, with a crushing sense

---

[1] Matt. xxvii. 4.

[2] The thirty pieces of silver—between £3 and £4 of our money—the price, according to Exodus xxi. 32, of a slave.

of divine retribution, with the horror and anguish of an awakened conscience, and apparently despairing of mercy, he went and hanged himself.[1] And it appeared as if the very tree on which he sought death threw him off. The cord with which he bound himself broke, and falling headlong—over a precipice perhaps—" he burst asunder in the midst, and all his bowels gushed out.[2]"

It was a terrible death to die, especially for one brought up in the religion of Jehovah. There is only another case of the kind in Scripture. It is remarkable it is also that of a traitor—that of Ahithophel, the betrayer of the cause of king David, the Judas of the Old Testament history.[3] Suicide was only too common in pagan Greece and Rome. There it was thought the proper and even manly thing to put an end to one's life when it

---

[1] Matt. xxvii. 5. Oecumenius (*Enarrationes in Acta Apostolorum*, ch. II.) refers back to Papias, a disciple of John, the tradition that Judas "moved about in this world, a terrible example of impiety, being swollen in body in such a degree that where a chariot would easily pass he was not able to find a passage. His eyelids were so swelled out that he could not see the light. . . After suffering many torments and judgments he died in his own field." Lange curiously supposes that Judas "attempted first to retire to a hermit life as anchoret," and then having found this life unendurable he went on his way of self-destruction (*Life of Christ*, vol. IV. 122).

[2] Acts i. 18. Hackett (*Illustrations of Scripture*, p. 266) says that he found "a precipice on the face of the hill from twenty-five to forty feet in height, with olive trees growing near the edge, and a rocky pavement at the bottom, so that a person falling from above would probably be crushed and mangled as well as killed."

[3] 2 Sam xvii. 23.

seemed to have nothing more to offer, when its burdens or its trials became too great to bear. And with paganism reviving and spreading amid our nineteenth century civilisation, suicide is increasing and is not looked upon with the horror it ought ever to inspire. The question is even seriously discussed whether there be not circumstances in which it is justifiable, as if such a sin could by any circumstances whatever be whitewashed and turned into a virtue. Believing that there is a God we justly look upon it as crowning Judas' guilt, as crowning any man's guilt, however great otherwise it may be, that he should thus abandon the sacred trust of life, and rush presumptuously and unbidden into the divine presence. In such a case the verdict usually required by charity is that the doer of the act was not in his sound mind when he did it. But taking the sceptic or the atheist even on his own ground, and allowing that there is no God and no judgment day to reckon with, we are bound to say that suicide is the basest and most cowardly of acts. It is a man running away from the battle of life because he has been worsted, and refusing to live because the selfish terms on which he demands to have existence are not met.

But what was to be done with the money Judas

had thrown on the *sanctuary* floor? It is significant how the priests discuss the question. They do it as men to whom the externals of law and creed are everything. Gathering up the silver pieces they said, "It is not lawful for us to put them into the treasury, for it is the price of blood."[1] It was according to them lawful to use those silver pieces to buy the services of a traitor, but not to put them to the sacred uses of the Temple. It did not matter how they soiled their consciences, but the Temple treasury must not be defiled. With the money they might buy a field in which to bury strangers—that is, pious pilgrims from heathen lands who happened to die in Jerusalem—but it must not be allowed to desecrate God's house. Men's consciences were of less account and less sacredness than the outward and material building in which God was worshipped; and apparently there was the least possible sanctity, if any at all, attaching to a graveyard for foreign Jews or Gentile proselytes.[2] They could plot against the Son of

---

[1] Matt. xxvii. 6, 7.

[2] Meyer (*Matthew*, vol. II., p. 249) thinks that it was intended as a burial place for foreign Jews, not Gentile proselytes, otherwise they would have been more specifically indicated. The prophecy he believes to be taken from Zechariah, XI., 12, 13, and that it was by some slip of the memory Jeremiah was inserted. Lange (*Com. on Matthew*, p. 505) holds the opposite view.

God, and hire the man that should betray Him without a sense of guilt at all, while they would have regarded it as a sin to fail in the smallest point of outward or ceremonial observance. It is singular how human nature inclines still to such artificial standards of conduct and moral judgment. Morality and religion are externalised; and men who would count it sacrilege to rob a church, or to be guilty of any outward irreverence, have no qualms of conscience while they may be robbing God and profaning His name every day by their lives and their conduct. And so absorbed do they become in the outward, the formal, and the conventional that it is difficult to bring them to any real sense of sin.

It was no doubt kind and thoughtful of these priests to lay out the money that had thus

---

Edersheim (*Life and Times,* vol. II. 575) believes that the "Potter's Field which was afterwards bought with the blood money was also the place where Judas had tragically ended his life. It was, he conjectures, near to where the Kedron and Hinnom valleys merge, and where jagged rocks rise perpendicularly, and there may have been some gnarled and stunted tree on which the woful deed might be done." According to Weiss (*Life,* III., 345) it was the "field of blood" because it was the place stained by Judas' blood when he committed suicide, and the place in which the first grave opened was that of the traitor himself. Robinson (*Biblical Researches in Palestine,* vol. I., 353) agreeing with Edersheim, describes the "Potter's Field" or Aceldama as at the eastern end of the ridge of the hill to the south of the valley of Hinnom opposite Mount Zion near to where that valley meets with the valley of Jehoshaphat. He says that the hill is steep and in many parts rises in rocky precipices, and that the rocks and the whole hill side are full of excavated tombs.

come into their hands in purchasing a burying place for strangers.¹ The proposal had this at least to recommend it, that it was a cheap way of carrying out a charitable object. It cost them nothing. The Potter's Field was a comparatively waste and worthless piece of land. It was the exchange they were pleased to have for the price at which they themselves had valued Jesus' blood. They would probably feel relieved when the money that might have come to burn their fingers, as well as those of Judas, was got rid of in such a satisfactory way. The strangers would esteem them the more highly that they had been so thoughtful for their dead. When the priests heard of Judas' tragic death they would be happy in the thought that they could use his own money to provide him with a grave. Probably Judas himself was the first to be buried in this new place of graves, this Aceldama or "field of blood," which tradition still points out as a monument to the truth of this part of the Gospel story.²

The evangelist Matthew, true to his characteristic

---

¹ In Acts i. 18 Judas is said to have purchased the field himself. Here in Matthew it is the priests who do it with Judas' money. But it is only the hypercritical who can see a discrepancy here.

² Tradition places the Potter's Field or Aceldama on the steep face of the southern hill opposite Mount Zion, which bounds the valley of Hinnom. For centuries it appears to have been used as a burying place for strangers or pilgrims.

manner, is careful to point out how prophecy was fulfilled in this singular transaction. "Then was fulfilled that which was spoken by Jeremy the prophet, saying, And they took the thirty pieces of silver, the price of Him that was valued, whom they of the children of Israel did value. And gave them for the Potter's Field, as the Lord appointed me."[1] Here is one of those minute difficulties or discrepancies in Scripture which have not yet been satisfactorily explained, but which should disturb no one unless he is concerned to maintain a very mechanical conception of the inspiration and inerrancy of Scripture. It is in Zechariah (xi. 12 13) and not in Jeremiah that the Old Testament quotation is to be found. And the quotation is a free one from a chapter in which, as it seems to us, the prophetic vision of the coming Christ, the Branch, as Zechariah loves to call Him, is not so clear as in some other passages from that prophet. But if the evangelist saw this prophetic meaning in the words, we may well yield to him. He stood nearer the times of those old prophets, and he had learned in the best of all schools—that of Christ Himself, how to interpret their predictions.[2]

---

[1] Matt. xxvii. 9, 10.

[2] Lightfoot is of opinion that here we have a mere mistake of

The character, career and end of Judas present one of the most difficult moral problems. For centuries he has been looked upon as the worst of men. In our own day there has been a certain reaction in his favour. Dante, who may be regarded as representing the general feeling of Christendom in his time, and for generations before and since, places him in the lowest circle of all in his Inferno. The emperor of the kingdom dolorous and he occupy the circle together, as if he were next to him in enormity of transgression, and pre-eminent above all sinners of mankind. He dwells in the mouth of Satan, who crunches him between his teeth. His face is hidden in the awful cavity, while his feet are plying wildly without. The Judecca, the name given to his abode, is a place where fire and ice maintain eternal feud; and his is the soul which beyond all others in the Inferno has the greatest pain.[1]

The judgment all this implies in regard to Judas some writers in our modern times have been disposed to call in question, and to modify,

---

memory, Jeremiah being put in the prophecy regarding the Potter's Field instead of Zechariah (*Horae Heb. in Ev. Matt.*, p. 307). Others suggest error in transcription, and others that Jeremiah was the name given to that division of the Old Testament from which the quotation was taken.

[1] Dante, *Inferno*, Canto XXXIV.

if not reverse. Reversed altogether it cannot be so long as men have respect to what our Lord, who knew what was in man, so plainly said of him, "Have not I chosen you twelve, and one of you is a devil."³

De Quincey's theory is well-known.⁵ It has seemed plausible to many. Judas had followed Jesus believing in His promised kingdom. He saw His power manifested in His miracles. He marked how He could move the people so that they were ready to take Him by force and make Him a king.⁴ But one year, two years, three years passed, and still there was no sign of the kingdom. Judas desired to hasten matters. He determined at last to precipitate a crisis. That Passover should see the revelation of his Master's expected power and glory. When his Master entered Jerusalem amid the hosannas of the multitude his hopes were raised to the highest point. Day after day however passed, and his Master seemed to do nothing to fulfil those hopes. At the supper in the Upper Room he resolved on the step that was to end the uncertainty. He was to put his Master into the hands of the Jewish rulers;

---

¹ John vi. 70.
² De Quincey's Works (*Masson's Edition*) Vol. VIII., 181.
³ John vi. 15.

and judging his Master by himself he expected that He would confound His most bitter and most formidable foes, extricate Himself from their hands, and make such a display of Himself and His supernatural power as would lead to the establishment of His kingdom. Events did not proceed as Judas anticipated. When he saw his Master a spectacle of pity given over to shame and torture and death, he was overwhelmed with disappointment and despair. Innocence and Divinity so meekly and patiently enduring, He that saved others not saving Himself—this Judas could not understand. The career of Jesus was ending so differently from what he had expected. All his hopes regarding it were blighted and destroyed. His suicide was that of one with a broken heart.

But however much of truth and plausibility there may be in this theory, it is not the one the evangelists support. They tell us Judas was an unworthy disciple, and that it was Satan's entering him that made him a traitor.[1] They state that the Master had seen the traitor in him long before he came to play that tragic part, and that He had sought to warn him from his evil course again and again.[2] They suggest to us that

---

[1] Luke xxii. 3.
[2] John vi. 64, and xiii. 26.

he was a selfish, covetous, ambitious, worldly-minded man.[1] They do not hesitate to say that he was a thief,[2] helping himself out of the bag which he carried as treasurer of the little company, doing sometimes what many thieves would scorn to do, stealing what Jesus would have given to the poor. They make plain that his avarice was uppermost when he bargained with the priests about the betrayal and unblushingly asked—"What are you willing to give me, and I will deliver Him unto you?"[3]

It is a problem how such a man came to be a disciple. Undoubtedly Jesus chose him as He did the others. He must have had the qualities which, outwardly at least, made him eligible. We cannot suppose that he was a deceiver from the first, or that he had come among the twelve as a spy or an enemy in disguise, of set purpose to play a traitor's part in the end. We think rather that Judas was a self-deceived man. He meant to be religious. There was very much in Christ that had a real attraction for him. But self continued uppermost. It did not yield to the influence, or to the direct

---

[1] John xii. 4-6
[2] John xii. 6.
[3] Matt. xxvi. 15.

appeals of the Master. He was willing to follow the good so long as it lay in the direction of his self-interest, but when the two parted it was to the self-interest he clung. The treasurership of the band exactly suited him. There was no competition for that office; and in it he was continued with a large measure of unsuspecting confidence of which he was unworthy.

As self would not yield, and covetousness and worldly ambition grew by what they had to feed upon, the inward rupture between Judas and his Master became more and more distinctly felt. The gulf widened. Jesus knew His false disciple through and through, and the false disciple came to feel more and more distinctly that he was found out. He could not but be aware that the Master did not like him, and did not trust him, and that so long as Judas was Judas, an unchanged man, the estrangement must continue. When there was strife among the Twelve as to which of them should be the greatest, we may be sure he would be in the heart of it. Any dissension there might be such a spirit as his would be sure to embitter; and one knows not how many old sores a jealous self-asserting nature like his may have given him to carry within. And his management of the bag may also have roused some measure of distrust and ill-feeling.¹ Renan thinks that spite had a good deal to do with Judas' conduct, and also that "the treasurer overcame the apostle."²

Three years was a long time for such a man to abide in the fellowship of Jesus. What a trial of patience it must have been for our Lord! It was tolerating in His innermost circle the man who should at length secure the cross for Him. It is not wonderful that by and by that association was more than Judas could endure. The open rupture was only a question of time and of mood. And the mood and the time came with the night of the Supper. Judas felt that he could no longer bear such holy company, and that there was nothing more for him to hope for from such a Master. He was also shrewd enough to know that a catastrophe was at hand, and he meant to be on the winning side. His fellow disciples seemed to him blinded, but he thought he knew where his advantage lay. He would make himself useful to those who, as he believed, were about to triumph. He would sell his services for what they might bring; and when the triumph of

---

¹ These and other causes accounting for Judas' remarkable character and development are admirably treated in the chapter on *Judas* in Professor Bruce's "*Training of the Twelve.*"

² Renan, *Life of Jesus*, p. 264.

the priests came he expected he would not be forgotten. His Master's loss should be his gain.[1] And so from the table in the Upper Room he went out—"and it was night."

Are Judas-like men so rare after all? How many under the influence of self are every day proving traitors to duty and to their most solemn professions? Judas' act of betrayal touched directly the person of Christ, and this has given it the pre-eminence in guiltiness that it has. But the spirit is the same which, for personal gain or pleasure or self in any form, sacrifices a friend or a cause or a principle to which one has distinctly pledged himself.

We believe there have been worse men than Judas. There have been men who have committed the greatest crimes, and have not been troubled with remorse or with pity for their victims. To escape those stings of conscience and the horrors of despair which were his tragic experience in the end Judas, it has been well remarked, should have been either a better or a worse man. If he had been a better man he would not have done

---

[1] Jeremy Taylor remarks that Judas sold his Master for the sum at which he valued the ointment that he saw poured on Jesus' head—reckoning the piece of silver to be equal to ten *denarii*, three hundred pence! (*Life and Death of Jesus Christ*, Part III. ad Sect. 15, 11.)

his wicked deed. If he had been a worse the doing of it would not have tortured him as it did. To such a man the words of Jesus have a specially significant application, " Woe unto him! it had been good for that man if he had not been born." [1]

---

[1] Matt. xxvi. 24.

THE VIA DOLOROSA

The trial was now over. Pilate had given sentence that it should be as the multitude required. Preparations for carrying out the crucifixion decreed were forthwith entered upon. Usually with us several days, weeks indeed, are allowed to elapse between the capital sentence upon a criminal and its execution. Jeremy Taylor states on the authority of Suetonius that there was a Tiberian law, made some twelve years before, requiring that ten days should elapse between a capital sentence and its execution.[1] But the conquered subjects of Rome were not treated as her citizens. They were often, like slaves, dealt with in a very summary way. According to Jewish law and custom, no one could be executed on the same day on which his sentence was pronounced. No time was lost in executing the sentence passed on Jesus. He was forthwith

---

[1] Taylor's *Life and Death of Jesus Christ*, III., xv., 28.

hurried on His way to Calvary. He was not a Roman citizen. Even if He had been, it is questionable whether, as one condemned for being a mover of sedition, He would have been allowed a right of appeal. Notorious robbers, or leaders of factions, or movers of sedition, might be punished immediately after their trial.[1] The Catiline conspirators were declared as public enemies to have forfeited their citizenship, and therefore to have no right of appeal, and they were strangled in prison on the afternoon of the day on which they were tried.[2] Yet it must be added that this act formed one of the charges on which Cicero afterwards was banished.[3] Usually the time for appealing, or the time elapsing between a sentence of capital punishment and its being carried out, was two or three days,[4] and it appears in the later Justinian code to have been lengthened to ten days.[5] But there was much arbitrariness in this part of Roman criminal procedure; and a governor like Pilate would see nothing improper or unjust, least of all in the case of one who could claim no Roman rights,

---

[1] Modestine, *Digest*, 49, 1, 16.
[2] Froude, *Julius Caesar*, p. 164.
[3] Froude, *Julius Caesar*, p. 214.
[4] Marcian, *Digest*, 49, 4.
[5] Justinian, *Novella*, 23, 1.

in his being led at once from the bar to the place of punishment.

It appears also that this promptitude in executing a capital sentence was in accordance with Jewish as well as Roman usage, and even with Jewish sentiment. Usually, according to the Talmud, a day was required to elapse between the sentence and its execution; but if the accused were condemned on a Friday (the Jewish week being understood), seeing it was not lawful for him to be executed on a Saturday or a Sabbath, he might be executed immediately after the trial, as they thought it not right to keep him waiting too long.[1] Rabbi Abahou said, "It would aggravate the punishment not to execute the condemned at once."

The multitude, in this instance at any rate, were impatient to see their victim on the cross. And what cared the Roman governor? Compelled to yield to their clamour, he was rather desirous to be done with the troublesome business as soon as possible. As for the Jewish priests and rulers, they had already shown their disregard of law, humanity, everything sacred or just, while they sought to compass Jesus' death. It was the Passover time. One

---

[1] Schwab's *Talmud*, vol. X. pp. 68, 268.

might have expected that they would have been unwilling to have their most sacred festival associated with a thing so abhorrent and so defiling as a public crucifixion. But they were as eager for their prey as the mob could be, and it was so ordered that the day on which the Passover should be slain should witness the shedding of the blood of the great Paschal Lamb. Probably in less than an hour after receiving His final sentence at the Praetorium, Jesus was to be seen in the agony of His cross on Calvary.

Pilate's last act as he left his chair of judgment on the Pavement was to order two thieves to join Jesus on his *via dolorosa*. It seemed a needless and wanton humiliation that He should have to travel to Calvary and to die there in such company. Probably they were Barabbas' companions in crime.[1] They were doubtless men who had been lying in prison under sentence of death. And Pilate seemed in the mood to give the mob the entertainment of more executions than they had asked for. He would forthwith on this day empty the dungeons of Jerusalem of its greatest criminals, cover Calvary

---

[1] So Andrews (*Life*, p. 460), who adds that an early tradition gives them the names of Titus and Dumachus, and says that Jesus met them in Egypt, and predicted to them that they should both be crucified with Him.

with crosses, and provide such a carnival of blood and horror as should satisfy the most bloodthirsty.[1]

We are tempted here to anticipate what Jesus afterwards made of His degrading company. What was intended as an insult and humiliation was turned into an honour. Jesus gained in one of those two thieves the first glorious triumph of His cross. The Friend of sinners found in one who seemed among the chief of sinners the companion He loved to have for Himself on His way that day to Paradise.

The cross they brought Jesus was, we may be sure, of the roughest description. Very likely it consisted simply of a strong upright post, not much over the height of a man, with two cross pieces nailed to it so as to form the shape of the letter V, and with a rough wooden pin about the middle of the beam offering a cruel seat for the body of the sufferer. The condemned man was expected to carry the cross on which he was to die, this being one of the refinements of cruelty and insult to which he was subjected. It was laid upon his shoulders,

---

[1] Weiss (*Life*, III. 362) thinks that Pilate, by joining the two thieves to His company, meant to insult not Jesus, but the Jews. Their king should die between two malefactors.

and to its outstretched arms it often happened that his own were bound.[1]

Thus we can imagine to ourselves Jesus going forth bearing His cross.[2] We can see Him moving on, wearing His own simple Galilean dress (for they had taken off the purple robe, and put His own raiment on again[3]), the crown of thorns still on His brows (there is no word of that being removed), and His arms bound to the arms of the cross He is carrying. He is stooping heavily under His burden. It seems as if He would faint and die under it before He reaches the place of execution. His two wretched partners in suffering and in this open shame are bearing Him company. Each carries a cross like His own, and with a whitened board hung from his neck, telling in large black letters what his name and his crimes are.[4] Each is attended by his executioners—four Roman soldiers to each acting as a guard; while before and behind are the rest

---

[1] Edersheim, *Life of Christ*, II., 583. Geikie, *Life and Words of Christ*, 706.

[2] Not merely the *patibulum* or cross beam, as has been supposed, but the whole of the great and heavy instrument of death. Zoeckler's *Cross of Christ*, p. 93.

[3] Matt. xxvii. 31. Mark xv. 20.

[4] This whitened board with the name and crime of the condemned man written in large letters on it was sometimes borne before him on his way to execution by an inferior officer. Suetonius, *Caligula* 32.

of the detachment under the command of the centurion whose duty it is to see the crucifixion carried out.[1] The great multitude who have been clamouring for this feast of slaughter, and whose numbers are increased as street after street is traversed, follow in the rear, or hasten on in front to secure for themselves the best places from which to view the dreadful spectacle.[2]

What the actual route was which was taken by the mournful procession can only be conjectured. Jerusalem has been so often destroyed and built upon again that it is very difficult to identify localities. Over its site city has been piled upon city in the course of the centuries. They tell us that London, as the Romans knew it, is some sixteen or seventeen feet below the surface of the London of to-day. To reach the Jerusalem and the way of sorrows which Jesus trod, or even the skull-like eminence on which He died, much deeper excavations have to be made. This explains why most of the holy places there, Calvary not excepted, are matters of uncertainty and controversy. What is certain in the present case is that the distance from the Praetorium to the place of

---

[1] Tacitus, *Annals*, III. 14.
[2] Edersheim remarks that processions usually took the longest road to the place of execution (*Life of Christ*, II., 583).

crucifixion must have been about a mile, that the procession had to traverse a considerable part of the city, and that the place called Calvary or Golgotha where the cross was erected was without the gate. Along that way the thorn-crowned Monarch of all lands and ages moved on to His death and to His triumph in meekness and in majesty, if also in pain and sorrow, marking the way as He went with His blood.

Over this *via dolorosa* of our Lord the Christian imagination has often been fondly at work. Incident after incident has been invented to fill in the lines of the infinitely pathetic picture. Thus we have the legend of Veronica,[1] the maiden who weeps as she sees the Man of Sorrows on His way, carrying His heavy load, His raiment so stained, Himself so weary and worn, and who, in the kindness of her heart, approaches and wipes the bloody sweat from His brow, receiving upon the napkin she uses the impression which it ever afterwards retains of the blessed Saviour's face.

Then, as if to supply and illustrate a lesson of a totally different kind, we have the remarkable legend which appears in so many forms of the

---

[1] In the apocryphal writings, the *Mors Pilati* and the *Vindicta Salvatoris*.

Wandering Jew.[1] Ahasuerus—for such is his name, according to perhaps the best known form of the story—is a shoemaker who, as Jesus is passing by, comes forth from his dwelling. Jesus asks to be allowed to rest for a little on his doorstep. The shoemaker scornfully refuses, strikes Him, causes Him to totter under His cross, and bids Him hasten with quicker steps upon His way. Jesus replies, " Because thou grudgest me a moment of rest, I shall enter into my rest, but thou shalt wander restless till I come again." From that moment Ahasuerus must needs follow the Christ and see Him die. Thereafter he must wander over the world, visiting many lands, passing through many a fearful experience and peril, and unable to find rest or death anywhere. A parable we have here, specially suited, no doubt, to mediaeval minds, but not without instruction for our own as to the restlessness and misery of those who turn away the suffering Saviour from their doors, or who have no place for Him in their hearts and their lives.

These two legends, so contrasted, illustrate well the varied impression Jesus bearing His cross still

---

[1] In Baring Gould's *Curious Myths of the Middle Ages*, different forms of this legend as existing in different countries are given, pp. 1-31.

makes upon men. As Jeremy Taylor when writing on this very event in the history of the Passion says, "Sin laughed to see the King of heaven and the great Lover of souls, instead of the sceptre of His kingdom, to bear a tree of cursing and of shame. But piety wept tears, and knew they would melt into joy when she should behold that cross, which loaded the shoulders of her Lord, afterwards sit upon the sceptres, and be engraved and signed upon the foreheads of kings."[1]

But art has done even more than legend here. One of Doré's most striking pictures is that of Christ leaving the Praetorium. It is one of the largest that ever left a painter's hands. In it there are several hundreds of figures, some of them lifesize. Christ is seen descending for the last time the steps of the Praetorium. He is wearing His seamless white robe, and the crown of thorns is still upon His head. He stands alone, sublimely apart, while a vast assemblage is looking on. He appears like the Man of Sorrows He is, sorrowful unto death, yet divinely majestic; meek and lowly, yet a dignity not of this world in His whole aspect and bearing. A halo is round His head; and it is so treated by the artist that it throws an unearthly radiance about

---

[1] Jeremy Taylor's *Life of Christ*, III. 15.

the crown of thorns, imparting to it a kind of transfiguration. Near Jesus are the chief priests who have had so large and guilty a hand in this divine tragedy. In the foreground are the excited mob, many of them pressing eagerly forward to feast their eyes upon their victim, while others seem as if now they would willingly be away from the scene. The Roman guard is seen sternly urging the crowd back with their glittering spears, and clearing a way for their Prisoner. In the distant background, amidst an ominous darkness that appears to be gathering about them, Pilate and Herod are to be observed making friends with each other—the governor in his *toga* of dusky red, with an air about him as if he were still uneasy, and not without a tinge of remorse, but the more eager on that account to disclaim all responsibility. Nor must we omit to mention that close by the great central figure are the mother of our Lord, in tranquil grief and in an attitude of resignation, some sympathetic friends and disciples, and Mary Magdalene, with her tearful face turned aside, and apparently sinking to the ground, in danger of being trodden upon by the rude soldiery. Through a crowd, that seems as if the cry "Crucify him" were upon their lips, the divine Sufferer is seen passing on with the majesty of God, and at the same time with the sensitiveness of man. And over the whole vast picture a mysterious darkening air is thrown, as if of gathering clouds presaging the tempest of divine wrath which was to break forth upon the infatuated people who rejected and crucified the Son of God.

That picture sets forth the pathetic scene with wonderful fidelity, though there are some things that must be set down purely to the artist's imagination. Certainly Pharisees were there with the look of malignant satisfaction on their faces, now that the object of their relentless hatred had been brought so low. Sadducees were there who used to listen with cynical disdain to His lofty spiritual teaching, bestowing upon Him now their contemptuous pity. Roman soldiers were there, fraternising with the Jewish people, and delighted that for this time at least they were playing a popular part and pleasing the multitude by the insults and tortures they had been and still were inflicting upon their Prisoner. And we are willing to believe that the licence is justified which the painter has used by throwing upon the canvas figures of an opposite character—the sympathising Nicodemus, the disciple whom Jesus loved, the Magdalene who could die for Him, and the mother whose heart was pierced by His sufferings as by a sword.

Of these sympathising friends, however, the sacred record says nothing. We cannot doubt that some of them were present; but, perplexed and paralysed by the turn things had taken, they had not the courage to declare themselves. Alone, trusting only in the Father, and upheld by His own great love which the greatest suffering and self-sacrifice could not exhaust, Jesus entered upon His way of sorrow, took up the cross men gave Him, and went to die upon it on Calvary. No human friend appeared to defend Him or His cause. No angel visibly came to His aid. No fire descended from heaven to consume those who had mocked and scourged Him, and who were now to put Him to the cruellest death. There was not even that ominous cloud-threatening sky which the artist has given to his work. The sun shone as usual. The hour had not yet arrived when nature should throw her thick veil of darkness over the last agonies of her Lord. She gave no sign, even when to her divine Maker the rude and cruel cross was brought, and when the crowd broke out into a yell of fiendish satisfaction as they saw it laid upon Him.

Yet to complete the picture we should like

to have of the whole pathetic scene, we would willingly put into it the great sympathetic grateful throng, who in their own grief and sorest need have turned to the divine Man of Sorrows bearing the cross of sin and shame for them, and have blessed Him for the help and the hope He has thus brought. We like the conception so far of that other French artist, Beraud, who in his picture of the scene has represented the Saviour travelling on and bending under His heavy load, with His foes and executioners behind Him, but with a great band of devout sympathisers and worshippers in front. In that representative band there are the old man whose face is made radiant as he directs his dying look upon his suffering Saviour, the orphan children praising His name and thanking Him for the loving care and the home His bearing the cross has provided for them, the wounded soldier who finds healing and soothing as he looks upon the Sufferer, the young bride entreating His benediction upon her new life, and the slave too holding up his chains and gazing wistfully and gratefully upon Him who suffered Himself to be bound that all might be free.[1] A countless throng indeed have

---

[1] The painter, as a good Roman Catholic, has not scrupled to be guilty of the anachronism of putting a priest and a couple of

gazed, and are still gazing upon this thorn-crowned Jesus bearing His cross; they are blessing Him through their tears for their comfort and salvation, while Jesus is moving onward through their midst, in triumph and in joy, leaving His foes behind or fallen.

With Jesus thus going forth the shame of His cross has begun. The cross was indeed the accursed tree. To touch it was pollution, to carry it was deepest disgrace. Reputable men shrank back from it, as indicating contact with the greatest criminality. Religious men remembered it had been said, "Cursed is every one that hangeth on a tree."[1] Self-righteous Pharisees saw in it the foulest contamination. And Gentiles shared in these feelings of abhorrence. Cicero wrote that death by the cross was a punishment the very name of which should never come near the thoughts, the eyes or ears of a Roman citizen, far less his person.[2] It was a punishment for slaves, for alien and rebellious subjects whom Rome despised, for the vilest malefactors; and it was that given to Jesus.

But what was all that men, with their poor

---

nuns in the forefront of this devout band. But we can overlook that for the value of his conception otherwise.

[1] Gal iii. 13.
[2] Cicero, *Pro Rabirio*, V.

perverted notions of honour or purity, saw in the cross, as a thing of horror and a thing telling of the curse, compared to what Jesus must have seen? To Him it spoke of sin, of its awful penalty and curse. It symbolised the atoning death He was to die. As He took it up He in very deed made Himself of no reputation, He beggared Himself of His wealth of righteousness. He consented to be numbered with the transgressors, He humbled Himself to the guiltiest sinner's place. The shame and punishment of our sins He made His own. This was what was worst of all to endure. To pass with His humiliating burden through a scowling and hostile crowd, to be exposed to every one's gibe and sneer, to insult and injury at every step—this was trying, especially for one with a keenly sensitive moral nature. But to take up and carry in the face of the universe the burden of a world's guilt, and that which should be its expiation, and to do this, knowing and feeling all as only the God Man could—this was humiliation and suffering altogether beyond our powers to conceive and realise. To take up the cross as Jesus did, purely under the compulsion of His own love, and in the fullest consciousness that those who laid it upon His shoulders had no power at all against Him except what was given them from above, affords us another glimpse of His sublime resignation to His Father's will, and His boundless devotion to His redeeming work. The martyrs in His cause, who have resignedly carried the wood for their own burning, have but followed Him at an infinite distance.

We do not forget, however, that the cross Jesus took up at the Praetorium had its two sides for Him. While there was the shame and the suffering manifest enough at that moment, there was also the glory that was to follow; and for the joy that was set before Him He went forth to endure the cross, despising its shame.[1] Unfriendly faces all around, voices that reviled Him, passionate insulting outcries such as only a frenzied mob could utter, eyes gleaming with malignant delight at the sight of Him bending and tottering under His humiliating load, what were they all to Him with His soul fixed on God and the eternities? Pilate, Caiaphas, Pharisee, Sadducee, what were they with their seeming triumph for an hour in comparison with the things that must stand for ever? What were men, who would soon all be off the stage of time and reduced to so many handfuls of dust, compared with the everlasting

---

[1] Heb. xii. 2.

God He had been sent to glorify, and the souls He yearned to save?

Would that we had more of the virtue that still goes out of Jesus to enable us worthily to follow Him. What is wanted is the strength to stand alone while all the world may be against us, together with the self-denial and the courage to make light of loss, pain, and shame for His sake. These come only to those who have the vision, as He had, of the eternal and divine, the unseen and heavenly. With that vision given to them, with their souls' look and bent fixed towards God and the things that abide, they are the less moved or appalled by the sights and sounds of this world. They can look above man and beyond time. The cloud o witnesses belonging to the higher world inspires them and concerns them more than the crowd of their struggling and sinning fellow-mortals around them on earth. They dare to do the right, and they follow the great Cross-bearer, rejoicing in the assurance that, beyond all crosses for His sake, there is the crown of life that fadeth not away.

SIMON OF CYRENE.

Art and legend have done not a little, as we have seen, to fill up the pathetic picture for us of our Lord's carrying His cross to Calvary. But the evangelists have not been altogether silent on the subject. Doubtless much occurred on the way, which the Christian world would gladly have known, and which they could so well have told us. Two of them at least, Matthew and John, were in all probability eye and ear witnesses; and Mark and Luke must have often heard apostles and others, for whom the day of Jesus' death would have an imperishable memory, telling of all they had that day seen and heard.

Yet how sparing of incidents they have been except when their Master was specially concerned. John, at any rate, who was a witness of the trial in Caiaphas' house, was not likely to have been absent from the crowd that saw his Master going with His burden of shame to the place where He was to die. He must have been a keen and deeply interested observer of all that took place on the way. He must have had incidents and impressions of the scene, stored up in His mind and memory, which He would retain to His dying day, and which the Church would willingly have possessed. But from him we have not even one. He has nothing to add to what the other three evangelists have given. Each of those three has preserved for us the story of Simon of Cyrene, and of his touching service to Jesus; the third, the evangelist Luke, has added that of the weeping of the women. These two incidents are all that are recorded of a scene on which the Christian imagination has ever fondly dwelt.

Now had the men from whom we have the Gospel history been the writers they are sometimes represented to be—men who wrote for selfish and party ends, and who did not hesitate to invent, and to put forth myths when such were likely to be helpful—they could not have resisted the temptation to pile up the miraculous and the legendary at this tragical stage of their story. But they have written as if they did not even know of temptation of that kind at all. They have told their story as honest simple-minded men o whom the truth was dearer than their lives. From their ample stores of knowledge and experience they have selected just what was needed to fulfil their great purpose in writing, which was to lift up Christ crucified worthily, and as He really was, to the view of the world through all ages.

To the first of these two incidents, then, we now turn our attention. A brief verse from each of the Synoptists is all we have regarding it. Yet each is not just the echo of the others. Each puts the incident in his own way; and so we find, as might be expected, a touch supplied by one which is not given by the others. Thus we are helped to a complete picture in our own minds.

We see the melancholy procession on its way from the Praetorium to Calvary. Jesus is in its midst bearing His heavy cross. Accompanying Him are the two thieves bearing each a similar burden, and bound for the same tragic end. The soldiers are there in strong force, with their centurion at their head, charged with the safe guarding of the prisoners and the carrying out of the sentence of crucifixion. And the mixed multitude are there, priests, rulers, people of all classes and conditions, enlivening the way with their brutal pleasantries. Onward the procession moves through street after street, bringing people forth from their houses to enquire what it all means, and to add to Jesus' reviling foes or to His few silent friends, according as the sight happens to touch them. At length it reaches the gate of the city, and makes for the hill in the open country beyond the walls, where ceremonial defilement from malefactors dying was supposed no longer to be feared.[1]

At this stage in the journey Simon of Cyrene appears upon the scene. He has been in no way connected with the previous proceedings. He has seen nothing of the trial. He knows nothing of what the priests and the people, Pilate and Herod have been doing. Very likely he has never seen the divine Sufferer before, though he may have heard of Him in the distant country in North Africa from which he has been travelling. It is just possible, though of this we have no hint, that through men of Cyrene coming up in previous years to the Paschal Feast[2] he has learned something of the wondrous career of the Man of Nazareth. Such men we know

---

[1] Crucifixions among the Romans as well as among the Jews were wont to take place outside the city. Cicero, *In Verrem*, V. 66.

[2] Ptolemy Lagus planted a colony of 100,000 Jews in Cyrene. There was a synagogue of them in Jerusalem.

had an honourable place among those on whom the blessing of Pentecost came, and such a place as naturally leads us to suppose they had some sympathetic acquaintance previously with Jesus. Simon is coming out of the country as the evangelists tell us.[1] He is on his way into the city, rejoicing as he comes near the gate at the prospect of ending a very long journey, and of being in time to join in the Passover celebrations. He is on pilgrimage to the holy city, and a crowd of high and sacred feelings are filling him. He is coming up to observe the most sacred of Jewish feasts, probably for the first time in his life. And here is the divine Paschal Lamb coming forth to meet him, on His way to be slain on Calvary. Could he ever have hoped to see such a sight? Could it be supposed that one looking as he was for the consolation of Israel would see at once in that most melancholy sight the fulfilment of his grandest hopes? Jesus bending and ready to fall under His heavy cross, and going to die upon it—could this be the consolation and the glory of Israel? Could He be the long looked-for Messiah? Or was it true

---

[1] Lightfoot supposes him to have been working in the fields and bearing wood home ; Meyer that he was a slave ; Andrews, Geikie, and many others that he may have been a pilgrim who was coming up to the Paschal Feast.

that the Paschal Lamb, associated with the great deliverance from Egypt's bondage, slain, roasted, eaten, was after all but the type of the true Messiah, and that Simon coming to observe the type was to find in that cross-bearing Jesus on His way to Calvary the veritable antitype? It was even so, as Simon, we have reason to believe, soon came to know.

One is struck with the instance here afforded of the unforeseen ways in which men may be brought into contact with Christ. Simon probably had no thought of meeting Him when he set out on pilgrimage. He came up to worship, but, like another from Ethiopia,[1] he was destined to return with the treasure of the Gospel; and his country of Cyrene was to be one of the first lands beyond Judea to receive the blessing of the knowledge of Christ.[2] He came to eat the Passover. A special providence it was for him that, as we have already remarked, he should meet at the very gate of the city as he was about to enter it, the true Paschal Lamb going forth to be offered up on the appointed altar on Calvary.[3] That apparently chance meeting

---
[1] Acts viii. 27.
[2] Acts xi. 20.
[3] Josephus (*B.I.*, VI., IX. 3) informs us that the Passover was slain from the ninth to the eleventh hour. So Jesus must have died as the first of these Paschal sacrifices were being offered.

turned the current of Simon's life for eternity.[1] An unexpected turn of events brings you in some way or other face to face with Christ: you meet Him bearing His cross, or revealing His saving power and life can never be again just what it has been. Either you take the cross, so to speak, from Christ's shoulders and make it your own, or you join the multitude who add to its weight and shame.

Simon met Jesus unexpectedly; and there are indications, we shall see, that his sympathies were with Jesus and not with His foes. Barabbas also came unexpectedly into contact with Him, but, we fear, with a different result. To Jesus he owed his release in a way he never could have anticipated. The multitude chose him in preference to the sinless Son of God. But he left his prison that morning, it is to be feared, notwithstanding the halo of beautiful romance modern writers of fiction have sought to throw around him, to join the ranks of the mob, and to show how worthy he was of their insulting and wicked choice. For a brief space of time he stood side by side with Jesus on the Gabbatha, but they met only to part again: he to receive the world's applause, Jesus

---

[1] Pressensé (*Life of Jesus*, p. 624) makes Simon a believer from the day of his carrying the cross.

to bear the world's sins, and to endure the cross at its hands.

Simon's is a different experience. Jesus evidently attracts his attention. To him He is no ordinary Prisoner on His way to death. He soon shows himself more than interested. As he sees Him under His cross, weary and worn with the marks of the cruel sport and scourging to which He has been subjected, his heart is touched. There is something in His look and bearing too that impresses him. His sympathy is stirred, and with it a certain undefined feeling of dislike and resentment towards the reviling mob. He has no wish to join them. The rude merriment they are indulging in, and the brutal spectacle to which they are looking forward have no attractions for him. He seeks to pass by,[1] and to hasten away from the dreadful scene.

But the soldiers and the mob are quick to perceive this. Immediately they find a new object for their hatred and contempt; and as Jesus is at that moment bending and ready to faint and fall under His cross they quickly take measures to pass the load from Him to the shoulders of this stranger. At once Simon is seized hold of.

---

[1] Mark xv. 21.

He is requisitioned by the military for service. The cross is taken from Jesus and laid upon him. He is compelled to bear it. The mob greets the act with their loud merriment and applause. They are just in the humour to enjoy seeing the cross, which Jesus is failing to carry with as quick steps as they could wish, put upon the broad shoulders of this foreign-looking, tawny-skinned man from North Africa. It gives them a cruel satisfaction to see this mark of ignominy put upon the stranger, who will not turn with them to add his raillery and insult to their own.

It is wonderful how an act of little or no importance in itself may reveal character and have momentous issues. Simon's passing by revealed a possible, if not an actual disciple. It annoyed the multitude. It drew their attention to him as one upon whom they were disposed to take a mean revenge by arresting his steps, and putting on him the humiliation of carrying the condemned Galilean's cross. Had he but mingled with them and united in their shouting and jeering he might have escaped, and his name would never have emerged from its obscurity. But his passing by singled him out, threw him into the fellowship of the divine Sufferer, and brought him the immortal honour which the greatest kings or heroes might covet, that of carrying the cross of Jesus.

Thus there are times and circumstances when a word or an act, otherwise of no particular consequence—the holding up of a hand, the writing of a name in a paper, the wearing of a badge, or the use of a watchword—the doing or not doing of any of these things, which in other circumstances might be of no importance, determines the place and the whole future of a man. It may be the very thing to put him among the friends or the foes of Christ, to bring him the cross of honour and suffering in His cause, or to number him with its persecutors and those who put Himself to open shame. Had Simon's passing by taken place an hour sooner or an hour later it might have had no special significance whatever. Happening when and where it did, however, it meant sympathy, then it led to association with Jesus, and it issued in salvation for Simon himself and for his family as well.

Are we claiming too much for Simon when we thus represent him and the significance and results of his passing by? We think not. Mark tells us he was the father of Alexander and Rufus[1]— two brothers, as we may conclude from the way

---

[1] Mark xv 21.

in which they are referred to, who were well known and highly esteemed members of the early Church. Paul in his closing words in the epistle to the Romans sends his salutations to "Rufus, chosen in the Lord, and his mother and mine."[1] This is one of the highest tributes which could be paid to Simon's wife that she had been as a mother to the great apostle of the Gentiles. It reveals the kind of woman she must have been that the great, tender, Christlike heart of the apostle found in her a kindred spirit—one to whom he could look up as sweeter, saintlier, more Christlike than himself. It would be strange indeed if the husband of such a woman and the father of two such sons, as had but to be named in order to be known wherever the Gospels were read, had not himself been a convert. The probability is that the burden he had that day to bear for Jesus was the thing that decided him in His service, and brought him into everlasting union with Him.

But Simon had to be compelled to take up this burden for Jesus. We might have wished this had not been necessary. We should have left it to be at least one bright human touch in the otherwise dark picture of our Saviour's passion

---

[1] Romans xvi. 13.

had Simon been so moved with pity as he passed by, at the sight of Him struggling along under His heavy cross, that he had freely offered to bear it for Him. When we think of the Man of Sorrows on His dolorous way, of the brutal soldiery, with the ruthless mob hurrying Him to His awful death, and then of what He had been, and of all the good He had done—how He had borne the sins and sorrows of others, and lightened every man's burden but His own, it seems incredible that there should have been no one to befriend Him in His day of sorest need, no one to spare Him a single indignity, no one to bear His cross for Him, even for a little, but this Simon who had to be compelled.

True, neither he nor any other could lighten Jesus of the heavier load which weighed upon His soul, and of which the cross was but the outward symbol. Yet it was something to relieve for a while the wearied aching bodily frame, and to enable Him to reach Calvary without further torture by the way. But Simon required to have this honour thrust upon him, the honour of doing a service for which every Christian heart has felt tenderly grateful ever since. Nor need we much wonder at this. It was a humiliation, a ceremonial defilement to have to touch the cross. To have to take up the cross of a supposed malefactor, just as he was about to enter the city to take part in the most sacred observance, was for Simon to be covered with contempt and shame, and subjected to the greatest indignity. It was hardly to be expected that the passing stranger and pilgrim should at once be found ready for this. Even the disciple whom Jesus loved could follow in the procession—we find him afterwards standing by the cross—but he had neither the courage nor the devotion to step forward and offer to relieve for a little his Master of His load.

Simon was richly rewarded for his service. His carrying the cross became his greatest privilege, his shame was turned to his immortal honour. Amidst the jeers of the mob he had the cross of Jesus laid upon him. Soon the procession, arrested for a little, moved forward again. But Simon with his humiliating burden had Jesus by his side. The two walked onward together. Can we doubt that a kindly relationship was established between them—a kinship so that Simon's soul was drawn out in growing sympathy and love towards Him whose cross he was bearing—and that Jesus found in him a trophy of the conquering power of His cross even while He was on the way to endure it?[1] If the penitent thief was so moved by what he saw of Jesus on the cross that the divine Sufferer became transfigured in his view from appearing a malefactor like himself into being a divine King with a paradise for His friends, what may we not suppose was the effect on Simon walking side by side with Him to Calvary amidst the reviling multitude, and carrying the cross on which He was to die?

Simon became, we may well believe, more and more interested in, and touched by the incomparable Sufferer. He felt the spiritual influence, the divine magnetism that went forth from Him. His emotions were such as he could not explain. There was a secret happiness and joy which welled up from a fountain within never unsealed before. The humiliating load became lighter, the rough road smooth as the softest grass for his feet. The jeering of the mob he heeded not, while he was absorbed and entranced by the presence and fellowship of Him whom he was relieving of His accursed load. The journey, that might have seemed to another as if it would never end, seemed all too short to him; and when he laid down his burden at Calvary we can imagine him laying down that reluctantly

---

[1] Stalker (*Trial and Death of Jesus*, p. 134) thinks he may be the same Simon of Acts xiii. 1.

which he took up only under compulsion. For all he had had to endure he felt immeasurably recompensed by the very presence and gracious regard of the Sufferer by his side; and it gave him a secret joy that he was relieving Him of His burden for the time, and making the way of sorrow and death easier for Him. And what a privilege was that of Simon, as he reached Calvary, to see with his own eyes how for sinners Jesus died, and to know more fully and poignantly than any other in the world could, by the personal experience he had had of it, what the cross, with its cruel weight and shame and woe must have been to Him who endured it for our sakes!

In Simon of Cyrene we see what all the followers of Jesus in some measure are. They walk with Him as He now unseen carries His cross through the world and the ages. Of them it may be said, as of Simon, that while passing by they have been arrested and turned aside, and made to bear the cross and shame of Jesus. But it is the burden and the conflict they take up for Jesus that establishes their deathless union and fellowship with Him. They share His cross, and they are destined to sit with Him upon His throne. And in one respect at least they are more favoured than he. Simon carried the cross with his face towards Calvary. He was unable to foresee all that might come of it, all the glory that was to follow it, all the streams of grace, pardoning mercy and salvation that should yet flow from it. But now, as they bear the cross after their Lord and Saviour, they can look back upon Calvary and all the blessings and triumphs there won. As they struggle on with their burden of present reproach, labour, and conflict in His service, they may know that they are walking with Him, not as He is wearily travelling from the judgment bar of His foes to His cross, but as He is moving on with the step of a divine conqueror from Calvary to glory.[1]

---

[1] De Costa (*Four Witnesses*, p. 415) offers an interesting explanation of Simon's service. He says that the cross, being ordinarily fastened to the shoulders of the condemned, was not likely to have been unloosed by the soldiers on the way. He is of opinion that Simon was only compelled by them to lift up the cross, which was proving too much for Jesus' physical strength, and to walk behind or beside Him bearing it up. This view also lends itself to spiritual uses and lessons such as we have indicated.

THE DAUGHTERS OF JERUSALEM.

It would have been strange indeed if, in that mixed multitude attending Jesus on His way to Calvary, there had been absolutely no evidence of sympathy with Him. Even the thought of that thorn-crowned Man of Sorrows bearing His cross has stirred pity and called forth tears in the case of a countless throng that have never seen Him. We can hardly imagine that the reality should have failed entirely to make a tender impression upon any of those who were eye-witnesses. So we are thankful for the touching incident which the evangelist Luke has preserved for us, and which he alone records as to the wailing of the women of Jerusalem. It supplies at least one pleasing human touch to the otherwise dark and forbidding picture of how the Son of Man fared at the hands of men when He was on His way to die for them. Alas for our poor fallen humanity, their treatment of Him seems, for the most part, more like that of fiends than like that of men. It reveals such depths of malice and such possibilities of evil that, when contemplating it, we seem to be beholding the wild play of malignity and sin among the abandoned and lost in the place of woe, rather than the conduct of men in a religious city observing its most sacred festival. It is a welcome relief to us therefore to learn that there were human hearts which were touched with compassion, that there were those who with their tears and lamentations followed the suffering Jesus to the place where He was to die.

There were women in the crowd, and they were not destitute of womanly feelings. They saw Jesus with His visage more marred than any man, and His form more than the sons of men. They marked the thorn-crowned brows, the blood-stained face and raiment, and the look of unutterable sorrow which He wore. They beheld Him moving wearily on, and ready to fall at times under His heavy and shameful burden. They were touched by the ruthless treatment He was receiving, the blows and insults with which He was hurried on His way, the awful death that was awaiting Him. Simon's service but increased their pity.

Those women were daughters of Jerusalem. It

was their husbands, fathers, or brothers that had raised the cry "Crucify him." They belonged to a city that, cursed by Rabbinism and Phariseeism, had been the least responsive to the public ministry of Jesus. It was not so much Jerusalem men and women who a few days before had greeted Him with hosannas, as the people who followed Him from Galilee.[1] When He entered in His triumphal way amid their acclamations, all the city was moved. Not with sympathetic gladness was it moved but with suspicion and alarm.[1] Jerusalem was the headquarters of all that was hostile to Jesus. Her priests and rabbis, self-interested and obdurate in their cold and unspiritual traditionalism, had shown themselves His bitterest adversaries. It was asked in scorn whether any of her rulers had believed in Him. Her religious sects though divided among themselves were united against Him. Her population, in general cold and self-complacent, full of religious pride and bigotry, were just the kind of people that could, without compunction, stand around and see such a one as Jesus die amid the horrors of crucifixion.

But in spite of all else nature asserted itself in her daughters. At the sight of the suffering Man

---

[1] Stalker's *Trial and Death of Jesus*, p. 140. [2] Matt. xxi. 10.

of Nazareth on His way to Calvary they broke forth into wailing. In their tears and lamentations nature paid Him this tribute that, whatever might be the charges against Him, whether they were true or false, His sufferings were such as to entitle Him to the deepest compassion. In the view of these women, Pilate, the Jewish rulers, the multitude might have been right in treating Him as they had done. Very likely they themselves had been lifting up their voices with those that clamoured for His death. There might have been also a Jewish law, as is alleged, forbidding sympathy with a condemned man. But notwithstanding all this, their tender womanly feelings proved too strong and overpowering to be restrained. There was that in the sufferings of Jesus and the divine way in which He was bearing them, which unsealed the fountain of pity and caused it to flow forth in spite of every obstruction. One, and then another and another took up the wailing, as if they were attending not an execution but a funeral.[1]

---

[1] Renan (*Life of Jesus*, p. 286) regards this whole passage about the wailing of the daughters of Jerusalem as unhistoric, and is sure that the words Jesus addressed to them could only have been written after the siege of Jerusalem. Keim (*Jesus of Nazara*, vol. VI., 131) also doubts Jesus having spoken to the women, though he admits His words are in keeping with the character and spirit of Jesus. But Luke's narrative here bears the clearest impress of naturalness and historic reality.

To women then, it is to be observed, the honour of paying this tribute of humanity is due. But the attitude of women to Jesus throughout His earthly career is altogether remarkable. We do not read of one of them ever doing Him an unkind act, or speaking an unfriendly or insulting word. It was not women who betrayed Him, or who forsook Him and fled when He was delivered up to His foes. It was not women who had any part in the brutalities of Pilate's judgment hall, in the mocking and scourging of Jesus; but it was they who were found offering the one refreshing draught of human sympathy which He received on His way to Calvary. On the other hand, it was women who solaced the Saviour with their fellowship, who ministered to Him of their substance, who anointed, one His feet with tears, another His head with the costliest ointment, who sorrowed over His sorrows while He went bearing His cross, and who were the first to seek Him and to be greeted by Him on the day of His resurrection.

But whatever debt Jesus thus owes woman He has infinitely repaid. He has brought her forth from her seclusion, and raised her from her state of subjection. He has made her the equal and the companion, instead of the slave of man. He has created for her the Christian home, and given her there love's throne. He has also thrown open to her His church upon earth and His kingdom above, as places where there is neither male nor female, but all are one in Himself. Wherever the Gospel of Jesus exerts its power, woman has most reason to call Him blessed.

Those tears and wailings of the daughters of Jerusalem did honour to their womanly hearts. But they did more. They afforded the most touching evidence of the greatness of the sufferings which called them forth. It would probably be doing those daughters of Jerusalem no injustice to say that their tears came from a mere emotional pity, without any genuine feeling of attachment. They wept for the suffering Jesus probably as children are wont to do at the sight of pain and anguish in others, apart from all consideration of who they are, and of what may be the cause of their suffering. Thus tears have been shed over the worst as well as over the best of men. They have flowed at the execution of the greatest criminals as well as at the burning of the most eminent saints and martyrs. They are but nature's sympathetic tribute to suffering humanity. They might not have been denied to Barabbas, had he been led forth to be crucified, any more than to Jesus.

These considerations, however, make the testimony of the women's wailing to the unique greatness of the suffreings of Jesus all the more striking and impressive. Those women had been consenting unto His death. They were the wives, sisters, or daughters of those who had been instant with loud voices requiring that he should be crucified. But they were moved, so to speak, in spite of themselves, in spite of all their prejudice and hatred. They could not be silent, but must break forth into piteous lamentations, even in the hour when the Sufferer was being assailed with the outpouring of the worst human passions. In short, His sufferings were so great and so pathetic, that they drew tears from the daughters of the sinful Jerusalem that was inflicting them. It is no wonder then that they have had such a power ever since to touch the hearts even of the greatest enemies of the cross. The world of humanity indeed is constrained to pay its tribute of sympathetic emotion to Him who meekly endured them, as to no other in the great army of sufferers.

It would have been well had the daughters of Jerusalem followed up their tears by action worthy of them. But, as we find, that was singularly awanting. They wept over the sufferings of Jesus, but they did nothing to alleviate them, or to bring them to an end. The tears shed did not avail to change hatred into love, or to turn the tide of evil. Too soon they were dried away, and the sinless Sufferer, who for the time called them forth, was allowed to go on to His awful death.[1]

What a great amount of such emotion there is still—emotion which is never translated into any worthy practical form! Tears too many there are that tell but of a passing fit of tenderness. Pity in plenty there is that can speak in touching accents, but the helping hand it should inspire is too often paralysed, or beyond its power to move. Tender sacred emotions fill the hearts of many under impressive religious influences to whom it hardly seems to occur that religion is seriously meant for their every day life. Many shed tears over the sufferings of Jesus, in the same way as they would over those of some fictitious hero or heroine in the last novel they have been reading, or the last sensational play they may have seen upon the stage.

Emotion which begins and ends with itself is a most dangerous thing. It is fascinating, and it is deceiving. It weakens the sense of duty,

---

[1] Sepp (*Life of Jesus*, vol. vi., 321) brings these wailing women into connection with those who offered Jesus drink to assuage His sufferings on the cross.

enfeebles the will power, and acts as a hurtful intoxicant upon the inner man. Hence the peril there is for very many from fiction and the drama. They go on imbibing large libations of mere sentiment and sensationalism. As a consequence they live in a state of intellectual and moral intoxication. They become dazed and insensible often to the ordinary duties and demands of life in this world, not to speak of the claims of religion and of the world that is to come. They can revel in scenes and situations the most thrilling and pathetic without their consciences being touched, or their being moved to do a single unselfish act, or to break off a single evil habit or sin that besets them, They can fatally and miserably content themselves with having in their own minds the emotional luxury of dreams of great, virtuous and heroic deeds without the trouble of doing them. They can also delude themselves with the idea that this aesthetic, artificially wrought up satisfaction will take the place of the happiness and rest within, which can come only from personal devotion to duty and to God. One can understand how many who thus live and dream and dissipate themselves in their artificial sensational world gradually waste away their moral strength and sensibilities, grow apathetic to every thing serious and sacred, and become practically wrecks so far as either this world or the next is concerned.

It is of vital importance that emotion should lay hold of our manhood, and that our manhood should be stirred to rise to its sacred appeals and demands. Emotion should be linked with reason and conscience and will. It should be as a force from above, ever inspiring and impelling to duty and to worthy Christian living. It is well that tender and sacred feelings should fill the heart, and that tears should flow at the sight of suffering, especially of suffering innocence. The daughters of Jerusalem did honour to their womanly affections, weeping while they saw Jesus bearing His cross. But they should have given Him more than the tribute of their tears. They would have brought everlasting honour to themselves had they with their pity given Him their heartfelt devotion, and had they done something to show how genuine it was. Where Jesus is concerned, it is true most of all, that tears and prayers and professions avail nothing unless our wills are won for Him, and unless the sacred feelings which find expression upon our lips are justified by the better conduct of our lives.[1]

---

[1] Some excellent remarks in the same direction here are to be found in Hannah's *Last Days of our Lord's Passion*, pp. 156-159.

We are not told what effect the women's wailing had upon the multitude, but we learn that it drew forth the most touching response from Jesus. Luke informs us expressly that Jesus turned to them, and addressed them.[1] For the moment doubtless this act arrested the procession. There was a brief pause in the onward march. Silence fell upon the multitude, and an awe probably for the moment like that which had fallen upon the band in the Garden. Every one was intent to hear what might fall from those lips, which all the outcries of the mob, and all the indignities and tortures they had seen inflicted had failed to open. The words heard in the temporary lull were the last words of Jesus to unrepentant Israel, full of pathetic expostulation and warning:[2] — "Daughters of Jerusalem, weep not for me, but weep for yourselves, and for your children. For, behold, the days are coming, in the which they shall say, Blessed are the barren, and the wombs that never bare, and the paps which never gave suck. Then

---

[1] Luke xxiii. 28—31.

[2] An interesting parallel to this scene we find in Josephus. He tells us of one Niger of Perea who had fought bravely against the Romans, and deserved well of his country, but fell a victim to party rancour. On his way to the place of execution this Niger addressed the people, and warned them of coming calamity because of their sins (Josephus, *B.I*, IV., VI. 1).

shall they begin to say to the mountains, fall on us; and to the hills, cover us. For if they do these things in a green tree, what shall be done in the dry?"

The speech of Jesus, especially during the time of His trial and sufferings, is as remarkable as His silence. He is silent before the council when they are bringing one after another of their false witnesses against Him; before Herod when that frivolous creature questions Him in many words, and when chief priests and scribes vehemently accuse Him; and before Pilate when the like occurs, answering him to never a word, so that the governor marvels greatly. But He speaks when His testimony to the truth is called for, or when some response is given to the appeal His sufferings make, as in the present case, by the wailing of these women who follow Him. He speaks when Pilate asks Him about His kingdom,[1] explaining to him its spiritual and unworldly character. In silence He moves on amid the noise and ribaldry of the mob attending Him on His way of death. He meekly endures their rude jests, their insulting outcries, without a word or look of repining or complaint. But the weeping of those tender-hearted women touches Him, and He

---

[1] John xviii. 30-37.

stops, pausing for a little on His dolorous way that He may respond to the tribute of their pity.

It is the same, we find, when He is dying on the cross. In silence He suffers, having no response but His own meek endurance to all the storm of human malice and abuse raging around Him. No sooner however has the penitent thief dying by His side turned from his railing, in which his companion in crime has been joining him, to speak words of thoughtful and even tender and reverential regard, than instantly he has the ear and the heart of Jesus. His humble request for remembrance when Jesus should come into His kingdom is far exceeded by the promise of fellowship that day with Himself in the joys of paradise.[1]

But it is the same still. When men are wrangling about Christ and His doctrines in the spirit of the rabbis who persecuted Him, or are treating Him like Pilate, who unjustly condemned Him, their voices prevail, His own is unheard. When they are bent, not on finding out the truth, but rather on making good their denials, He may be found answering to never a word. When they suffer themselves to be carried away

---

[1] Luke xxiii. 43.

by the prevailing tide of the hour, allow reason and conscience to be silenced and overpowered, and are ready to shout with the multitude, not knowing what they do, He preserves an ominous silence. But let there be the smallest movement of serious feeling and thought towards Himself, be it the tribute of sincere homage paid to Him for His worth and work, or only a tear genuinely shed over His sorrows, Jesus will respond to it, and the honest heart must be drawn more and more closely to His own. We may well believe that He, who was willing, so to speak, to step aside from the tumult of those who hurried Him to Calvary that He might address Himself to the wailing women of Jerusalem, is ready now to stoop from His divine throne to recognise and make response to the most unworthy penitent.

Turning now to the words which Jesus addressed to the wailing women, we are struck first of all with what they reveal of the patriotic spirit of Jesus, and of the place Jerusalem had in His heart. The pity the daughters of Jerusalem expressed for Him called forth a truer, tenderer pity in His heart for them and their children, in view of the awful calamities that were soon to overtake them. His own cross was heavy; but He was bearing it in His sinlessness, and He was sustained by the joy that was set before Him. Their coming cross, however, was to be so awful, and so unrelieved, as one coming upon a guilt-laden people ripe for their day of doom. The wrath and destruction about to descend upon them were to be for their nation like the fire consuming a dry and sapless tree.

Jesus' heart was moved at the woful prospect for the race and nation to which he belonged, and which He loved so well. It was His last opportunity before He should be stretched upon the accursed tree to utter a warning word, or to leave His public testimony behind Him, if haply the threatened calamity might be averted. What a heart of pity and love His melting words disclose! What a testimony they are, given by Him as He is about to be driven off the stage of this world, alike to His righteousness and His mercy! Jesus willed not that any should perish, but He willed rather to stand when He could, and as long as He could, between men and their doom.

Our wonder and praise, as we think of this truly divine pity of Jesus, increase when we recall how He had been treated by the city and people with which those daughters of Jerusalem were connected. Jerusalem had given Him little reason for affectionate remembrance. As a matter of fact, no city had been so cold, so unresponsive. Its rabbis had no welcome for the greatest of teachers. Its priests did not recognise His priesthood. Its rulers did not believe in Him. Its inhabitants, on one occasion at least, threatened to stone Him.[1] And now they seemed all with one accord clamouring for His death, and hurrying Him to Calvary.

But for all that Jesus loved the city. It was dear to Him as the place God had chosen for His habitation. In its Temple He recognised His Father's house.[2] Its history, so chequered, was after all that which He had come to crown with His own reign and work as the true King and Redeemer of Israel. Its name seemed engraven upon His heart. It is really remarkable how its future concerned Him, and how frequently it engaged His thoughts, and called forth His tenderest solicitude. O Jerusalem, Jerusalem, He exclaimed, as with a breaking heart, while He recalled what God had done for it, sending prophets and messengers, and at length His own Son, and while He thought of how its people had killed the prophets, and stoned them that had been sent unto

---

[1] John viii. 59.
[2] Luke xix. 46.

them, and were about to consummate their guilt in crucifying Himself.[1]

Four times within the week before His death He referred to the city, and each time in a tone of infinite pathos. As He came to it for the last time from Galilee, and sat in view of it on the Mount of Olives, He wept over it and said, "If thou hadst known in this thy day the things which belong to thy peace, but now they are hid from thine eyes."[2] On the afternoon of the day of His arrival, when they were pointing out to Him the goodly stones with which the Temple was adorned, He said, "See ye not all these things? Verily I say unto you there shall not be left one stone upon another which shall not be thrown down."[3] Later on when the disciples touched by His words asked for an explanation, He uttered His long prophecy about the siege and destruction of the city and the scattering of the Jewish nation.[4] Then here on the eve of His crucifixion when He was in the very act of bearing His cross, and when as the city's greatest Outcast He was going forth without its gates to die, it was Jerusalem with its

---

[1] Matt. xxiii. 37.
[2] Luke xix. 42.
[3] Matt xxiv. 2.
[4] Matt. xxiv. 3-51. Mark xiii. 5-37.

future that occupied His thoughts and stirred His tenderest feelings. The lips that had kept close amidst the storm of reproach and suffering opened to give the most touching evidence, in the words addressed to the women who bewailed Him, of how the sins and the coming woes of Jerusalem lay heavy upon His heart.

Those momentous words were a prevision of the appalling carnage and horrors which, a generation later, were to overtake the city He loved. They should be called blessed who had no sons or daughters to come after them, fated to perish miserably during those woful days. Retribution the most terrible should be stalking abroad, and the people should be seeking escape and refuge from it in the dens and caves of the earth, in the underground passages and sewers of the city.[1] They should prefer to be buried beneath the mountains than to be exposed to the sword of their infuriated and revengeful foes.[2]

---

[1] Josephus, *B.I.*, VI., IX., 4.

[2] Description of the horrors of the siege, with famine, plague, bitter party feud, massacre, incendiarism, devastation, scourging the doomed city and its guilty inhabitants will be found in Josephus, *B.I.*, Books V. and VI. The dire retribution on the various guilty actors involved is vividly portrayed in Farrar, *Life of Christ*, pp. 685, 686. Professor Graetz, a non-Christian Jewish writer in his recent history of the Jews (1891), says that more than a million Jews perished in the siege, and that many thousands were sold afterwards into slavery at an incredibly low figure. His graphic account of the siege is given in vol. II., ch. XI.

Were the women of Jerusalem so touched by the sufferings of Jesus that they could not be restrained from wailing and from tears? What then would they be were they to live to see the sufferings of their nation in its day of wrath? If the fire caught, scorched and burned the green tree so terribly, what would it do with the wood of the dry? If the sufferings falling upon an innocent person as He was were so great as to call for their lamentations, what cause for weeping there would be over the woes befalling a city whose sins and crimes were the wonder of the universe, and which was ready for destruction as dry wood for the flames![1]

But are we not too apt to forget that guilty Jerusalem and the Israel that rejected and crucified Christ are only representatives of, or other names for ourselves as guilty sinners? His love

---

[1] Graetz admits that the Jews did not understand at the time the importance of Jesus' death, but protests that it was not they but Pontius Pilate and his Roman soldiers who maltreated and murdered Him, while he writes of Him and of the momentous consequences of His crucifixion for the Jewish race in these remarkable words:— "Such was the end of the man who had devoted himself to the improvement of the most neglected, miserable, and abandoned members of his people, and who, perhaps, fell a victim to a misunderstanding. How great was the woe caused by that one execution! How many deaths and sufferings of every description has it not caused among the children of Israel! Millions of broken hearts and tragic fates have not yet atoned for his death. He is the only mortal of whom one can say without exaggeration that his death was more effective than his life." *History of the Jews*, vol. II., 165, 166.

and pathetic solicitude for Jerusalem, and His patriotic feeling for Israel were only, as it seems to us, the colours in which at the time Jesus chose to clothe His love and solicitude for the sinning world for which He was on His way to die. Jerusalem with Him but stood for the world that should reject Him. The love He had for it, with all its blackslidings and sins, is but the form in which He expresses the yearning of His heart for human souls. His sorrow over its doom is His sorrow over ours, if we should go on our way as impenitent sinners. Even those warning and imploring words He utters in regard to it while bearing the cross which it gave Him, are in a measure the Gospel appeal to us all. They are impressive words meant for ourselves, bidding us repent and believe, that we may be saved from the wrath and judgment which otherwise must fall on us. The pity they breathe towards those whose sins were giving Him all His woes, like the prayer He lifted up for His murderers while He was hanging on the cross, is the divine compassion He has for all sinners of mankind. There is no better or more salutary exercise for us than to take all the terrible things that ever were or could be said against guilty Jerusalem, and to charge them home against ourselves. On the other hand, as penitent sinners, we cannot desire or hope for greater blessings, or a greater salvation than what Jesus yearned to bestow upon those who crucified Him.

"Weep for yourselves," said Jesus to the daughters of Jerusalem; "weep not for me."[1] What cause they had for the sorrow that wrought repentance. What wailing could be too great for a people crucifying their promised Christ, and thereby morally crucifying themselves! If only they had seen their sins as God did, and if they had had so much as a glimpse of the immeasurable calamities they were bringing upon themselves, theirs would have been the weeping of true broken-hearted penitents, and their sorrow would have been their salvation. Had those women wept and lamented for themselves as Jesus so pathetically desired them, they would have wept none the less but all the more for Him, and they would have given Him their hearts and their devotion for ever. They would have come to sympathise with Him and to trust in Him as they never otherwise could do, and their sorrow should have been turned into joy.

The cross of Jesus can be understood only when its great mystery of redeeming love is read

---

[1] Luke xxiii. 28.

with eyes filled with penitential tears. Whatever its woes are to others in the way of exciting compassion and calling forth sorrow, they are still more in this direction to those who look upon them as caused by their sins, and as the price paid for their forgiveness and salvation. We weep for the suffering Jesus all the more when we weep for ourselves. Our pity is intensified when we see that our sins gave to Him a crown of sharper thorns than that which was bound upon His brows, and that they inflicted upon His soul more humbling and painful stripes than those which fell upon His body. Our sorrow is sincere when we realise that our sins clothed Him with a more awful shame than that which the purple robe put upon Him, and all the mockery and insult He had to endure. Ours is the repentance not to be repented of when we mourn for our sins as having made for Jesus a heavier and more awful cross than that which men saw Him carry and die upon. Never indeed can we know the true pathos of the cross until we have seen it in this light, and have wept for ourselves as well as for Jesus in presence of its infinite mystery.

Tracing the history of our Lord's passion, as we have endeavoured to do, recalling the incidents of His arrest and trials, with all the shame and suffering with which they were accompanied, we have been led necessarily to review the conduct of those immediately concerned. But while sitting in judgment upon the guilty actors, it is for us to bear in mind that we are also sitting in judgment upon ourselves. The priests and rulers, Pilate, Herod, the Roman soldiers, and the Jewish multitude were after all but instruments; the sins which moved them were the real authors of Jesus' death. Their sins are represented in each one of our hearts, and they make us all partners in their guilt. But they become—to use the beautiful expression of Augustine—*beatae culpae*, when we sincerely repent of them, and are brought humbly and gratefully to accept of salvation through the death which they caused.

INDEX.

Accent, Galilean, 125
Accounts of Peter's denials—discrepancies, 130
Accuracy of the evangelists, 140, 190, 263, 274, 303
Aceldama, 273, 274
Action and emotion, 325-327
"Acts of Pilate," 261
Address to the wailing women, 328
Agony in the Garden, 26-62; its greatness, 44; its mystery, 43-62; its cause. 49; the spirit in which it was endured, 59
Albinus, 205
Alexander and Rufus, 311
Alford, 130, 259
Ambrose, 253
Andrews, 10, 130, 139, 287, 306
Angel strengthening Jesus, 47
Annas, 63, 84
Annas faction, 89, 90
Ananias, "the whited wall," 263
Antonia, 246
Apocryphal writings referred to, 190, 261, 291
Apology for the Jewish people, Jost's, 95, Graetz', 336; for Pilate, Stephen's, 238; for the Sanhedrim, Mill's, 95
Appeal, Right of, discussed, 284-286
Arnold (Edwin), 231, 239
Arrest in the Garden, 63-82
Art, Gethsemane in, 44, 74
Art, Via Dolorosa in, 293, 297
Arbitrariness of Roman criminal procedure, 285

Atheism and persecution, 85
Atonement and the Incarnation, 52
Attitude of women to Jesus, 322
Augustine, 130, 340
Augustus, The emperor, 260
Avarice of Judas, 279
Band led by Judas, 66; falling to the ground, 70
Baptist, John the, 163, 167
Barbarities in the common hall, 248
Barabbas, 209; with Jesus on the Gabbatha, 210; never the world's saviour, 217; his release an acted parable, 219; place in modern fiction, 220
Bearing the cross *after* Jesus, 317
"Behold the Man," 251
Bema, or judgment seat of Pilate, 136
Beraud's *Christ bearing the Cross*, 297
Betrayers of the Christ, The Jews, 135
Blood-sweating, Cases of, 44
Brodrick. 62
Bruce (Professor), 281
Buffeting of Jesus, 105, 240
Burden and curse of sin on Jesus, 59
Caesar, Delivering Jesus to, 106
Caesarea, Scene at, 223
Caiaphas and the Council, 63, 89, 91
Canton (W.), 238
Captain of Temple guard, 65

INDEX.

Captors, Jesus' words to His, 78
Carlo Dolce, 44
Caspari, 27, 113, 135, 138, 259
Casuistry of the priests, 272
Celsus and Julian the Apostate, 48, 67
Chagigah, Offering of the firstlings, 138, 139
Charges against Jesus—ecclesiastical, not civil, 144
Chastising and liberty, 184
Christianity and the sword, 76
Cicero, 196, 241, 298, 305
Claudia Procula, 191
Clubs and swords, 65
Cock-crowing, 128
Coins, Jewish, 223
Common hall at Antonia, 248
Companions in death—thieves, not disciples, 72
Company round the fire in Caiaphas' house, 113
Compelled to bear the cross, 312
Compromise, Pilate's, 184, 187
Conscience and sentiment, 327
Country house called Gethsemane, 28
Court hours early, 133
Corelli, Marie, 220
Court of Sanhedrim, 91
Crimen maiestatis, 260
Cross, described, 288; its shame and suffering triumphed over in the Garden, 61
Crown of thorns, 248
Crucifixion, Hour of. 258; its shame, 241, 298, 313; outside the city, 305
Cup and the hour, 57
Cyrene, Jews in, 305; Simon of, 302

Da Costa, 130, 317
Danger from fiction and the drama, 326

Dante, 91, 276
Daughters of Jerusalem, 318-340
Delitzsch, 139
Denials of Peter, 130
Denney, 55
De Quincey, 277
Destroying and raising the Temple again, 99
Difficulty in identifying holy places in Jerusalem, 290
Disciples, sentinels at the gate, 30; sleeping in the Garden, 33; not understanding the cross, 37; Jesus' concern for them, 71; forsaking and fleeing, 80; witnesses of the trial and death, 110, 302
Discourse on the way to Gethsemane, 15
Discrepancies as to Peter's denials, 130; passover observance, 138; hour of crucifixion, 258; Jeremiah's prophecy, 275
Doré's *Dream of Pilate's wife*, 193; and *Christ leaving the Praetorium*, 293
Dorner, 52
Dream of Pilate's wife, 191
Dreams, Roman belief in, 196
Duccio's *Arrest in Gethsemane*, 74

Earthly and Messianic kingship, 149
Edersheim, 11, 86, 128, 135, 138, 139, 273, 289
Elijah, Waiting for, 14
Ellicott, 44, 50, 71, 113, 141, 211, 248, 289
Employment of Roman soldiers in the arrest, 65
Emotion and duty, 327
Eusebius, 141, 259, 261
Evangelists sparing of incidents, 302; record end of none of guilty

INDEX.

actors but Judas, 263; independent and accurate, 111, 262
Ewald, 73, 110, 135, 138, 211
Execution on feast days, 106
Extradition, Practice in regard to, 160

Farrar, 249, 259, 335
Fathers roused from their slumbers for the trial, 87
Fear of the people, The priests', 199; Pilate's, 260
Fines for humiliating treatment of accused persons, 98
Five sons of Annas, 84, 263
Forewarning of divine retribution, 335
Four references to Jerusalem by Jesus during Passion week, 334
Fourth Gospel's silence about Gethsemane, 31; Judas' end, 262; incidents on the way to Calvary, 303
Fourth Gospel, Incidents special to: band in the Garden falling backward, 70; trial before Annas, 87; sent bound to Caiaphas, 87; officer smiting Jesus in Caiaphas' court, 97; private interviews with Pilate, 147, 255; "Behold the Man," 251; "Behold your King," 259
Friedlieb, 87
Froude, 285

Gabbatha or the Pavement, 136, 182, 210
Galilee and Judea, 159
Galilee, hotbed of disaffection, 159
Gallio and Pilate, 152
Gardens on Olivet, 10
Gazith, the usual meeting place for Sanhedrim, 87
Geikie, 17, 65, 90, 92, 129, 171, 245, 248, 266
Gerizim uprising, 211

Gethsemane, locality, 26; country house so called, 28; three hours agony in, 31-33; world's Gethsemane of suffering, 43; mystery of, 57; its transforming spirit, 61; in art, 44, 74
Gould (Baring), 12, 65, 88, 91, 98, 204
Graetz (Professor), 249, 335, 336
Greek used in the trials, 147
Green tree and the dry, 336
Grievance of Annas and the Sadducees against Jesus, 86
Guilty Jerusalem the type of the sinful world, 337, 340

Hackett, 56, 270
Hallel at Paschal feast, 12, 14 Jesus leading in the singing, 12
Handwashing of Pilate, 231-239
Hannah, 327
Hase, 32
Hasty procedure of the Jewish rulers, 199
Heathen edifices and ceremonial defilement, 137
Heathen custom of washing hands, 226
Heaven's interest in the Passion, 47; its sympathy with sorrow upon earth, 48
Herod Agrippa I. and II., treasurers of the Temple, 174; Agrippa I. insulted at Alexandria, 249
Herod Antipas, his palace in Jerusalem, 157; coming to the feasts, 160; judgment hall, 161; had never seen Jesus before, 162; his treatment of John the Baptist, 163; more pagan than Jewish, 163; asking for a miracle, 164; babbling about religion, 168; at enmity with Pilate, 174;

made friends, 174; his downfall and end, 179, 263
High priest's palace described, 88, 111
High priest rending his garments, 102
Hilgenfeld, 32
"His blood be on us," 231
Honour thrust on Simon of Cyrene, 313
Hour of the crucifixion—Mark and John, 258
Hour's respite for Peter between second and third denial, 123
Hours, Roman and Jewish reckoning of, 258

Illegalities and irregularities of the Sanhedrim trial, 92-95
Incarnation in relation to the Agony, 52
Informal trial before Annas, 86
Informers and the dread of being reported to Caesar, 260
Innocence of Jesus, Testimonies to, no fault in Him, 152; Pilate's efforts to obtain release, 184, 197, 207, 213, 220, 250, 259; Pilate's washing his hands, 221
Intercessory Prayer, 16

James, one of the three in the Garden, 30
Jameson (Mrs.), 44, 74, 244
Jeremy the prophet—difficulty, 275
Jerusalem unresponsive to Jesus' ministry, 320, 333; difficulty of tracing its holy places, 290; Jesus' love for it, 333; His lamentations over it, 334; the horrors of its siege and destruction, 228, 335
Jesus singing on His way to Gethsemane, 12; agonizing in the Garden, 26; interpreting His own sorrow, 46; His relation to the world's sin, 50; His sublime resignation, 59; His last miracle done to an enemy, 74; words to the band arresting, 78; bound with cords, 79; alone on His way of trial and death, 83; condemned on His own confession of divinity, 102; treatment by His guards in Caiaphas' house, 104, 105; His vision of glory there, 107; explaining His kingdom to Pilate, 147; remitted to Herod, 155; sent back to Pilate, 181; His silence before the Sanhedrim, 95; before Pilate, 153; before Herod, 165, 169; in the common hall, 249; set at nought by Herod's men of war, 171; His innocence, 177, 232; His being scourged and crowned with thorns, 240; side by side with Barabbas, 212; His private interviews with Pilate, 147, 255; condemned, 241; His *via dolorosa* 284; Simon His companion, 310; daughters of Jerusalem bewailing Him, 321; hushing the tumult while He speaks to them, 328; predicting Jerusalem's doom, 334
Jesus and Socrates, 48, 97, 267
Jewish abhorrence of images, 223
Jewish law as to appeal, 284
Jewish non-Christian writers on the trial and death of Jesus, 95, 336
Jewish police and Roman soldiers, 65
Jewish tumults during Pilate's governorship, 222-225
Joanna, wife of Chuza, 190

John and Peter following at a distance, 82; witnesses of trial in Caiaphas' house, 100; and of the crucifixion, 303
John's priestly descent, 111
Josephus, 27, 85, 87, 89, 106, 132, 136, 137, 157, 160, 171, 172, 179, 186, 205, 225, 228, 234, 242, 258, 263, 264, 307, 328, 335
Jost, 89, 95
Judas leaving Upper Room by himself, 10; his bargain with the priests, 11, 279; his surprise and discomfiture that Jesus did not resist, 67; his terror in the Garden, 80; his despair on seeing Jesus condemned, 266; his confession to the priests, 268; his suicide, 270
Just man, Plato's prophecy of his fate, 252
Justinian, 285
Justin Martyr, 261

Kedron, Brook, 12
Keeper of the high priestly robes, 174
Keim, 10, 32, 45, 65, 71, 89, 100, 147, 259, 321
King of the Jews abandoned to be crucified, 259
Kingship worldly and spiritual, 148
Kiss, The traitor's, 69, 264
Knowledge of the cross through penitence, 338

Lange, 16, 272
Lanterns and torches, 66
Latin and Greek Christians and site of Gethsemane, 91
Leading members of Sanhedrim, 89, 90
Legend of Pilate's suicide, 238; of Veronica, 291; of Wandering Jew, 292
Lightfoot, 264, 276, 306
Livy, 204, 244
Lower and upper house in Sanhedrim, 91
Luke's Gospel, Incidents special to: bloody sweat, 43; angel strengthening, 47; hour between second and third denial, 123; the Lord's looking upon Peter, 128; trial before Herod, 158; daughters of Jerusalem, 303
Luther, 214, 247

Malchus, 23; his kinsman, 124
Mark, the young man who followed and fled, 29, 84
Mark's Gospel, Incidents special to: the two cock crowings, 120, 128; multitude asking for the act of release, 202; Barabbas lying bound in prison, 210
Matthew's Gospel, Incidents special to: Jesus standing before the governor, 140; Pilate's wife's dream, 191; Pilate washing his hands, 227; multitude crying "His blood be on us," 228; traitor's suicide, 262
Meeting-place of Sanhedrim, 88
Mercenaries and not Roman soldiers scourging and mocking Jesus, 249
Message from Pilate's wife, 190
Messianic claims, 102, 107, 148
Meyer, 272, 306
Midnight Temple services, 11
Mill, 14
Mill (John S.), 96
Mockery of Jesus in Caiaphas' house, 104; by Herod's men of war, 171; by Pilate's soldiers in the common hall, 248

Modern mood as to physical aspects of the Passion, 243
Modestine and Marcian, 285
Moral difficulty to acceptance of Christianity, 179
Motives for hasty procedure of the priests, 87

National crime, Jesus' death a, 95, 259, 336
Nature's tribute to Jesus' sufferings
Naturalistic explanations and their failure, 71
Nerva, 260
Niger of Perea, 328
Numbered with the transgressors, 214
Numbers employed in the arrest, 65

Obedience of Jesus to His Father's will, 59
Oecumenius, 270
Officer striking Jesus during trial in Caiaphas' house, 97
Olive trees cut down, 27
Opportunism, Roman. 187
Oracles, Roman belief in, 196
Origen, 49, 67
Orr, Professor, 55
Ovid, 226

Palace of Herod, 157
Papias, 270
Paschal Lamb, type and antitype, 306
Paschal meal and the Supper, 138
Passover according to the Synoptists and John, 138, 139
Passover customs referred to, 14, 139, 197
Passover sacrifices offered at the hour Jesus died, 307
Patriotism of Jesus, 331

Paul's tribute to Rufus and his mother, 312
Penitence and knowing the mystery of the cross, 338
Persecuting spirit of Sadduceeism 85
Pertinacity of Jewish rulers, 153, 169, 188, 201, 260
Petavel, 28
Peter's avowals of devotion, 18; blundering sword stroke, 74; following at a distance, 82; denials, 110; witness of the trial, 84
Philo, 225, 249, 254, 260
Physical, Jesus' sufferings more than merely, 49
Pilate's aid sought for the arrest, 65, his residence, 135; the Praetorium, 136; his character 140; his opportunism and spirit of compromise, 184—187; examines the Prisoner himself, 140; his sending Jesus to Herod, 155; his repeated efforts and pleadings to release Jesus, 204; his meetings with Jesus privately in the judgment hall, 147, 255; his tributes to Jesus' innocence, 152, 184, 227, 250; his failure to understand Him, 147, 255; his washing his hands, 221—239; his pity for Jesus scourged and mocked, 251; his dread of being reported to Caesar, 260; his surrender to the multitude, 241; his report of our Lord's case, 261; his end, 238, 264
Plato, 252, 267
Possibilities of evil in man revealed, 105, 167, 248, 319
Praetorium, 135
Preparation, The, 139, 258
Price of blood, 272

Pressensé, 113, 308
Priests leading in the outcries, 89; fearing defilement, 137; afraid of the people, 199; propaganda among them, 214
Problem of Judas, 276
Procession to Calvary, 290
Prophecy fulfilled, 275
Protesting and yielding, 240

Quaestors, Pilate without, 140
Quorum of Sanhedrim, 89

Rein, 160, 203, 242
Relation of Jesus to the world's sin, 50
Release, 202; custom at Passover time, 203; origin of custom, 204
Renan, 76, 101, 151, 158, 248, 259, 281, 321
Repeated attempts to release Jesus, 152, 184, 197, 207, 225, 253, 259
Resistance anticipated to the arrest, 66
Responsiveness of Jesus, 329-331
Revolutionary tribunals, 89
Robinson, 27, 112, 273
Roman governors in Judea, 141
Roman governors and their wives, 190
Roman mode of reckoning the hours, 258
Roman respect for Jewish laws and institutions, 254
Roman shields and standards, 222, 225
Roman soldiers and Jewish offenders, 242
Roman restraints upon the Sanhedrim 132
Sadducees severe and persecuting, 85
Sanhedrim, quorum, 89; president, 89; not lawful before dawn, or on a feast day, 63; held in Caiaphas' house, 87; usually in Gazith, 87; leading members, 91; two meetings, 105; irregularities and illegalities in its procedure, 92—94; condemning Jesus for claiming divinity, 105; unanimity, 106; no power to punish with death, 132; appeal to Caesar, 132
Schwab, 92, 143, 286
Scourge, The, 240; its severity, 245
Scourging, The place of, 246; a military as well as civil punishment, 241
Sejanus and Pilate, 140
Self dominant in Judas, 280
Sending forth of the Seventy, 21
Sepp, 266, 325
Simon of Cyrene, 302: a Jewish pilgrim, 306; meeting Jesus at the gate, 306; endeavouring to pass by, 309; compelled to bear the cross, 312; his fellowship with Jesus in suffering, 314; a convert and type of Jesus' followers, 316
"Sleep on now and take your rest," 40
Smith (Professor G. A.), 159
Soldiers, not lictors, scourging Jesus, 242
Sophocles, 226
Spirit willing and flesh weak, 35
Spirit in which the agony was endured, 59
Stalker, 315, 320
Steinmeyer, 113
Stephen (Sir J. F.), 239
Strauss, 32, 101, 144, 263
Stroud, 44
Substitution and redemption, 58
Suetonius, 136, 289
Suicide and secularism, 271
Sympathizers with Jesus, 297

INDEX.

Synagogue of Cyrenians, 305
Synoptists and John as to Passover, 138; Gethsemane, 31; Peter's denials, 112; incidents on the way to Calvary, 303
Tacitus, 132, 140, 144, 147, 190, 260, 290
Talmud, Jewish (canonical literature of Judaism, witness to Jewish laws, customs and institutions), 63, 88, 92, 93, 94, 100, 102, 103, 106, 125, 137, 143, 204, 286
Taylor (Jeremy), 185, 282, 284, 293
Tears, the tribute to suffering, 323
Temple, its police, 64; its sanctuary floor, 272; its treasurer, 174; its destruction, 334
Tertullian, 261
Thieves joined with Jesus, 287; one of the two a triumph of His grace, 288
Thirty pieces of silver, 64, 269
Thomas' picture of Judas, 266
Thomson, 27
Three appeals to the people, 213
Three, The chosen, 30
Three tributes to Jesus—of Pilate's wife, the Roman centurion, and the penitent thief, 192
Tiberias Romanized by Herod, 160
Tiberius, The emperor, 179, 190, 254, 260
Titus, The emperor, 27, 335
Titus and Dumachus, 287
Traditions—as to Gethsemane, 27; Pilate's wife, 190; the Potter's field, 273; Judas' suicide, 270; the two thieves, 287; Pilate's tragic end, 238
Traitor found among the disciples, 64
Traitor's kiss, how Jesus felt it, 69

Trials of Jesus—before Annas, 84; before Caiaphas and the Council, 87; before Pilate, 132; in Herod's judgment hall, 157; before Pilate again, 181; at bar of the Jewish people, 199
Trials for treason, 260

Ugolinus, 92
Upper Room, scene of the Supper, 9; supposed to be Mary's house, 9

Via Dolorosa, 290
Violence and inhumanity of the age, 247
Virgil, 226
Vox populi vox Dei, 215

Wace, 145
Walking with Jesus from Calvary to glory, 317
Warren and Wilson, 246
Washing hands—Jewish and Heathen, 226
"Weep not for me," 338
Weiss, 50, 84, 112, 175, 212, 228
Westcott, 17, 65, 130
"What is Truth?" 151
What woman owes to Jesus, 322
Whately, 85
"Whence art thou?" 255
Winer, 204
Women's treatment of Jesus, 322; their tribute to the greatness of His sufferings, 323; offering drink to Him on the Cross to assuage His pain, 325
Witnesses, False, at the Sanhedrim trial, 99; none produced before Pilate, 183; or before Herod, 168
Wünsche, 92, 125

Zechariah's prophecy about the Potter's field, 272, 275
Zöckler, 289

www.ingramcontent.com/pod-product-compliance
Lightning Source LLC
Chambersburg PA
CBHW031848220426
43663CB00006B/533